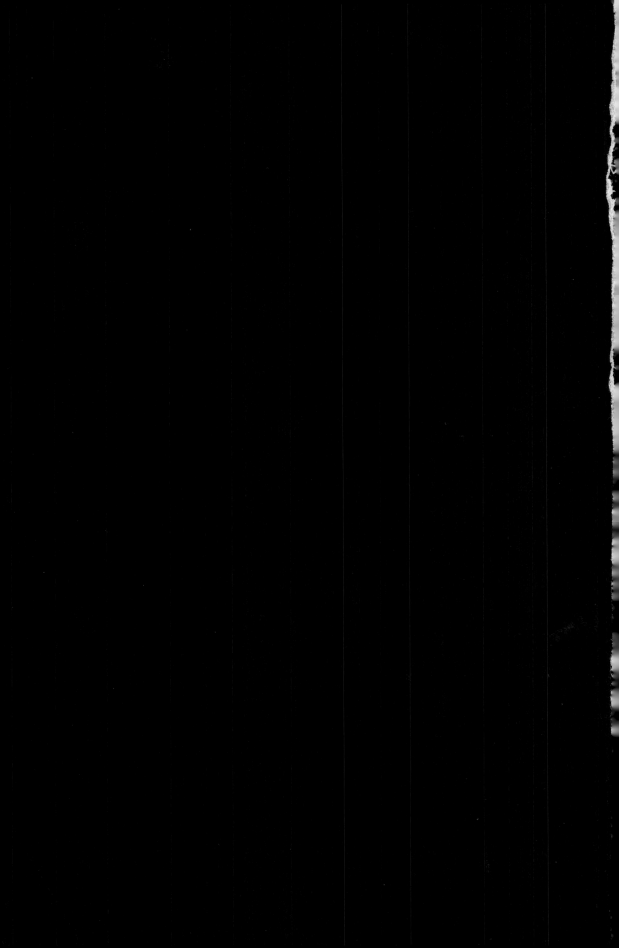

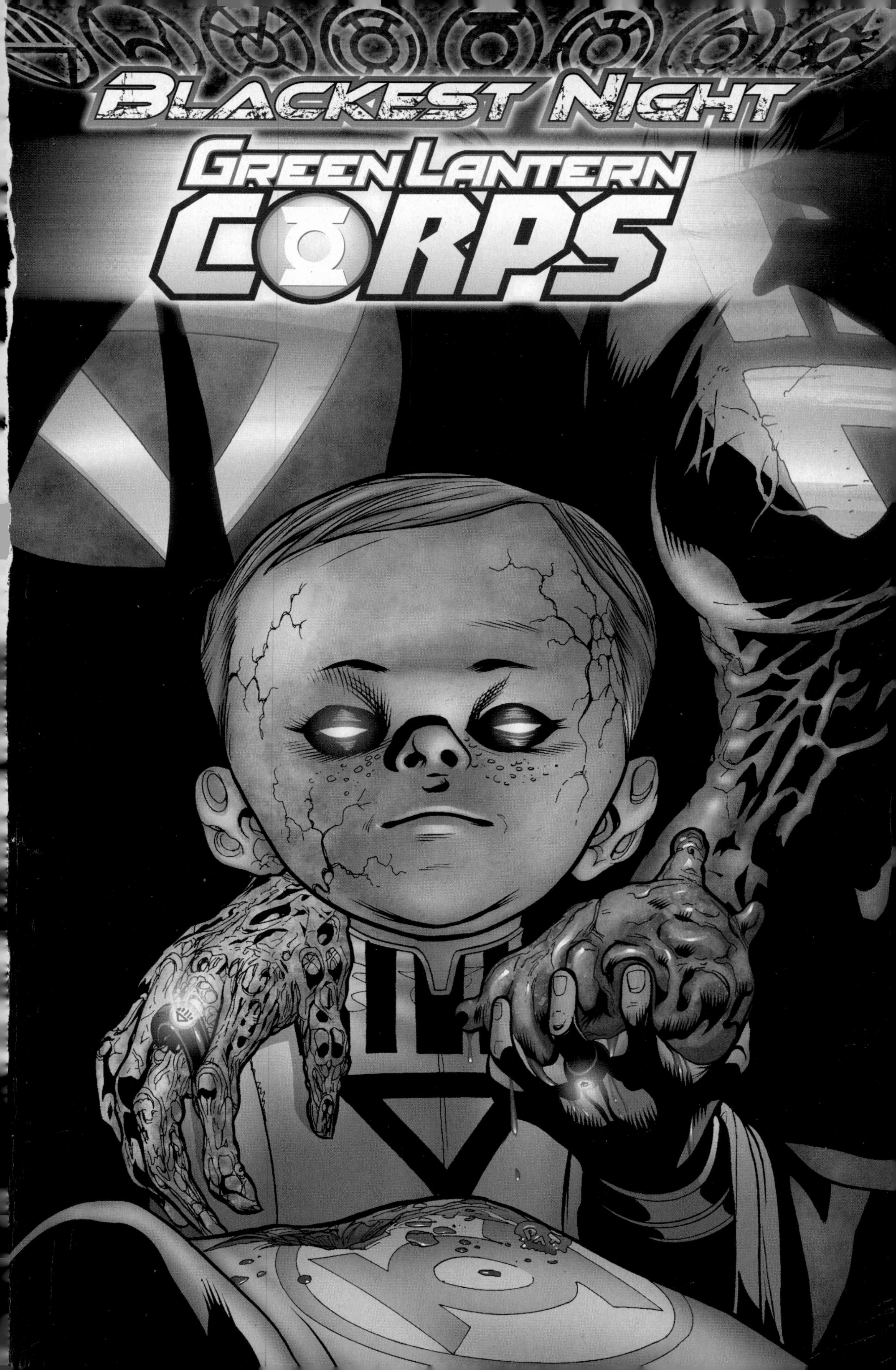
BLACKEST NIGHT
GREEN LANTERN
CORPS

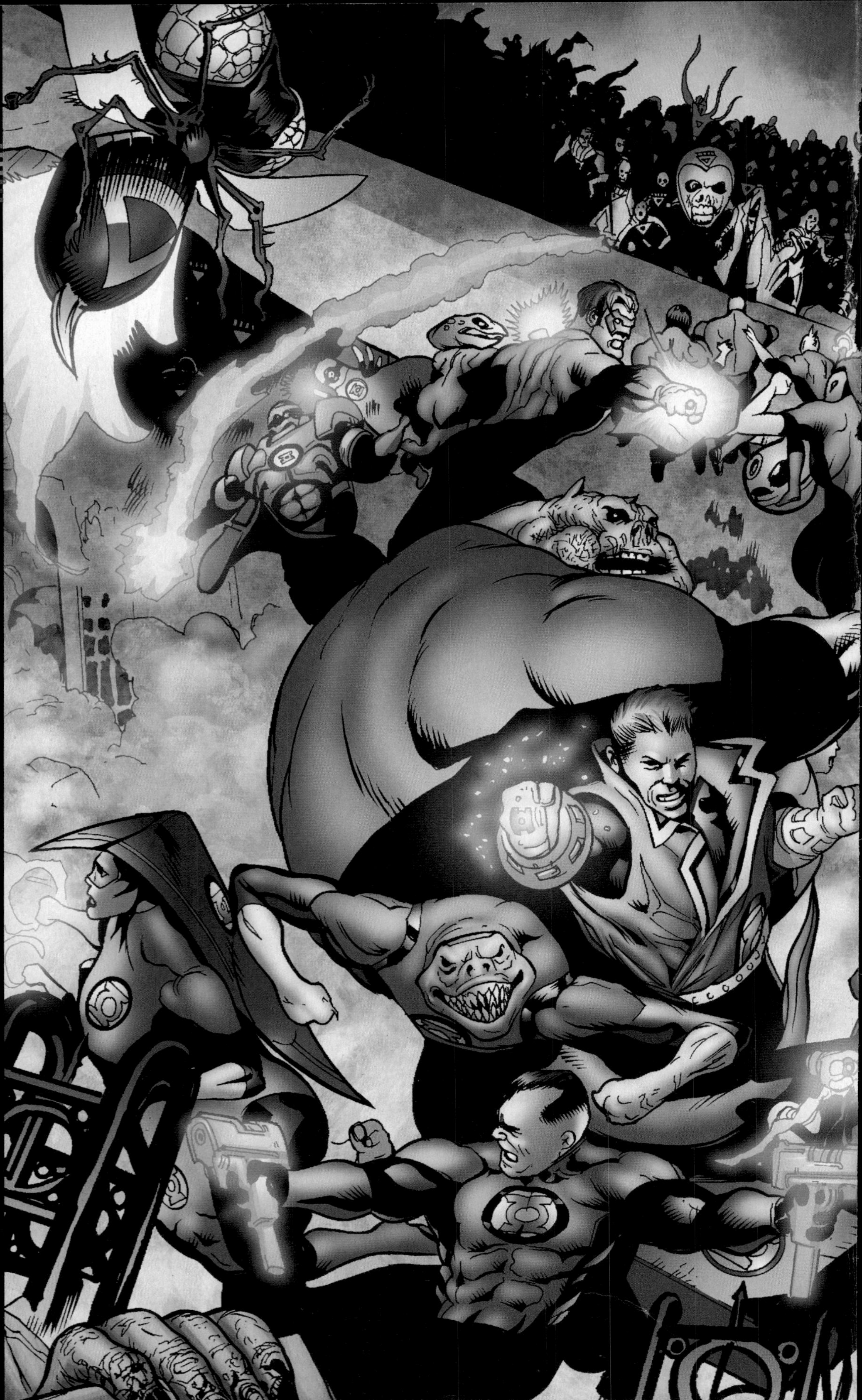

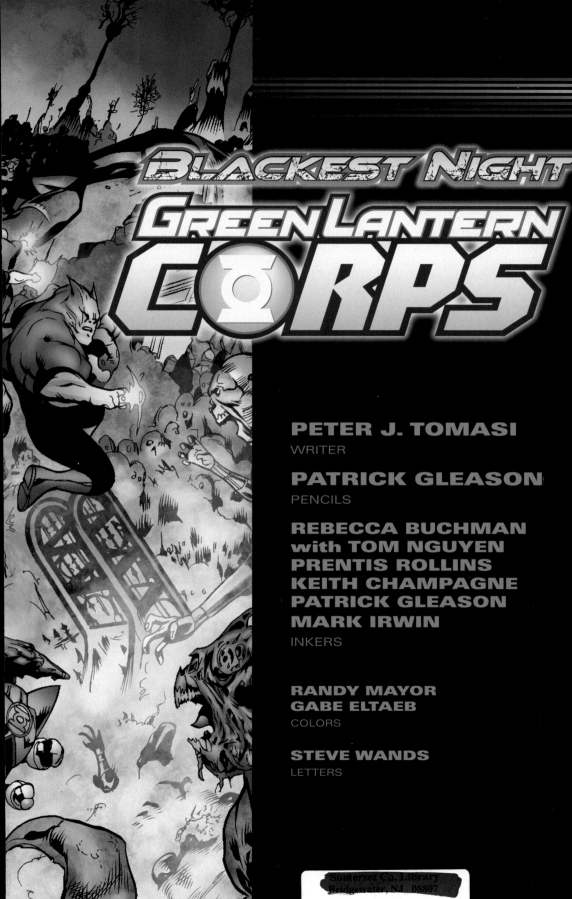

BLACKEST NIGHT
GREEN LANTERN CORPS

PETER J. TOMASI
WRITER

PATRICK GLEASON
PENCILS

REBECCA BUCHMAN
with **TOM NGUYEN**
PRENTIS ROLLINS
KEITH CHAMPAGNE
PATRICK GLEASON
MARK IRWIN
INKERS

RANDY MAYOR
GABE ELTAEB
COLORS

STEVE WANDS
LETTERS

Adam Schlagman *Editor-original series*
Bob Harras *Group Editor-Collected Editions* I Bob Joy *Editor*
Robbin Brosterman *Design Director-Books* I Curtis King Jr. *Senior Art Director*

DC COMICS I Diane Nelson *President* I Dan DiDio and Jim Lee *Co-Publishers*
Geoff Johns *Chief Creative Officer* I Patrick Caldon *EVP-Finance and Administration*
John Rood *EVP-Sales, Marketing and Business Development* I Amy Genkins *SVP-Business and Legal Affairs*
Steve Rotterdam *SVP-Sales and Marketing* I John Cunningham *VP-Marketing*
Terri Cunningham *VP-Managing Editor* I Alison Gill *VP-Manufacturing* I David Hyde *VP-Publicity*
Sue Pohja *VP-Book Trade Sales* I Alysse Soll *VP-Advertising and Custom Publishing*
Bob Wayne *VP-Sales* I Mark Chiarello *Art Director*

Cover by Rodolfo Migliari

BLACKEST NIGHT: GREEN LANTERN CORPS Published by DC Comics.
Cover, text and compilation Copyright © 2010 DC Comics. All Rights Reserved.

Originally published in single magazine form in GREEN LANTERN CORPS 39–47. Copyright © 2009, 2010
DC Comics. All Rights Reserved. All characters, their distinctive likenesses and related elements featured in this
publication are trademarks of DC Comics. The stories, characters and incidents featured in this publication are
entirely fictional. DC Comics does not read or accept unsolicited submissions of ideas, stories or artwork.

DC COMICS 1700 Broadway, New York, NY 10019 A Warner Bros. Entertainment Company

Printed by RR Donnelley, Salem, VA, USA. 6/9/10. First printing.

HC ISBN: 978-1-4012-2788-3
SC ISBN: 978-1-4012-2805-7

THE STORY SO FAR...

Billions of years ago, the self-appointed Guardians of the Universe recruited thousands of sentient beings from across the cosmos to join their intergalactic police force: the Green Lantern Corps.

Chosen because they are able to overcome great fear, the Green Lanterns patrol their respective space sectors armed with power rings capable of wielding the emerald energy of willpower into whatever constructs they can imagine.

Hal Jordan is the greatest of them all.

When the dying Green Lantern Abin Sur crashed on Earth, he chose Hal Jordan to be his successor, for his indomitable will and ability to overcome great fear. As the protector of Sector 2814, Hal has saved Earth from destruction, even died in its service and been reborn.

Thaal Sinestro of Korugar was once considered the greatest Green Lantern of them all.

As Abin Sur's friend, Sinestro became Jordan's mentor in the Corps. But after being sentenced to the Anti-Matter Universe for abusing his power, Sinestro learned of the yellow light of fear being mined on Qward. Wielding a new golden power ring fueled by terror, Sinestro drafted thousands of the most horrific, psychotic and sadistic beings in the universe, and with their doctrine of fear, burned all who opposed them.

When the Green Lantern Corps battled their former ally during the Sinestro Corps War, the skies burned with green and gold as Earth erupted into an epic battle between good and evil. Though the Green Lanterns won, their brotherhood was broken and the peace they achieved was short-lived. In its aftermath, the Guardians rewrote the Book of Oa, the very laws by which their corps abides, and dissent grew within their members.

Now Hal Jordan will face his greatest challenge yet, as the prophecy foretold by Abin Sur in his dying moments finally comes to pass...

The emotional spectrum has splintered into seven factions. Seven corps were born.

The Green Lanterns. The Sinestro Corps. Atrocitus and the enraged Red Lanterns. Larfleeze, the avaricious keeper of the Orange Light. Former Guardians Ganthet and Sayd's small but hopeful Blue Lantern Corps. The Zamarons and their army of fierce and loving Star Sapphires. And the mysterious Indigo Tribe.

As the War of Light ignited between these Lantern bearers, the skies on every world darkened. In Sector 666, on the planet Ryut, a black lantern grew around the Anti-Monitor's corpse, using his vast energies to empower it.

The first of the Black Lanterns, the Black Hand, has risen from the dead, heralding a greater power that will extinguish all of the light—and life—in the universe.

Now across thousands of worlds, the dead have risen, and Hal Jordan and all of Earth's greatest heroes must bear witness to Blackest Night, which will descend upon them all, without prejudice, mercy or reason.

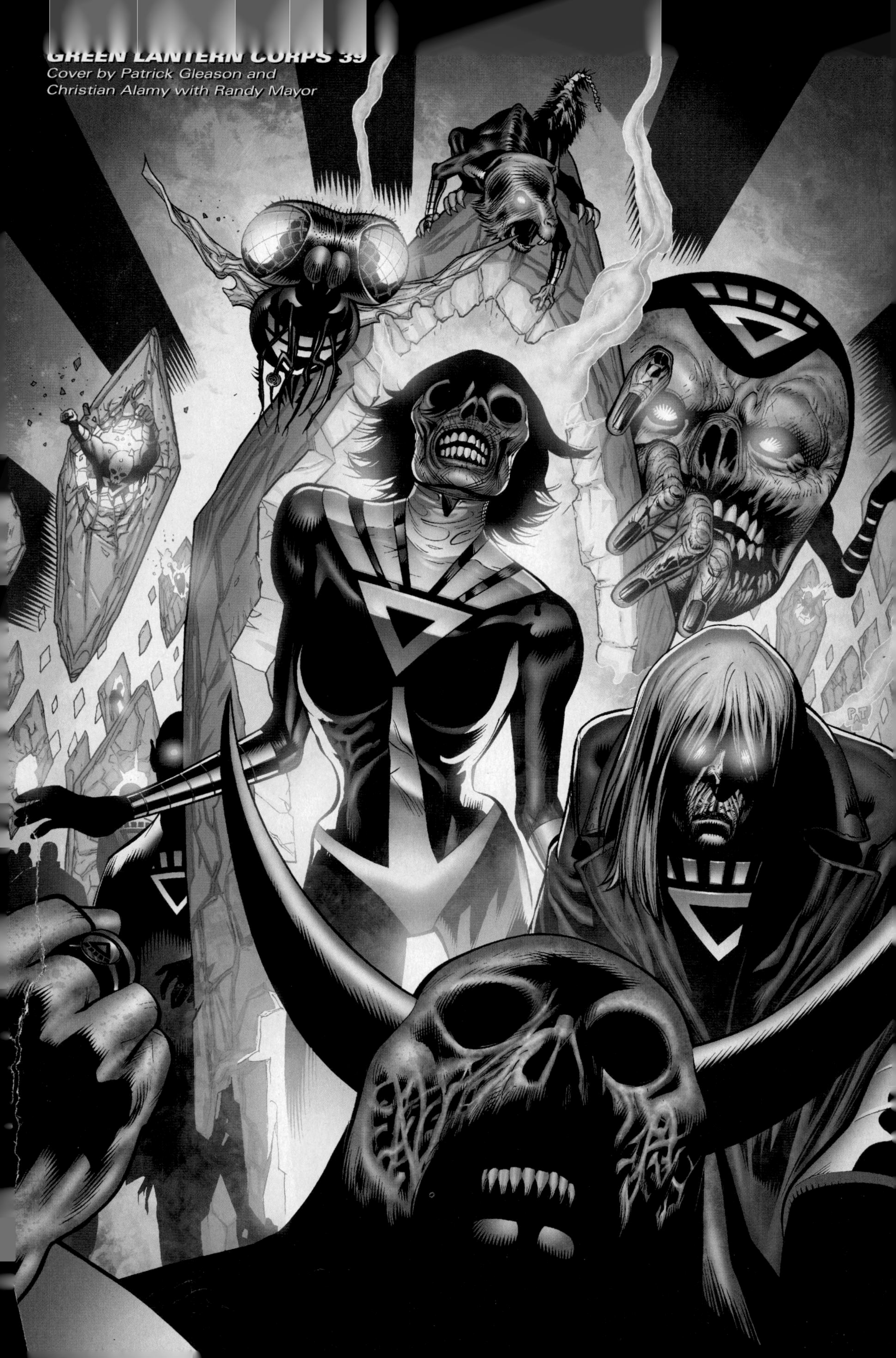

GREEN LANTERN CORPS 39
Cover by Patrick Gleason and Christian Alamy with Randy Mayor

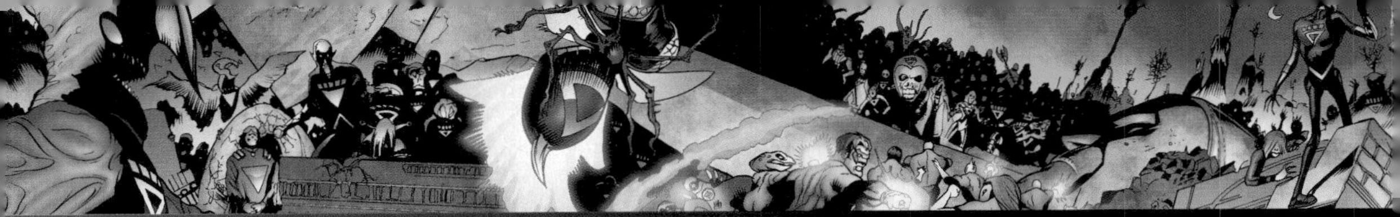

FADE TO BLACK

PATRICK GLEASON
PENCILS

REBECCA BUCHMAN
TOM NGUYEN
INKS

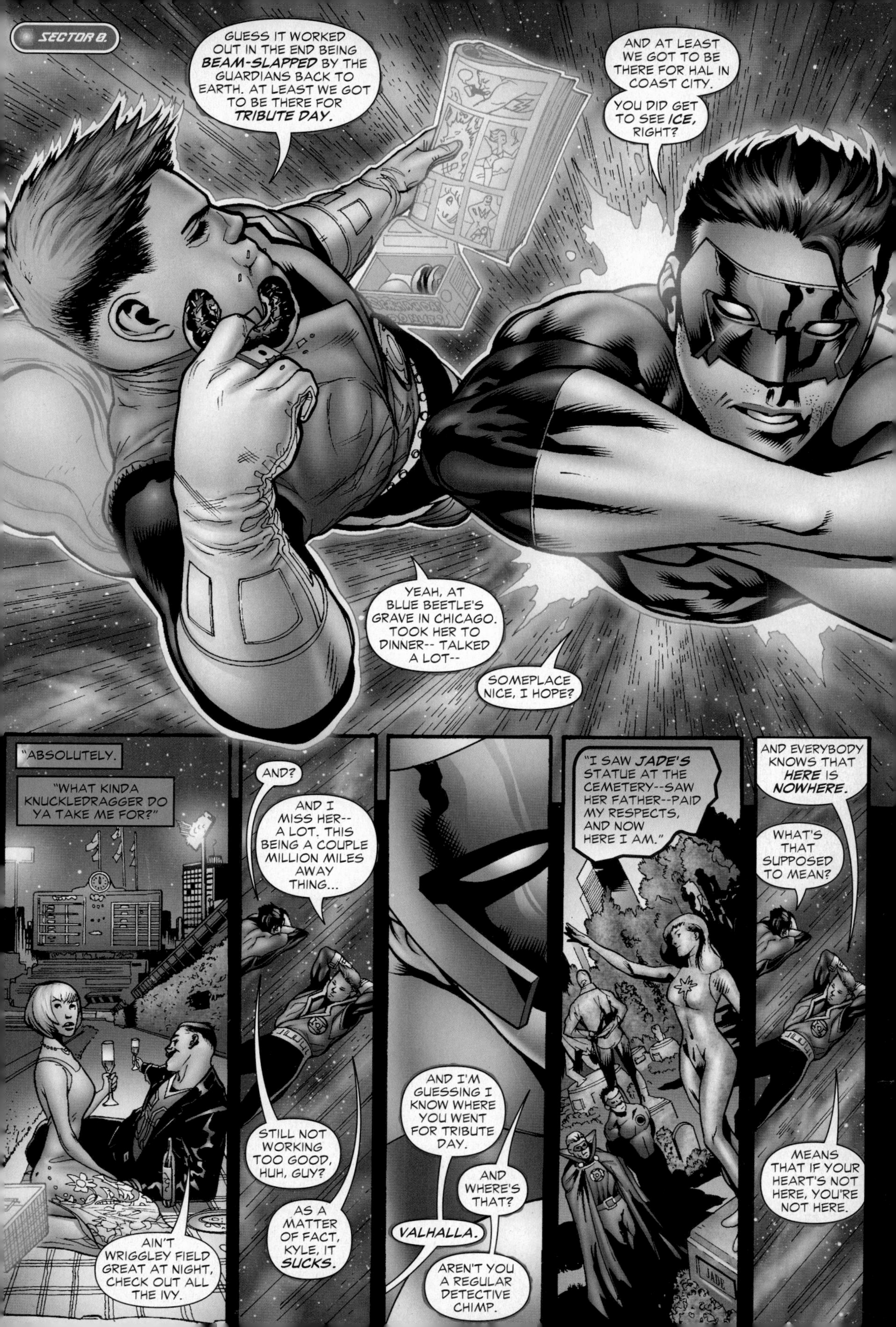
SECTOR 0.
GUESS IT WORKED OUT IN THE END BEING BEAM-SLAPPED BY THE GUARDIANS BACK TO EARTH. AT LEAST WE GOT TO BE THERE FOR TRIBUTE DAY.
AND AT LEAST WE GOT TO BE THERE FOR HAL IN COAST CITY.
YOU DID GET TO SEE ICE, RIGHT?
YEAH, AT BLUE BEETLE'S GRAVE IN CHICAGO. TOOK HER TO DINNER-- TALKED A LOT--
SOMEPLACE NICE, I HOPE?
"ABSOLUTELY.
"WHAT KINDA KNUCKLEDRAGGER DO YA TAKE ME FOR?"
AIN'T WRIGGLEY FIELD GREAT AT NIGHT, CHECK OUT ALL THE IVY.
AND?
AND I MISS HER-- A LOT. THIS BEING A COUPLE MILLION MILES AWAY THING...
STILL NOT WORKING TOO GOOD, HUH, GUY?
AS A MATTER OF FACT, KYLE, IT SUCKS.
AND I'M GUESSING I KNOW WHERE YOU WENT FOR TRIBUTE DAY.
AND WHERE'S THAT?
VALHALLA.
AREN'T YOU A REGULAR DETECTIVE CHIMP.
"I SAW JADE'S STATUE AT THE CEMETERY--SAW HER FATHER--PAID MY RESPECTS, AND NOW HERE I AM."
JADE
AND EVERYBODY KNOWS THAT HERE IS NOWHERE.
WHAT'S THAT SUPPOSED TO MEAN?
MEANS THAT IF YOUR HEART'S NOT HERE, YOU'RE NOT HERE.

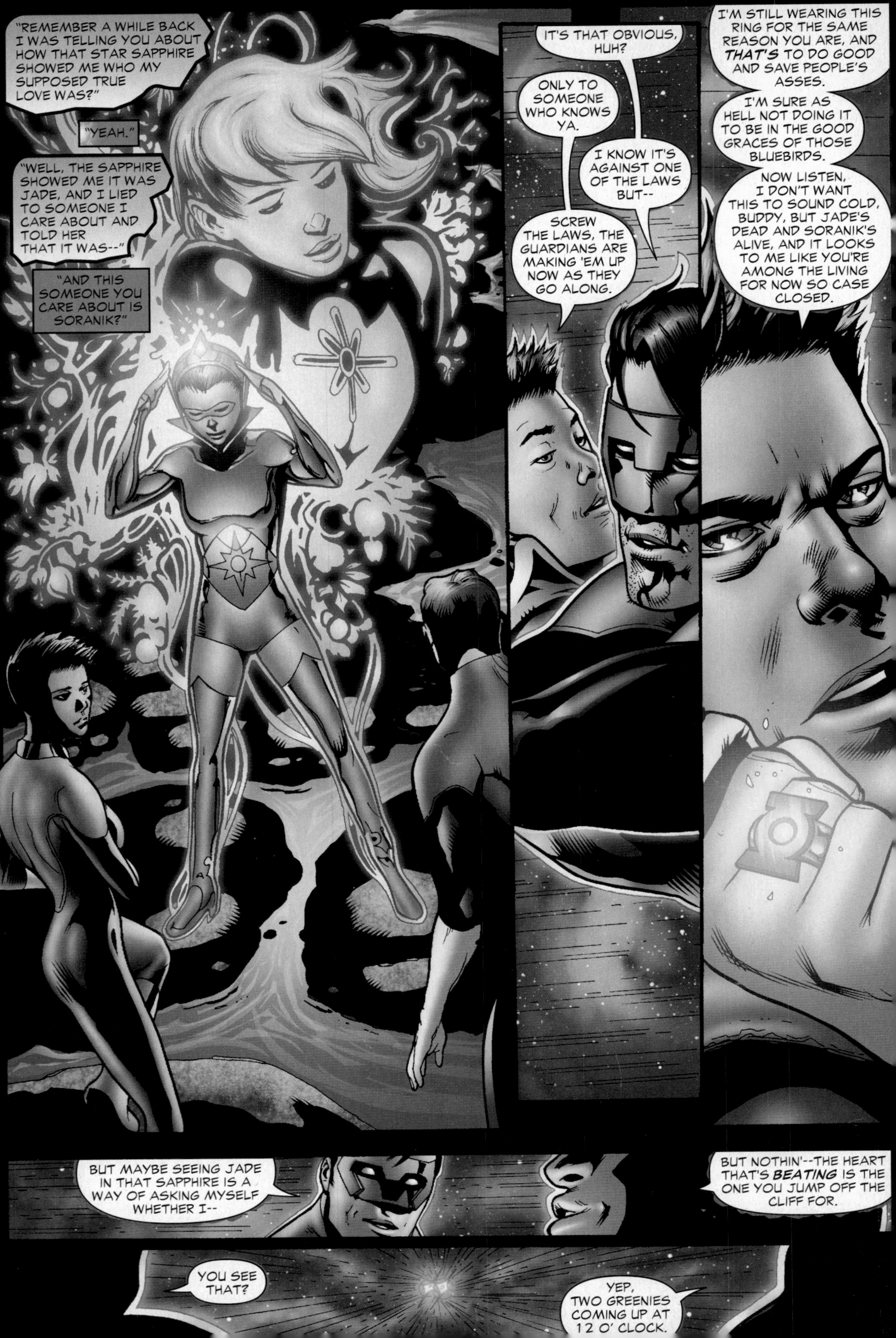
"REMEMBER A WHILE BACK I WAS TELLING YOU ABOUT HOW THAT STAR SAPPHIRE SHOWED ME WHO MY SUPPOSED TRUE LOVE WAS?"
"YEAH."
"WELL, THE SAPPHIRE SHOWED ME IT WAS JADE, AND I LIED TO SOMEONE I CARE ABOUT AND TOLD HER THAT IT WAS--"
"AND THIS SOMEONE YOU CARE ABOUT IS SORANIK?"
IT'S THAT OBVIOUS, HUH?
ONLY TO SOMEONE WHO KNOWS YA.
I KNOW IT'S AGAINST ONE OF THE LAWS BUT--
SCREW THE LAWS, THE GUARDIANS ARE MAKING 'EM UP NOW AS THEY GO ALONG.
I'M STILL WEARING THIS RING FOR THE SAME REASON YOU ARE, AND THAT'S TO DO GOOD AND SAVE PEOPLE'S ASSES.
I'M SURE AS HELL NOT DOING IT TO BE IN THE GOOD GRACES OF THOSE BLUEBIRDS.
NOW LISTEN, I DON'T WANT THIS TO SOUND COLD, BUDDY, BUT JADE'S DEAD AND SORANIK'S ALIVE, AND IT LOOKS TO ME LIKE YOU'RE AMONG THE LIVING FOR NOW SO CASE CLOSED.
BUT MAYBE SEEING JADE IN THAT SAPPHIRE IS A WAY OF ASKING MYSELF WHETHER I--
BUT NOTHIN'--THE HEART THAT'S BEATING IS THE ONE YOU JUMP OFF THE CLIFF FOR.
YOU SEE THAT?
YEP, TWO GREENIES COMING UP AT 12 O' CLOCK.

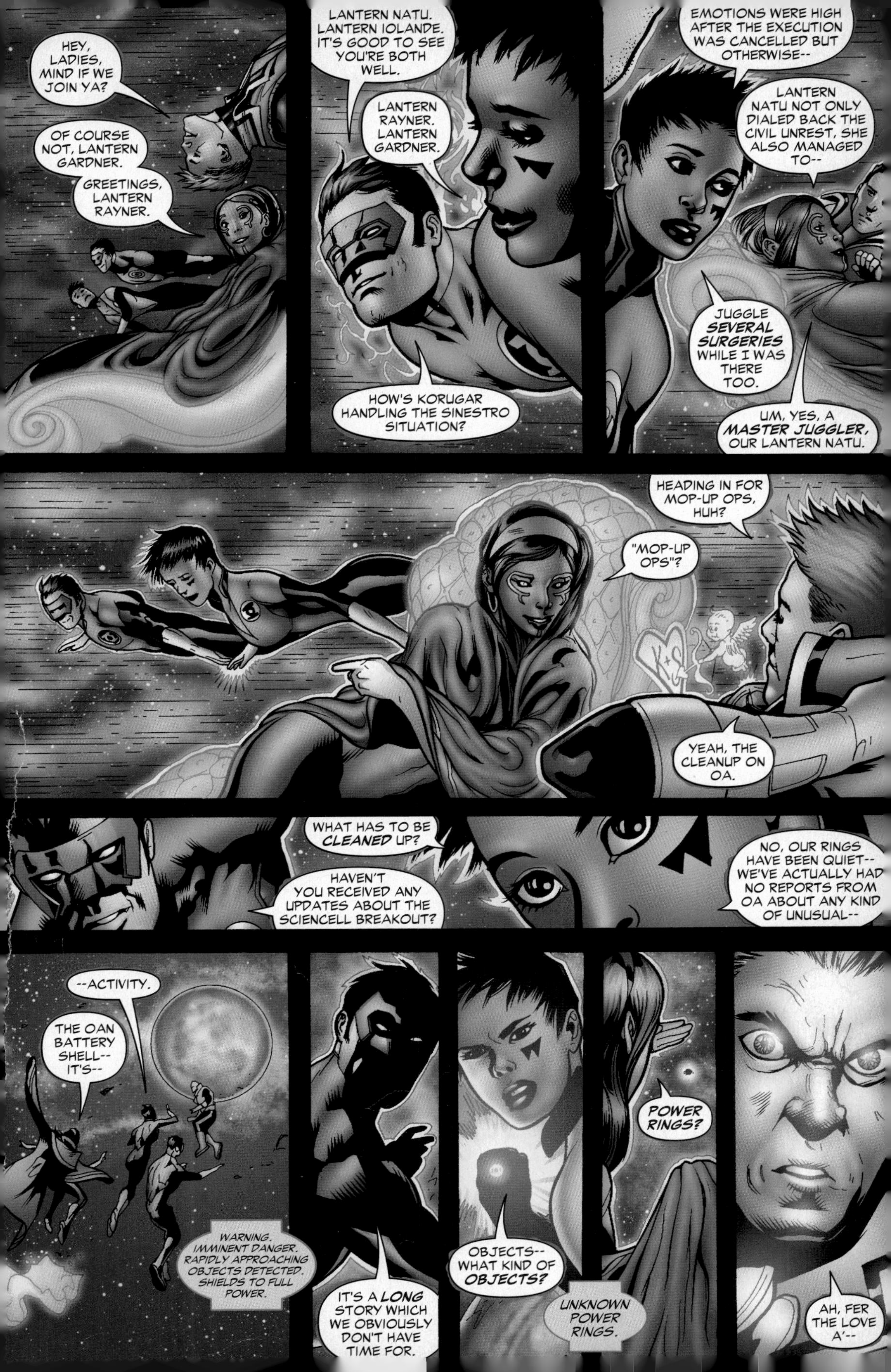
HEY, LADIES, MIND IF WE JOIN YA?
OF COURSE NOT, LANTERN GARDNER.
GREETINGS, LANTERN RAYNER.
LANTERN NATU. LANTERN IOLANDE. IT'S GOOD TO SEE YOU'RE BOTH WELL.
LANTERN RAYNER. LANTERN GARDNER.
HOW'S KORUGAR HANDLING THE SINESTRO SITUATION?
EMOTIONS WERE HIGH AFTER THE EXECUTION WAS CANCELLED BUT OTHERWISE--
LANTERN NATU NOT ONLY DIALED BACK THE CIVIL UNREST, SHE ALSO MANAGED TO--
JUGGLE SEVERAL SURGERIES WHILE I WAS THERE TOO.
UM, YES, A MASTER JUGGLER, OUR LANTERN NATU.
HEADING IN FOR MOP-UP OPS, HUH?
"MOP-UP OPS"?
YEAH, THE CLEANUP ON OA.
WHAT HAS TO BE CLEANED UP?
HAVEN'T YOU RECEIVED ANY UPDATES ABOUT THE SCIENCELL BREAKOUT?
NO, OUR RINGS HAVE BEEN QUIET-- WE'VE ACTUALLY HAD NO REPORTS FROM OA ABOUT ANY KIND OF UNUSUAL--
--ACTIVITY.
THE OAN BATTERY SHELL-- IT'S--
WARNING. IMMINENT DANGER. RAPIDLY APPROACHING OBJECTS DETECTED. SHIELDS TO FULL POWER.
IT'S A LONG STORY WHICH WE OBVIOUSLY DON'T HAVE TIME FOR.
OBJECTS-- WHAT KIND OF OBJECTS?
UNKNOWN POWER RINGS.
POWER RINGS?
AH, FER THE LOVE A'--

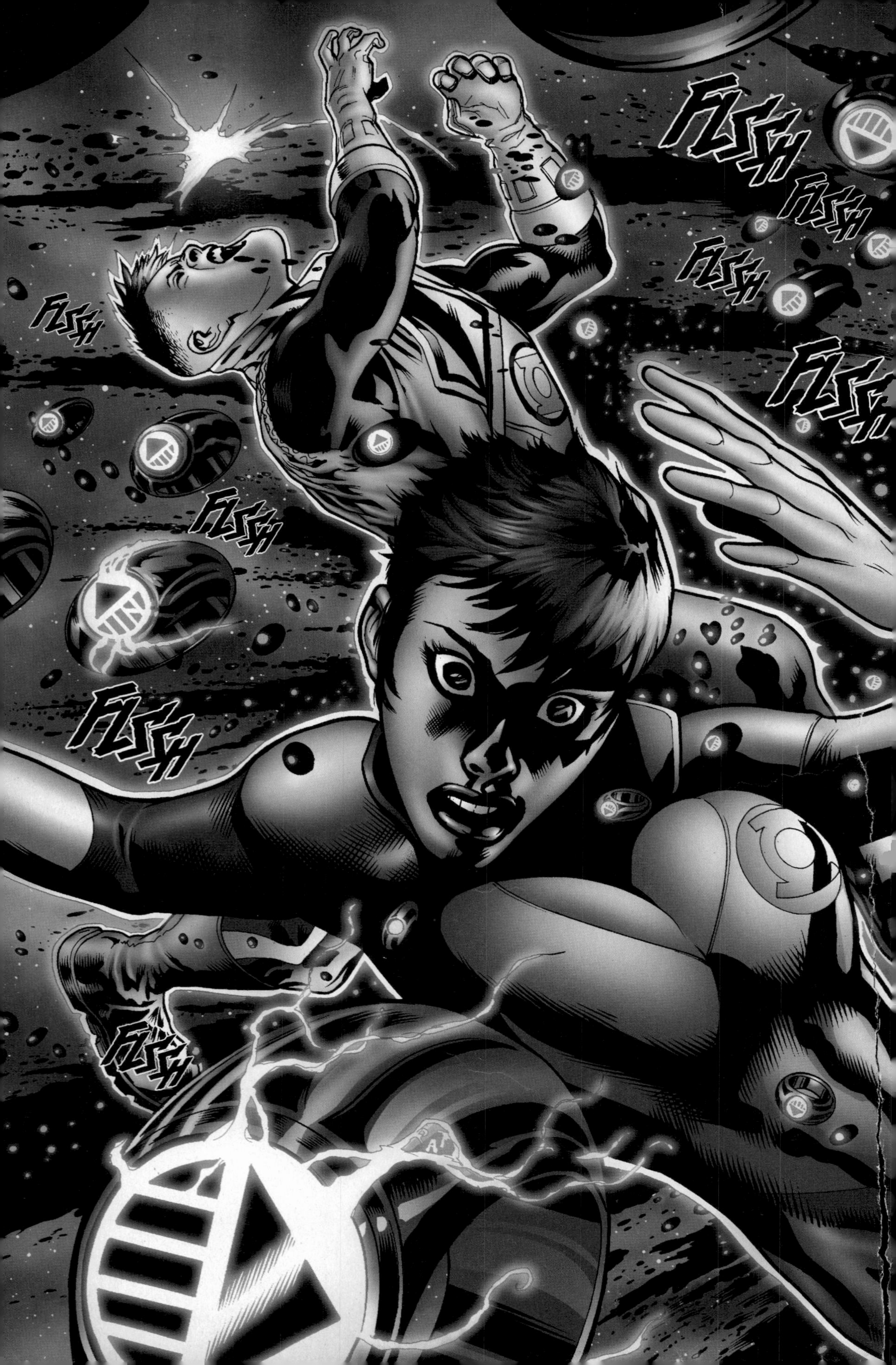
FZSH
FZSH
FZSH
FZSH
FZSH
FZSH
FZSH
FZSH

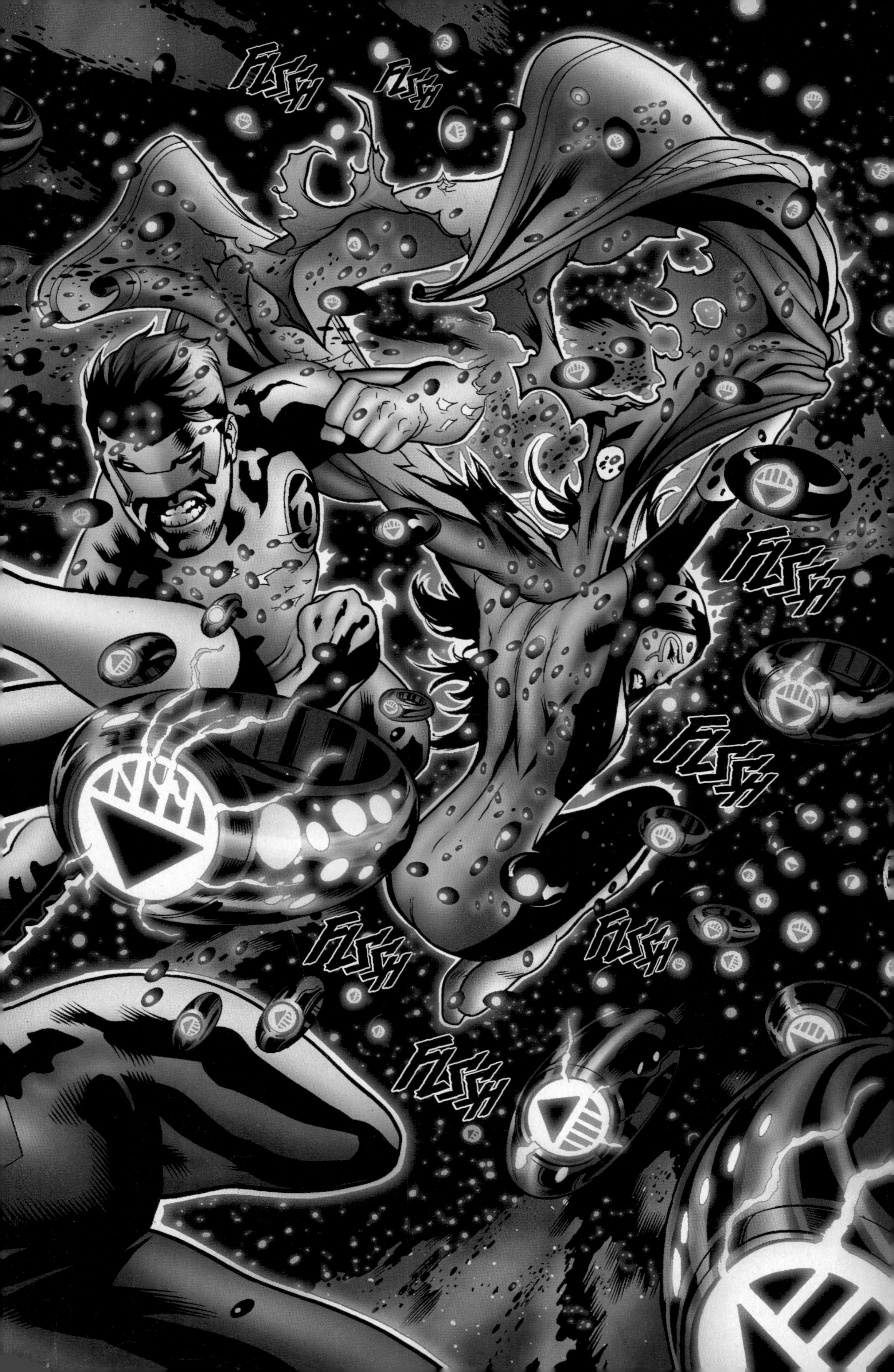
FZSSH
FZSSH
FZSSH
FZSSH
FZSSH
FZSSH
FZSSH

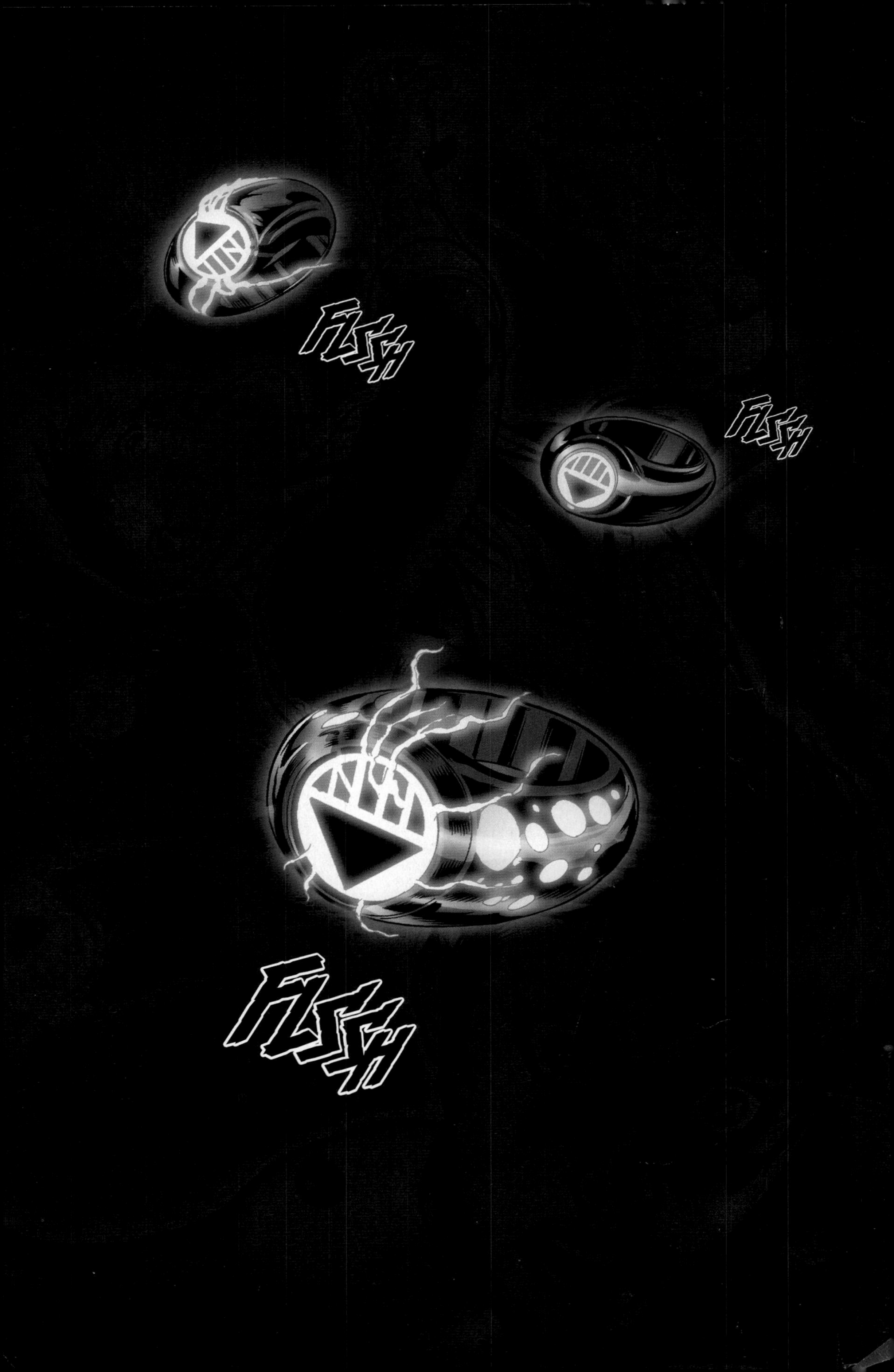
FLSSH
FLSSH
FLSSH

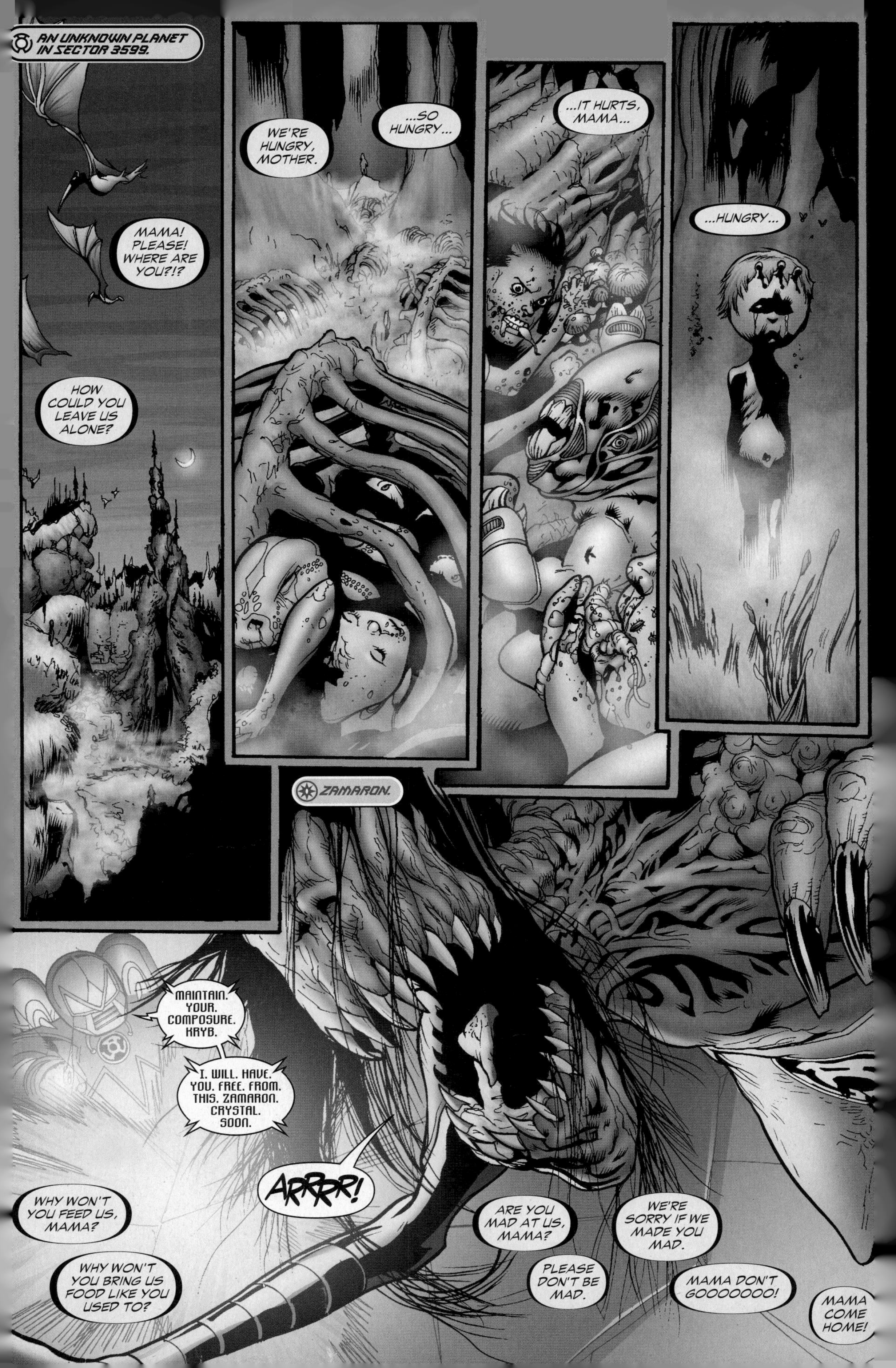
AN UNKNOWN PLANET IN SECTOR 3599.
MAMA! PLEASE! WHERE ARE YOU?!?
HOW COULD YOU LEAVE US ALONE?
WE'RE HUNGRY, MOTHER.
...SO HUNGRY...
...IT HURTS, MAMA...
...HUNGRY...
ZAMARON.
MAINTAIN. YOUR. COMPOSURE. KRYB.
I. WILL. HAVE. YOU. FREE. FROM. THIS. ZAMARON. CRYSTAL. SOON.
ARRRR!
WHY WON'T YOU FEED US, MAMA?
WHY WON'T YOU BRING US FOOD LIKE YOU USED TO?
ARE YOU MAD AT US, MAMA?
PLEASE DON'T BE MAD.
WE'RE SORRY IF WE MADE YOU MAD.
MAMA DON'T GOOOOOOO!
MAMA COME HOME!

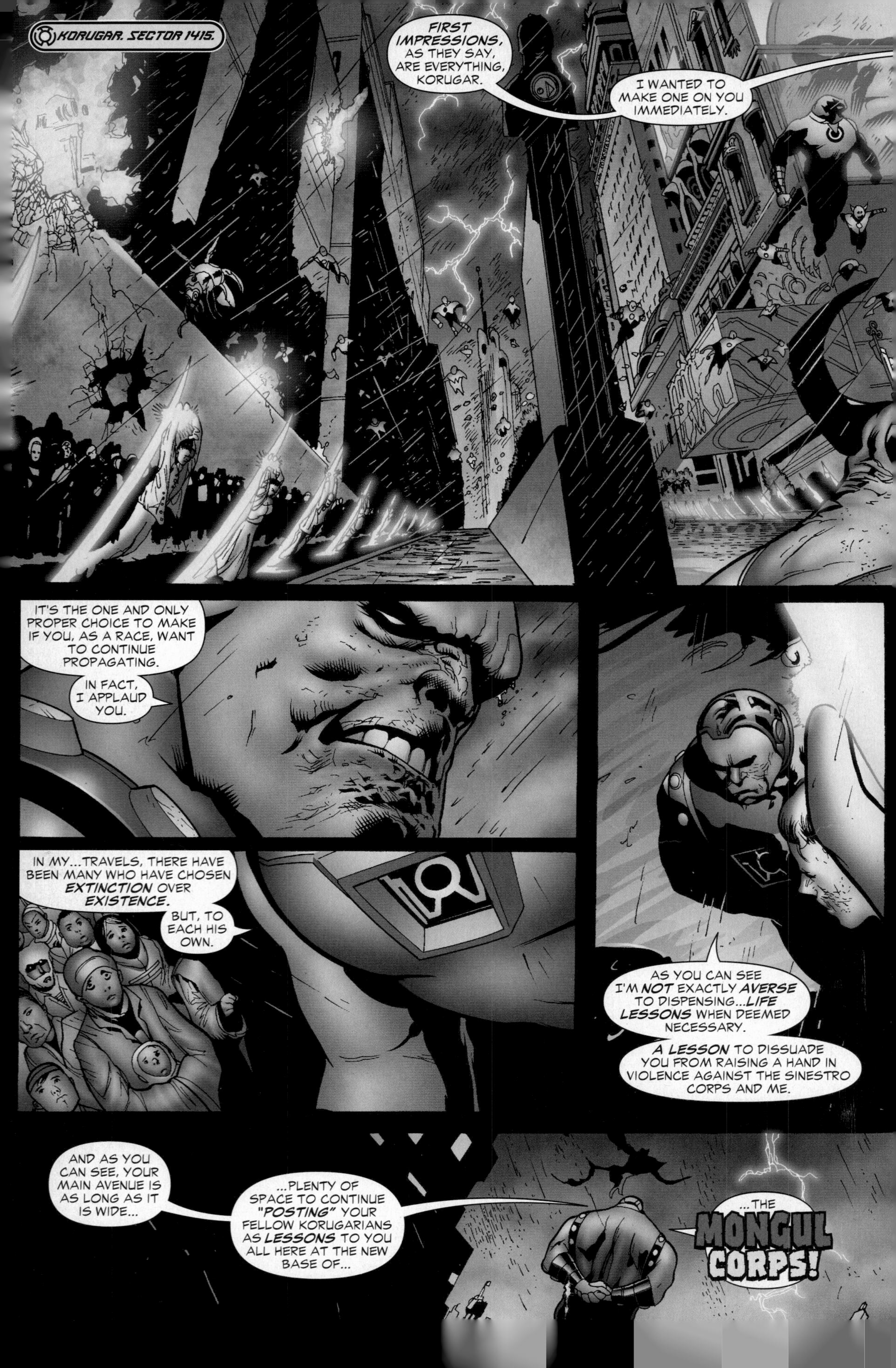
KORUGAR. SECTOR 1415.
FIRST IMPRESSIONS, AS THEY SAY, ARE EVERYTHING, KORUGAR.
I WANTED TO MAKE ONE ON YOU IMMEDIATELY.
IT'S THE ONE AND ONLY PROPER CHOICE TO MAKE IF YOU, AS A RACE, WANT TO CONTINUE PROPAGATING.
IN FACT, I APPLAUD YOU.
IN MY...TRAVELS, THERE HAVE BEEN MANY WHO HAVE CHOSEN EXTINCTION OVER EXISTENCE.
BUT, TO EACH HIS OWN.
AS YOU CAN SEE I'M NOT EXACTLY AVERSE TO DISPENSING...LIFE LESSONS WHEN DEEMED NECESSARY.
A LESSON TO DISSUADE YOU FROM RAISING A HAND IN VIOLENCE AGAINST THE SINESTRO CORPS AND ME.
AND AS YOU CAN SEE, YOUR MAIN AVENUE IS AS LONG AS IT IS WIDE...
...PLENTY OF SPACE TO CONTINUE "POSTING" YOUR FELLOW KORUGARIANS AS LESSONS TO YOU ALL HERE AT THE NEW BASE OF...
...THE
MONGUL CORPS!

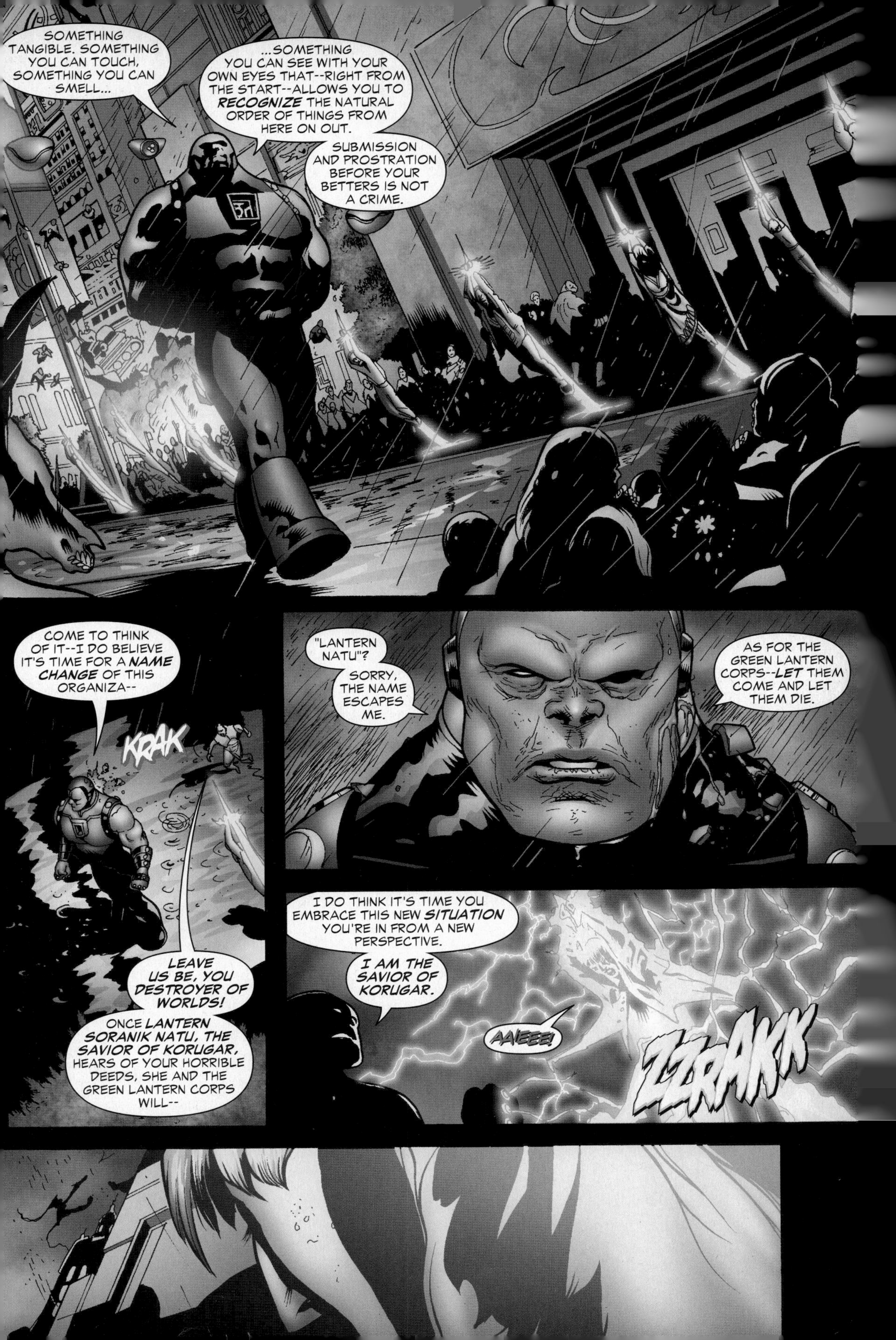
SOMETHING TANGIBLE. SOMETHING YOU CAN TOUCH, SOMETHING YOU CAN SMELL...
...SOMETHING YOU CAN SEE WITH YOUR OWN EYES THAT--RIGHT FROM THE START--ALLOWS YOU TO RECOGNIZE THE NATURAL ORDER OF THINGS FROM HERE ON OUT.
SUBMISSION AND PROSTRATION BEFORE YOUR BETTERS IS NOT A CRIME.
COME TO THINK OF IT--I DO BELIEVE IT'S TIME FOR A NAME CHANGE OF THIS ORGANIZA--
KRAK
LEAVE US BE, YOU DESTROYER OF WORLDS!
ONCE LANTERN SORANIK NATU, THE SAVIOR OF KORUGAR, HEARS OF YOUR HORRIBLE DEEDS, SHE AND THE GREEN LANTERN CORPS WILL--
"LANTERN NATU"?
SORRY, THE NAME ESCAPES ME.
AS FOR THE GREEN LANTERN CORPS--LET THEM COME AND LET THEM DIE.
I DO THINK IT'S TIME YOU EMBRACE THIS NEW SITUATION YOU'RE IN FROM A NEW PERSPECTIVE.
I AM THE SAVIOR OF KORUGAR.
AAIEEE!
ZZRAKK

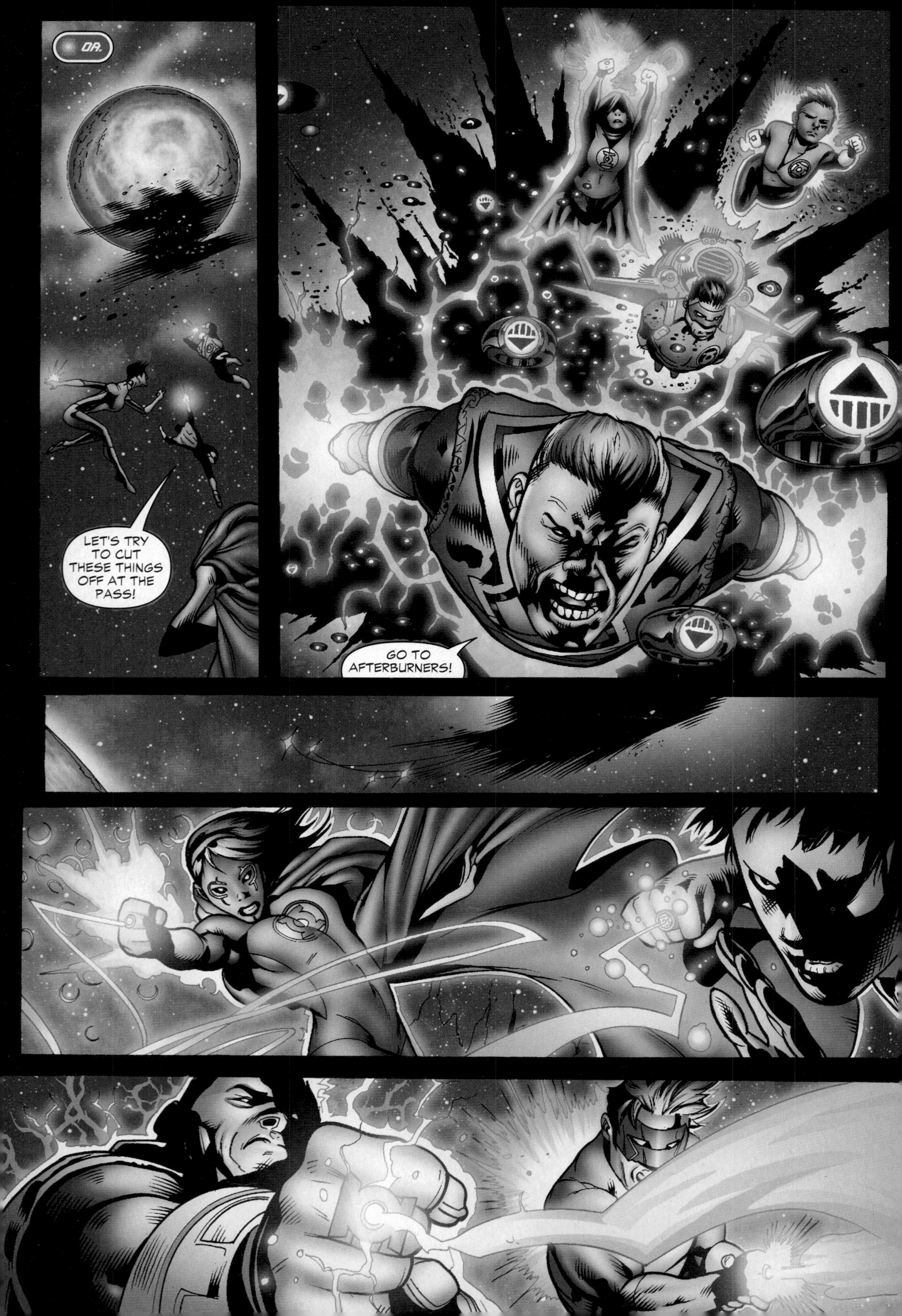
OA.
LET'S TRY TO CUT THESE THINGS OFF AT THE PASS!
GO TO AFTERBURNERS!

ALL RIGHT, LET'S SEE 'EM GET--

FLSSH

FLSSH

FLSSH

--THROUGH THAT.

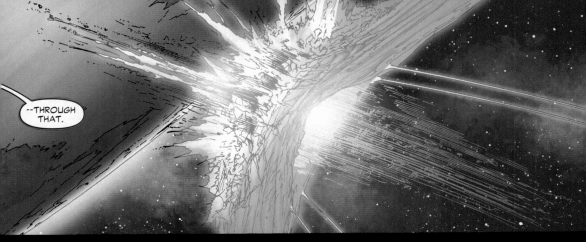

AW, CRAP.

AW, CRAP.

NOT SURE WHAT WE GOT HERE, BUT IT CAN'T BE GOOD!

LET'S GET DOWN THERE!

IOLANDE AND I ARE GOING STRAIGHT TO THE HOSPITAL TO GET THE PATIENTS TO SAFETY!

BE CAREFUL, KYLE.

YOU TOO.

THAT'S IT, "YOU TOO"? WHY DIDN'T YOU TELLA THAT NICE GIRL A: I LOVE YA SO MUCHA, NATU, I THINK I'MA GONNA DIE!

ZIP IT.

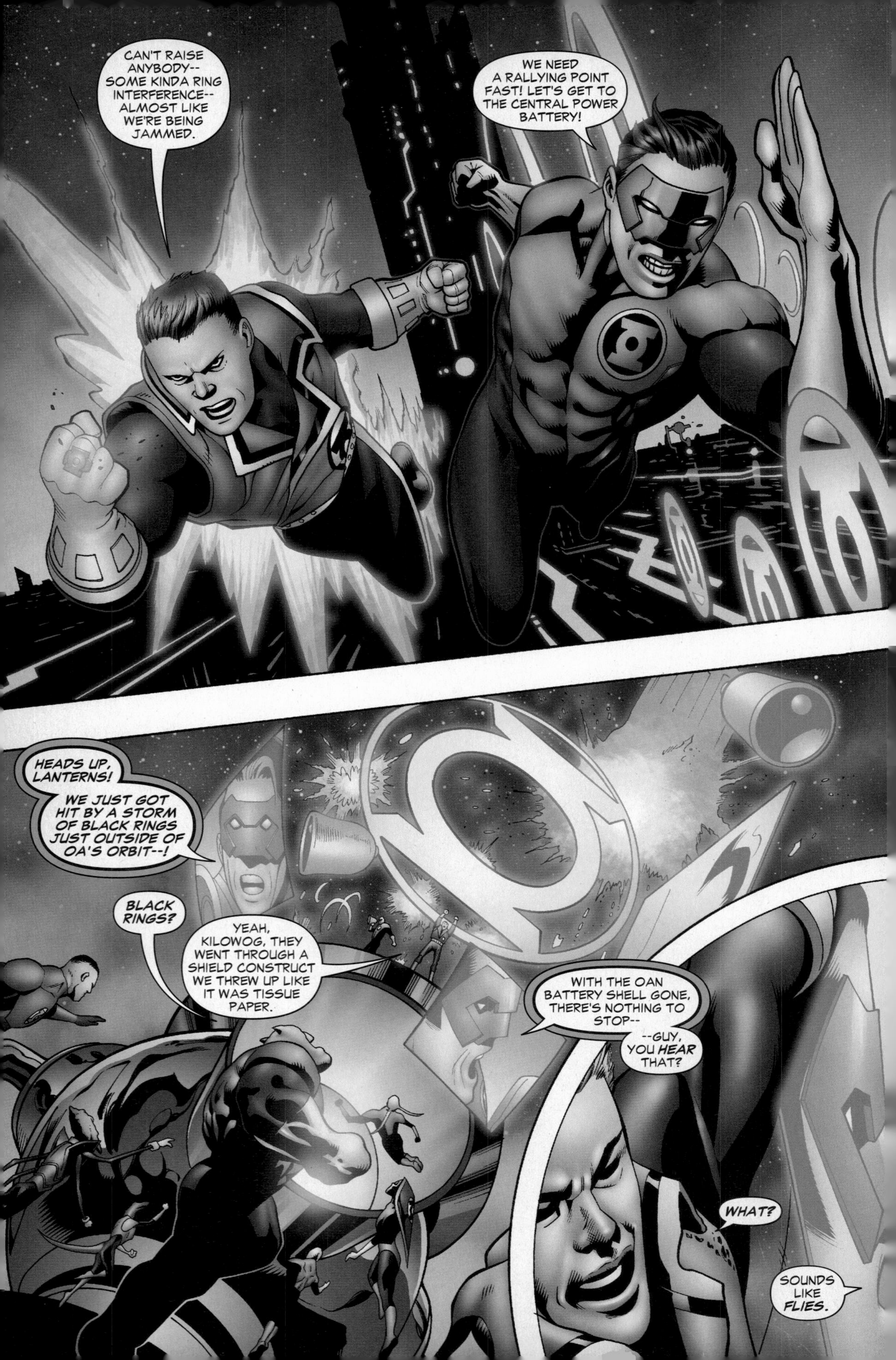
CAN'T RAISE ANYBODY-- SOME KINDA RING INTERFERENCE-- ALMOST LIKE WE'RE BEING JAMMED.
WE NEED A RALLYING POINT FAST! LET'S GET TO THE CENTRAL POWER BATTERY!
HEADS UP, LANTERNS!
WE JUST GOT HIT BY A STORM OF BLACK RINGS JUST OUTSIDE OF OA'S ORBIT--!
BLACK RINGS?
YEAH, KILOWOG, THEY WENT THROUGH A SHIELD CONSTRUCT WE THREW UP LIKE IT WAS TISSUE PAPER.
WITH THE OAN BATTERY SHELL GONE, THERE'S NOTHING TO STOP--
--GUY, YOU HEAR THAT?
WHAT?
SOUNDS LIKE FLIES.

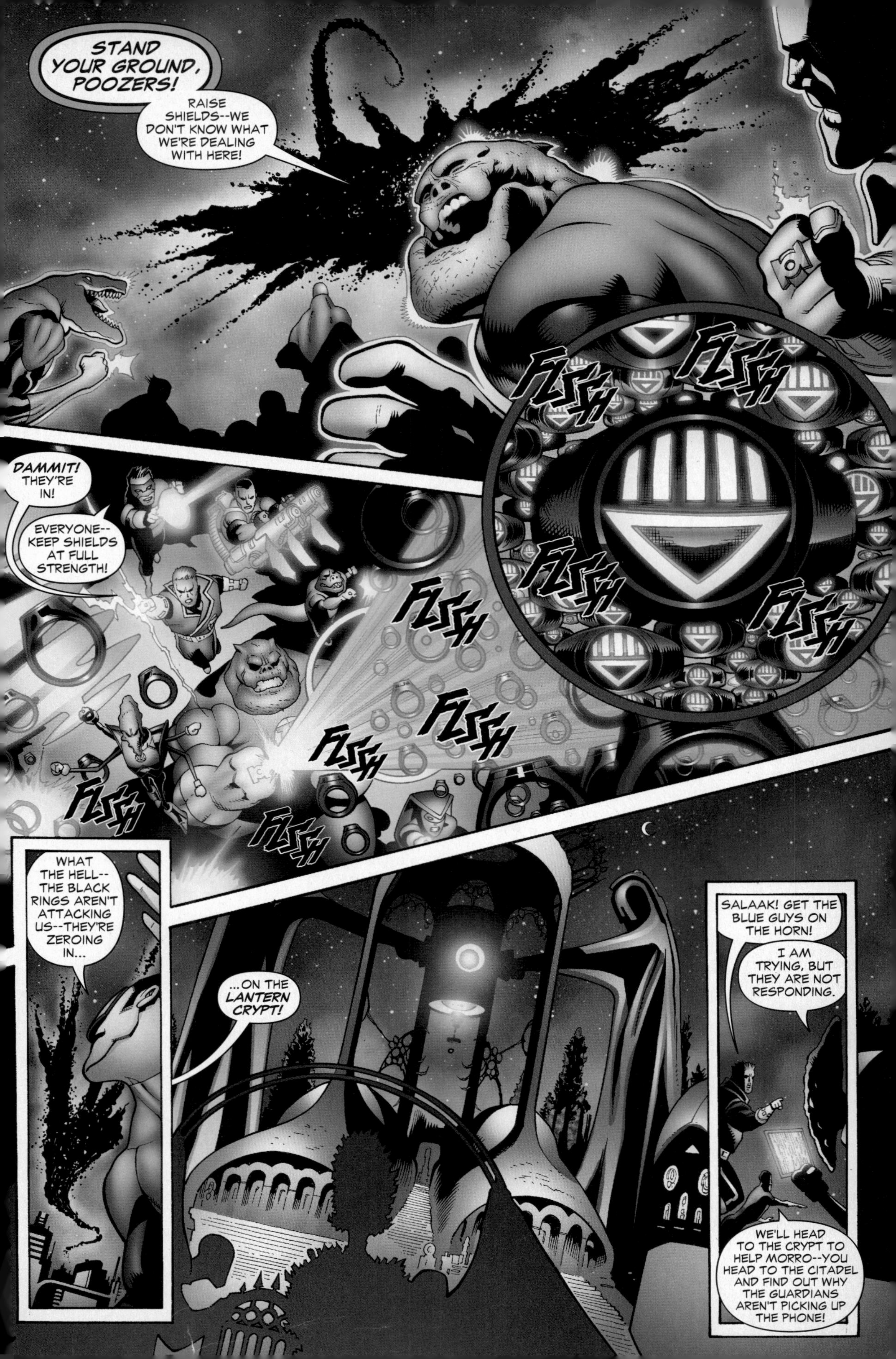
STAND YOUR GROUND, POOZERS!
RAISE SHIELDS--WE DON'T KNOW WHAT WE'RE DEALING WITH HERE!
DAMMIT! THEY'RE IN!
EVERYONE--KEEP SHIELDS AT FULL STRENGTH!
FLSSH
FLSSH
FLSSH
FLSSH
FLSSH
FLSSH
FLSSH
FLSSH
FLSSH
WHAT THE HELL--THE BLACK RINGS AREN'T ATTACKING US--THEY'RE ZEROING IN...
...ON THE LANTERN CRYPT!
SALAAK! GET THE BLUE GUYS ON THE HORN!
I AM TRYING, BUT THEY ARE NOT RESPONDING.
WE'LL HEAD TO THE CRYPT TO HELP MORRO--YOU HEAD TO THE CITADEL AND FIND OUT WHY THE GUARDIANS AREN'T PICKING UP THE PHONE!

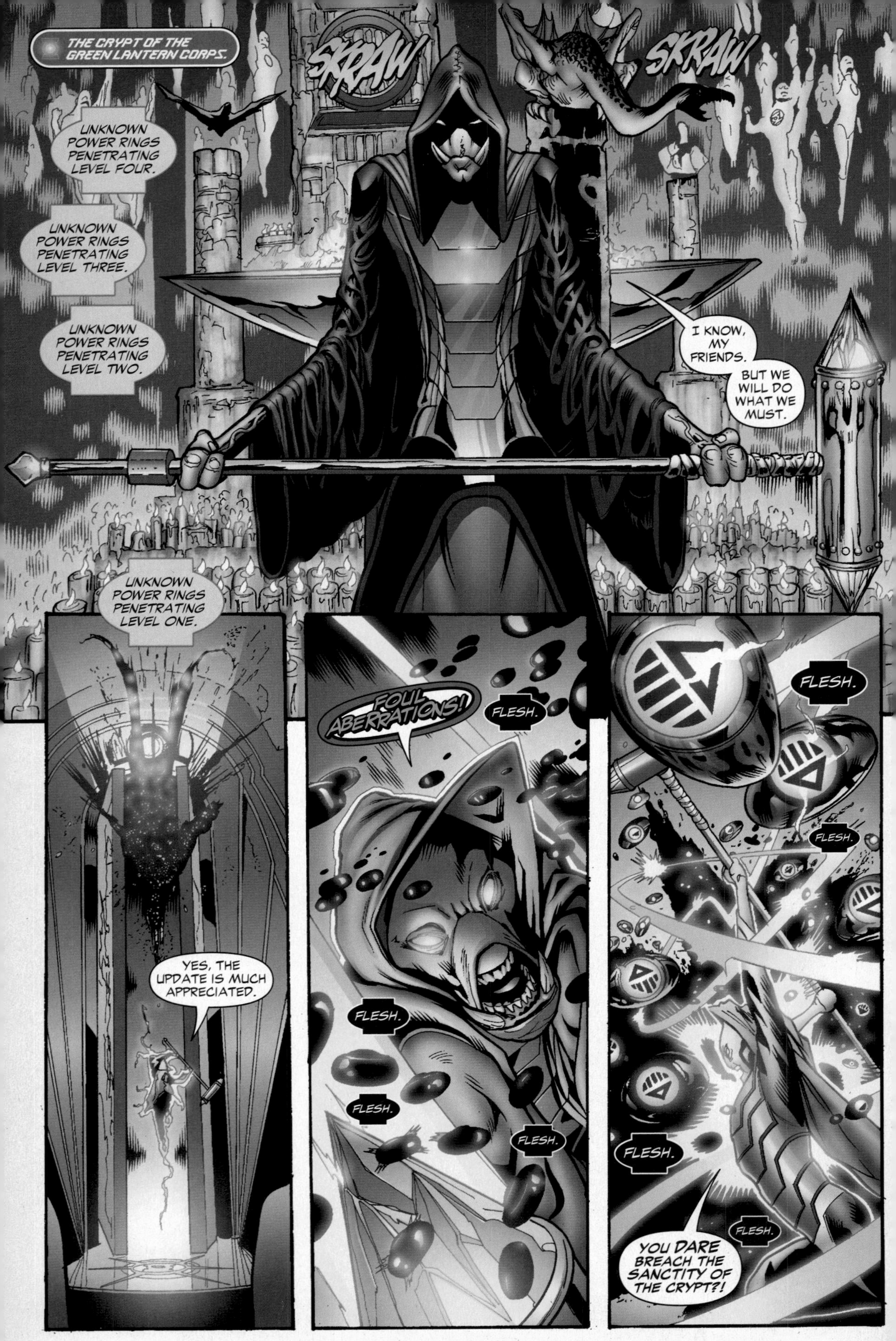
THE CRYPT OF THE GREEN LANTERN CORPS.
SKRAW
SKRAW
UNKNOWN POWER RINGS PENETRATING LEVEL FOUR.
UNKNOWN POWER RINGS PENETRATING LEVEL THREE.
UNKNOWN POWER RINGS PENETRATING LEVEL TWO.
I KNOW, MY FRIENDS.
BUT WE WILL DO WHAT WE MUST.
UNKNOWN POWER RINGS PENETRATING LEVEL ONE.
YES, THE UPDATE IS MUCH APPRECIATED.
FOUL ABERRATIONS!
FLESH.
FLESH.
FLESH.
FLESH.
FLESH.
FLESH.
FLESH.
FLESH.
YOU DARE BREACH THE SANCTITY OF THE CRYPT?!

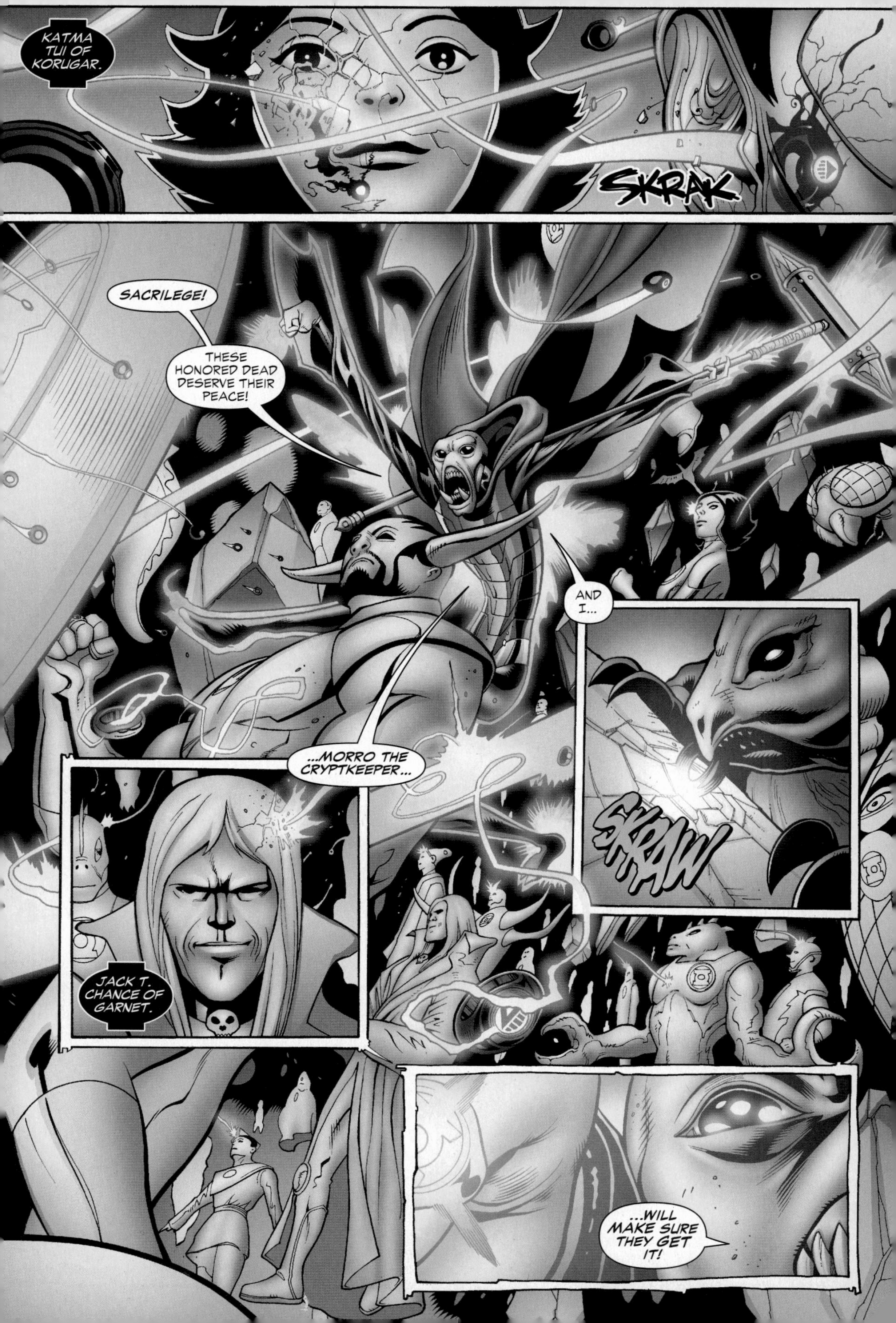
KATMA TUI OF KORUGAR.
SKRAK
SACRILEGE!
THESE HONORED DEAD DESERVE THEIR PEACE!
AND I...
...MORRO THE CRYPTKEEPER...
SKRAW
JACK T. CHANCE OF GARNET.
...WILL MAKE SURE THEY GET IT!

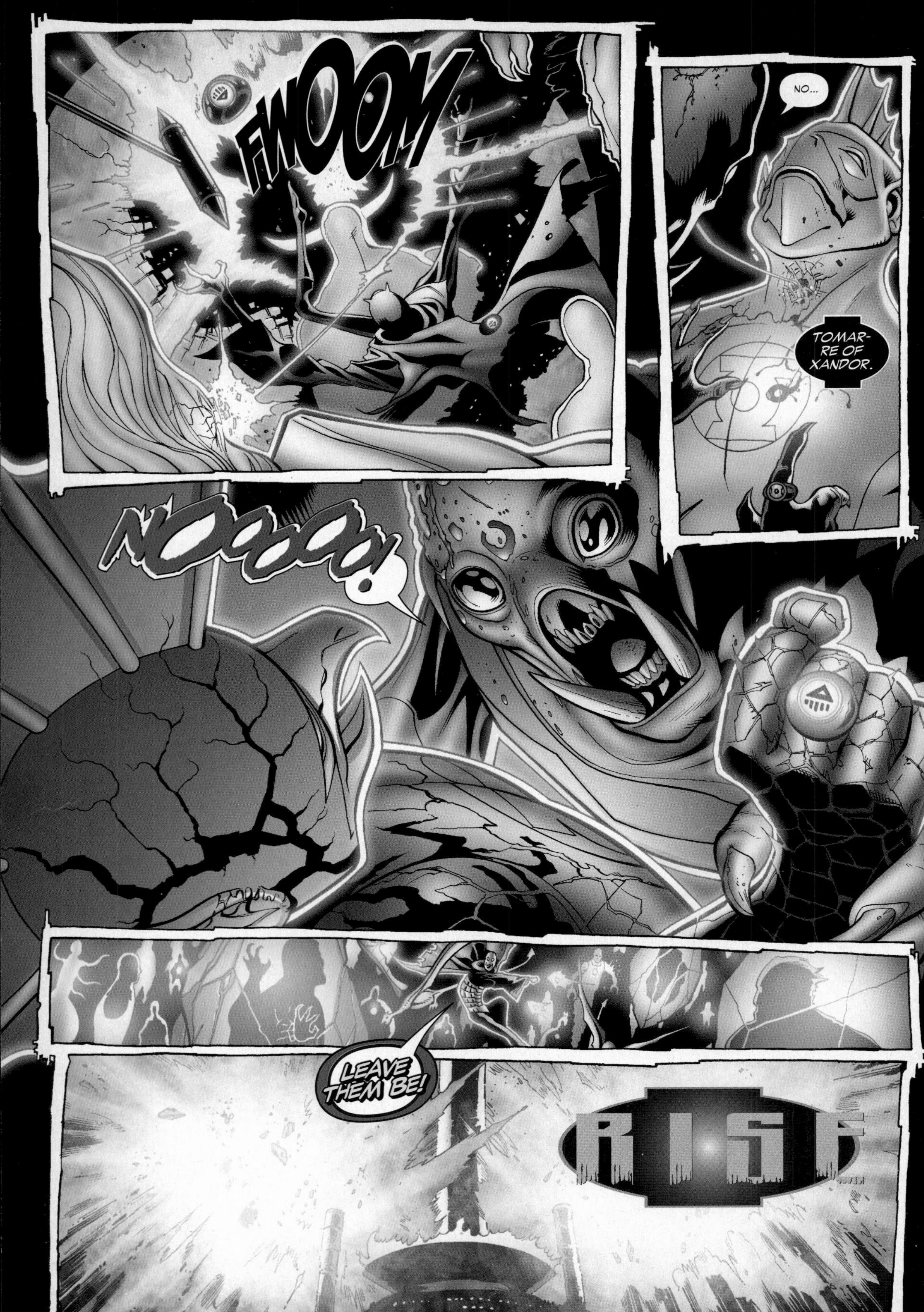
FWOOM
NO...
TOMARE-RE OF XANDOR.
NOOOOO!
LEAVE THEM BE!
RISE

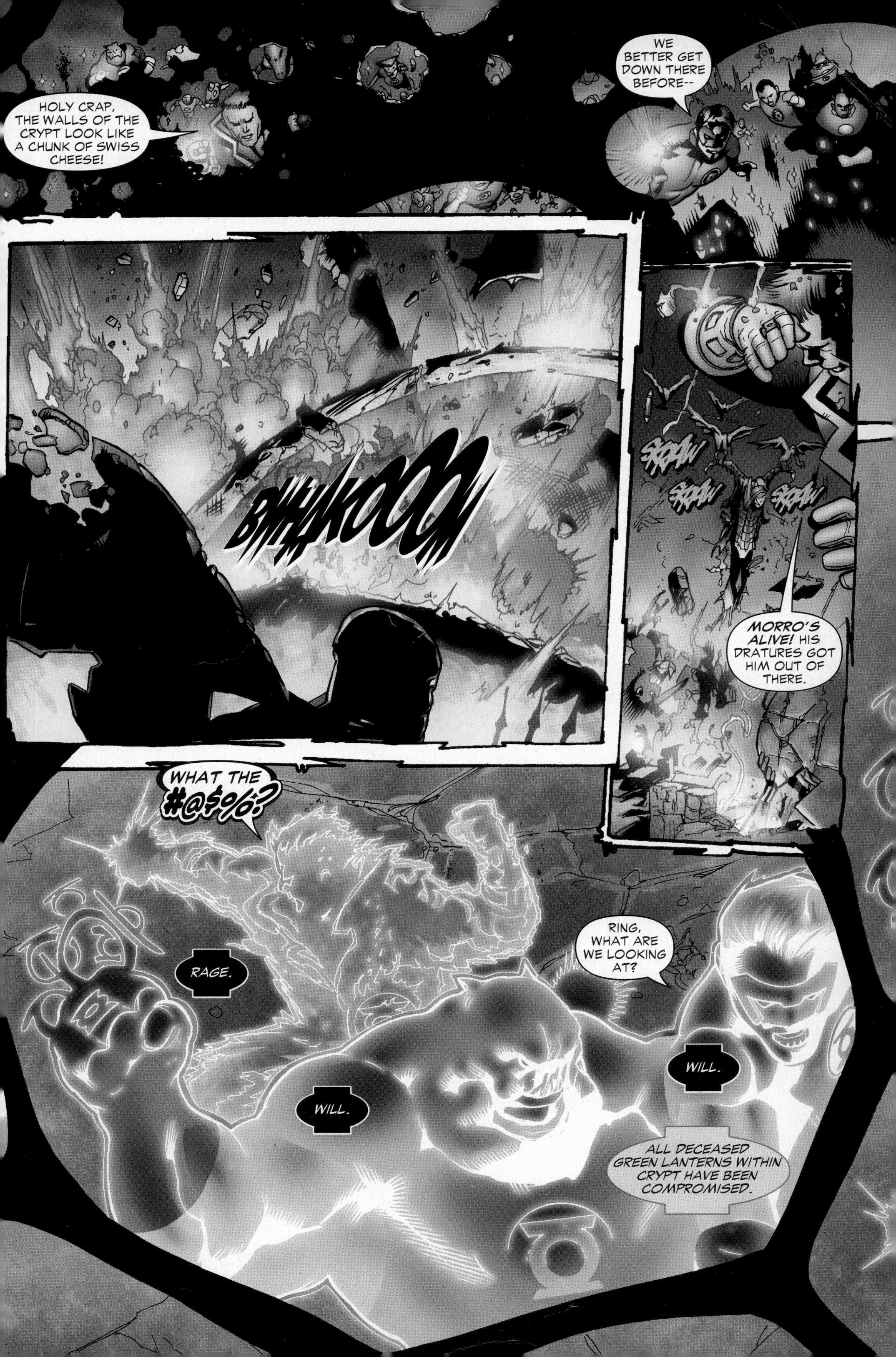
HOLY CRAP, THE WALLS OF THE CRYPT LOOK LIKE A CHUNK OF SWISS CHEESE!
WE BETTER GET DOWN THERE BEFORE--
BHHAKOOOOM
SKRAW
SKRAW
SKRAW
MORRO'S ALIVE! HIS DRATURES GOT HIM OUT OF THERE.
WHAT THE #@$%?
RING, WHAT ARE WE LOOKING AT?
RAGE.
WILL.
WILL.
ALL DECEASED GREEN LANTERNS WITHIN CRYPT HAVE BEEN COMPROMISED.

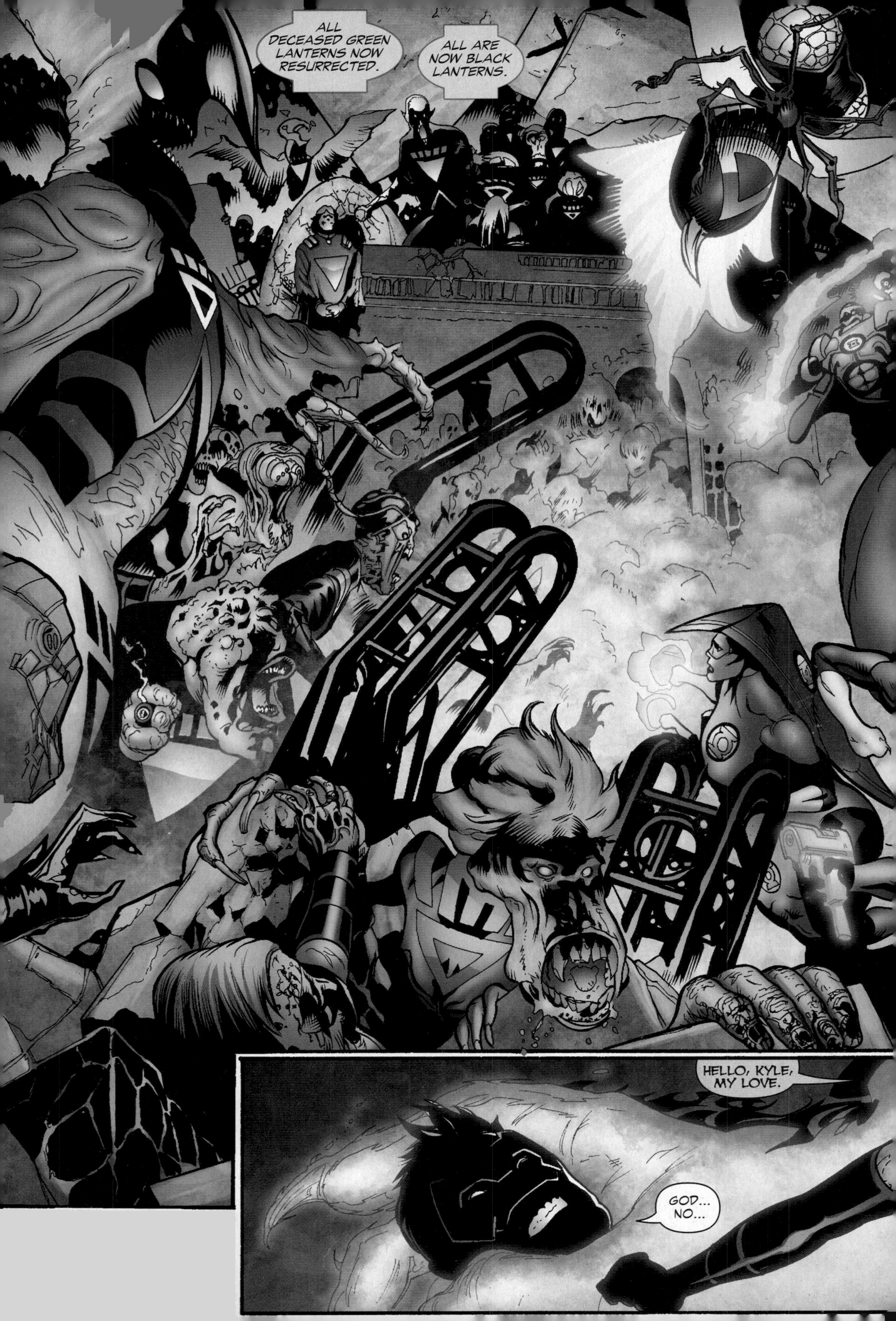
ALL DECEASED GREEN LANTERNS NOW RESURRECTED.
ALL ARE NOW BLACK LANTERNS.
HELLO, KYLE, MY LOVE.
GOD... NO...

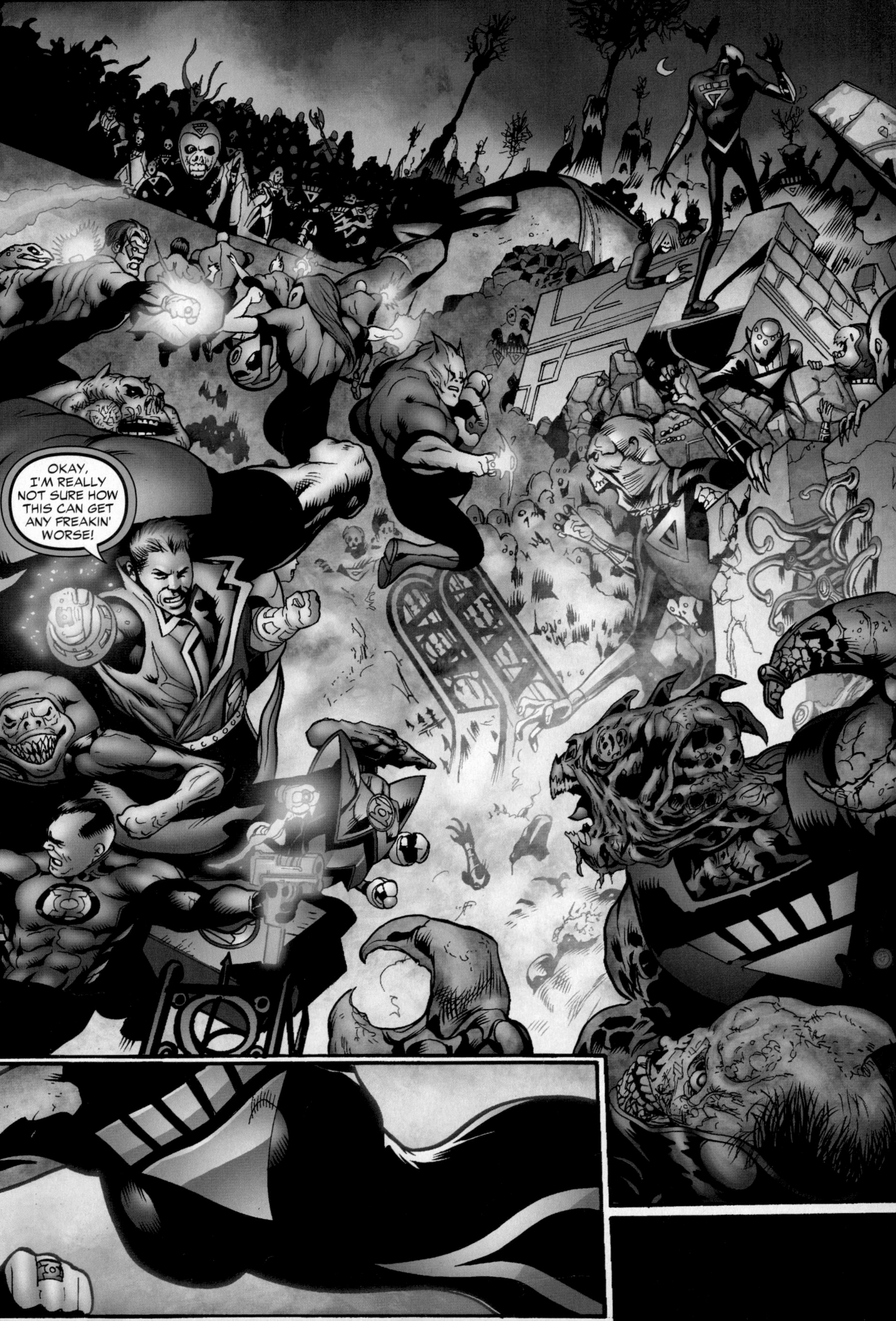
OKAY, I'M REALLY NOT SURE HOW THIS CAN GET ANY FREAKIN' WORSE!

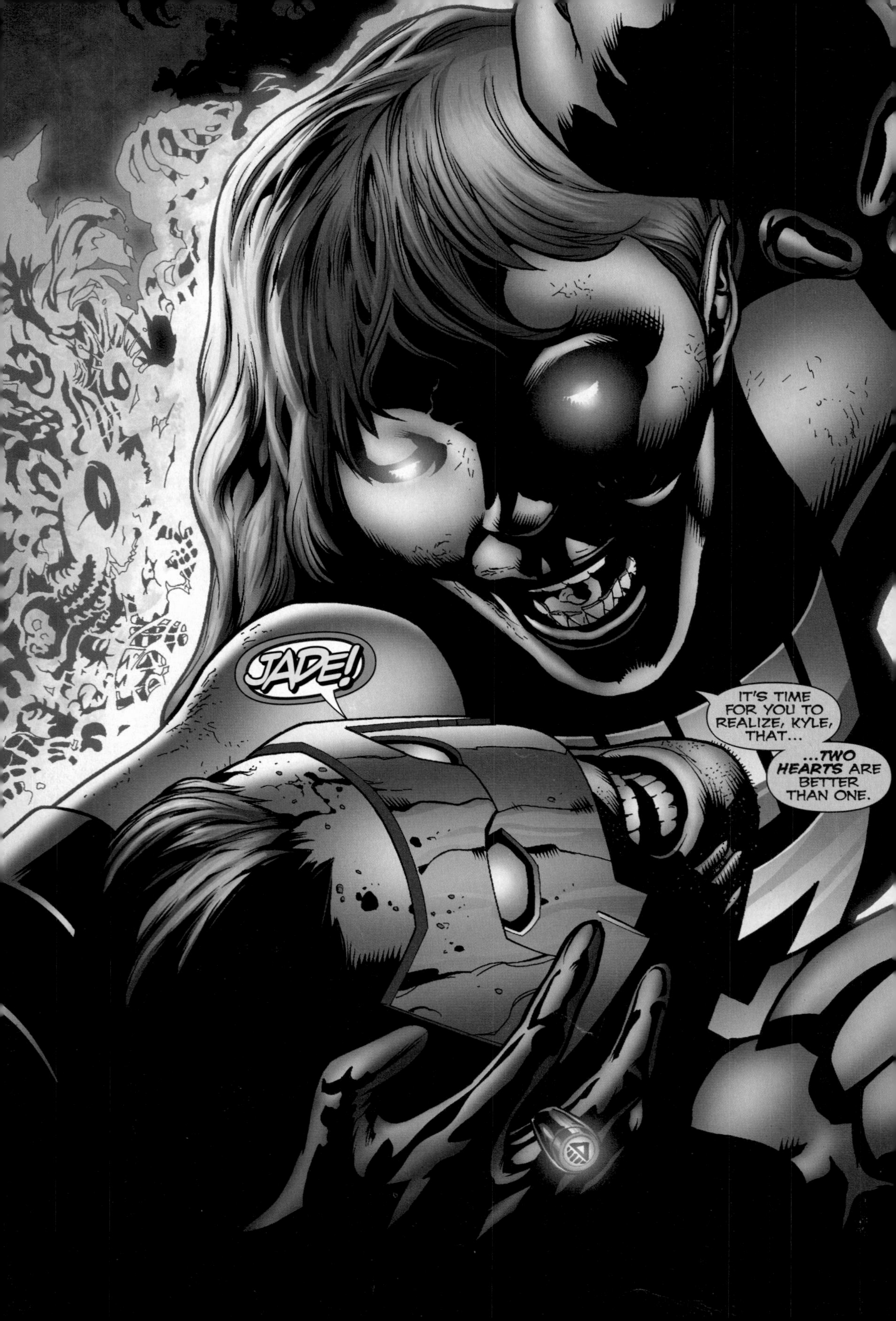
JADE!
IT'S TIME FOR YOU TO REALIZE, KYLE, THAT...
...TWO HEARTS ARE BETTER THAN ONE.

GREEN LANTERN CORPS 40
Cover by Patrick Gleason and
Rebecca Buchman with Randy Mayor

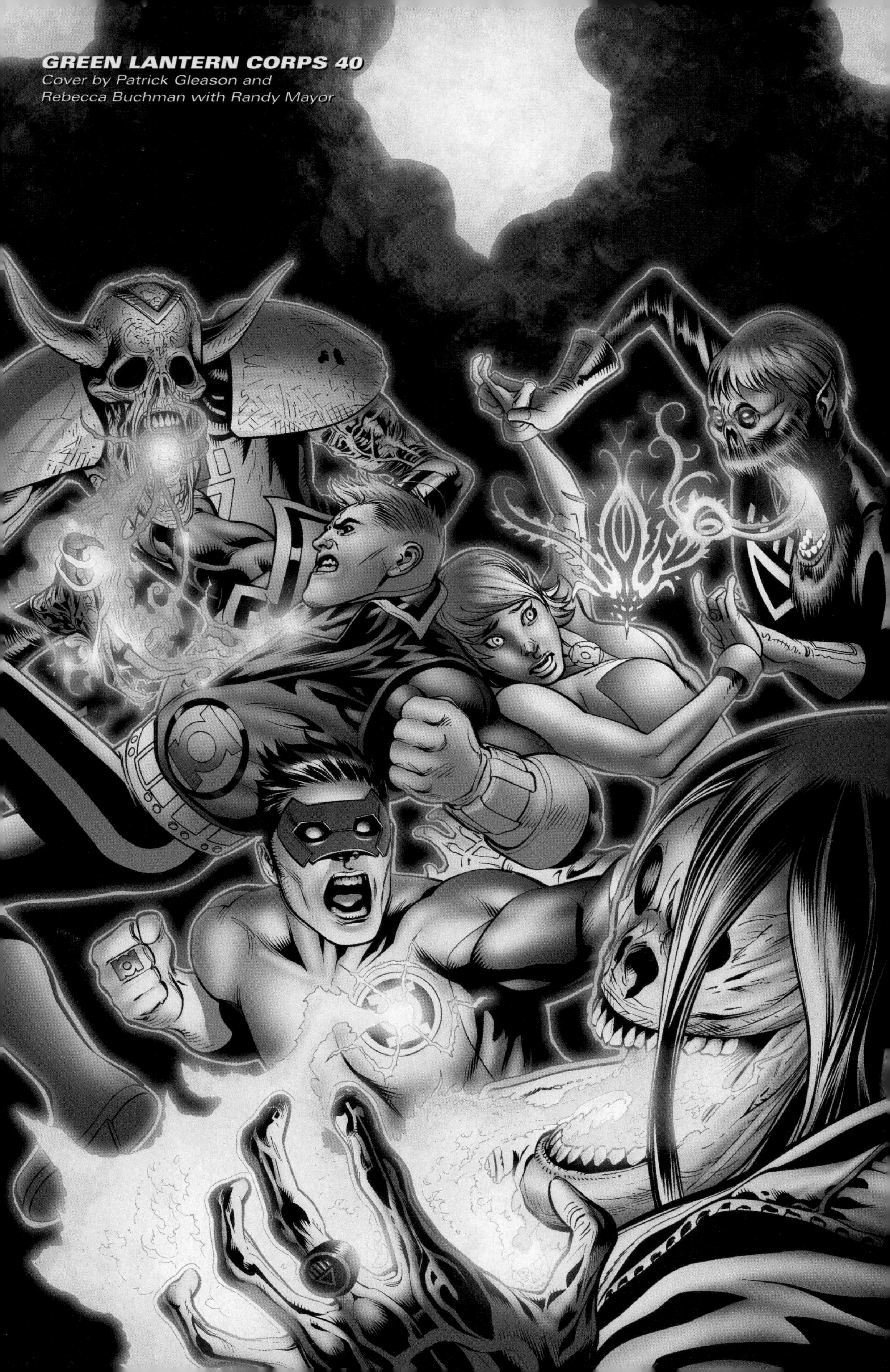

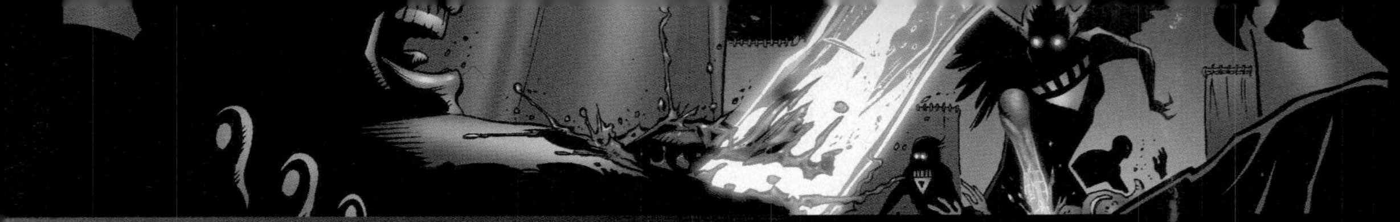

HEART OF DARKNESS

PATRICK GLEASON
PENCILS

REBECCA BUCHMAN
TOM NGUYEN
PRENTIS ROLLINS
INKS

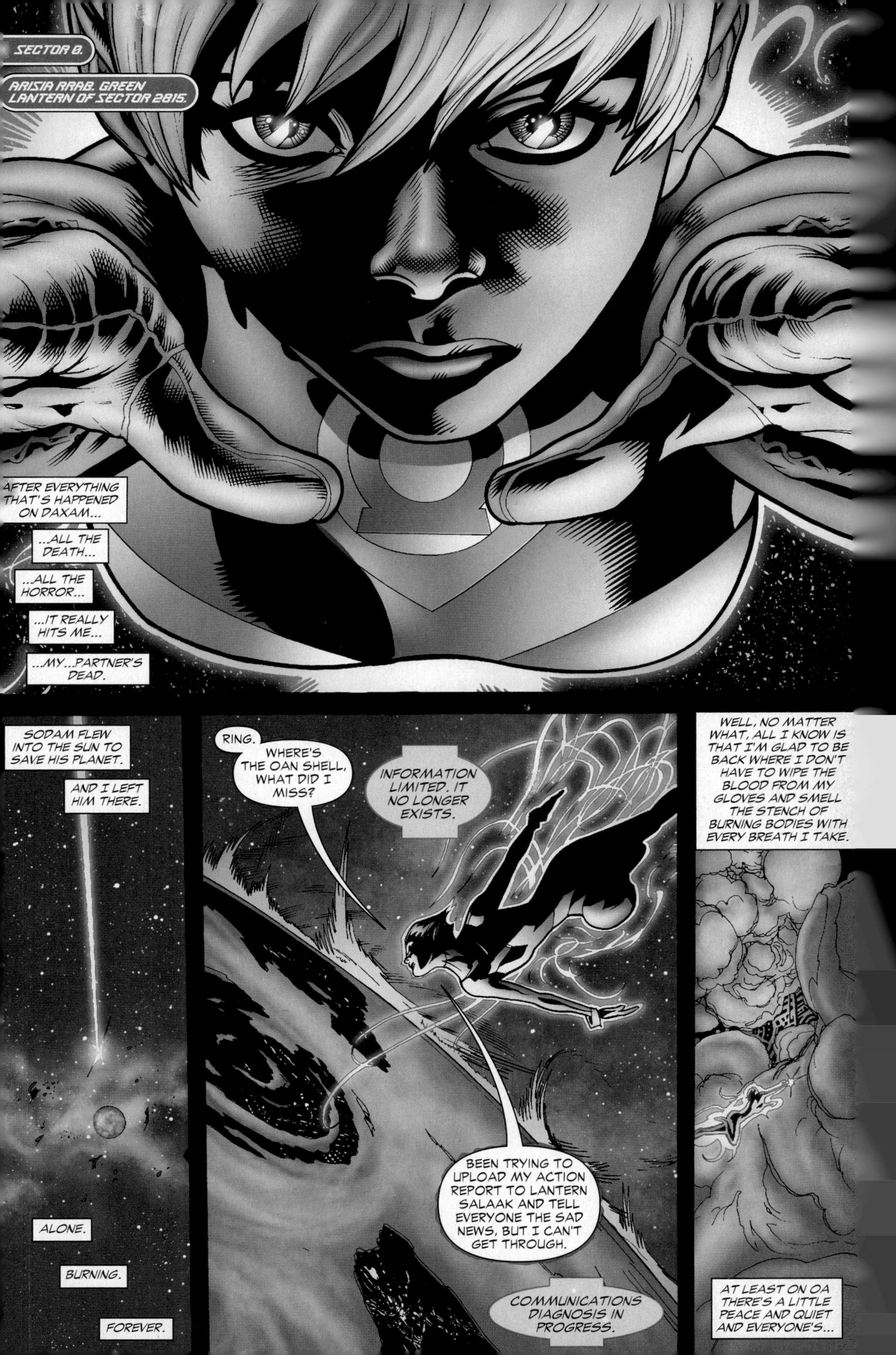
SECTOR 0.
ARISIA RRAB, GREEN LANTERN OF SECTOR 2815.
AFTER EVERYTHING THAT'S HAPPENED ON DAXAM...
...ALL THE DEATH...
...ALL THE HORROR...
...IT REALLY HITS ME...
...MY...PARTNER'S DEAD.
SODAM FLEW INTO THE SUN TO SAVE HIS PLANET.
AND I LEFT HIM THERE.
ALONE.
BURNING.
FOREVER.
RING.
WHERE'S THE OAN SHELL, WHAT DID I MISS?
INFORMATION LIMITED. IT NO LONGER EXISTS.
BEEN TRYING TO UPLOAD MY ACTION REPORT TO LANTERN SALAAK AND TELL EVERYONE THE SAD NEWS, BUT I CAN'T GET THROUGH.
COMMUNICATIONS DIAGNOSIS IN PROGRESS.
WELL, NO MATTER WHAT, ALL I KNOW IS THAT I'M GLAD TO BE BACK WHERE I DON'T HAVE TO WIPE THE BLOOD FROM MY GLOVES AND SMELL THE STENCH OF BURNING BODIES WITH EVERY BREATH I TAKE.
AT LEAST ON OA THERE'S A LITTLE PEACE AND QUIET AND EVERYONE'S...

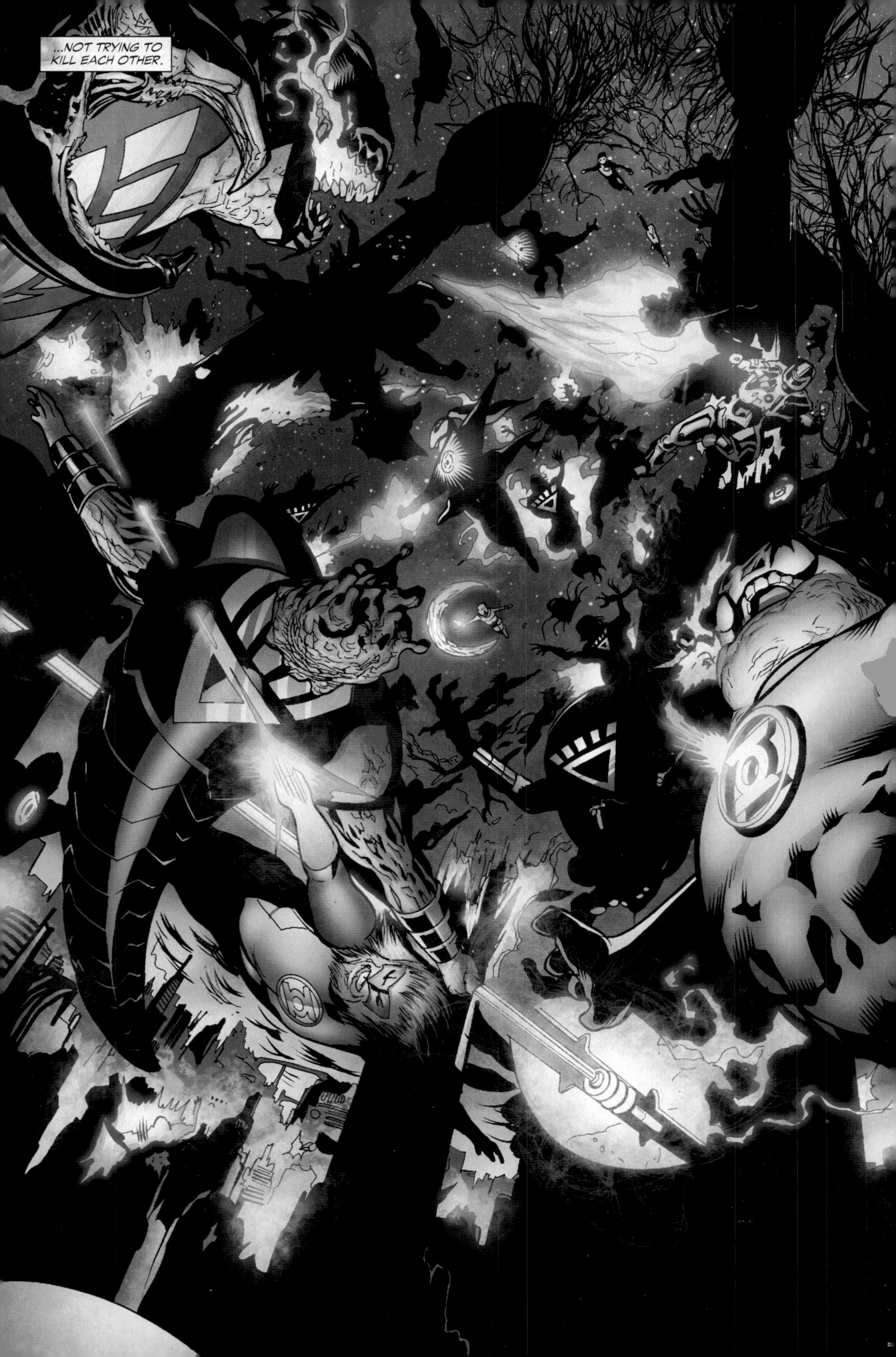
...NOT TRYING TO
KILL EACH OTHER.

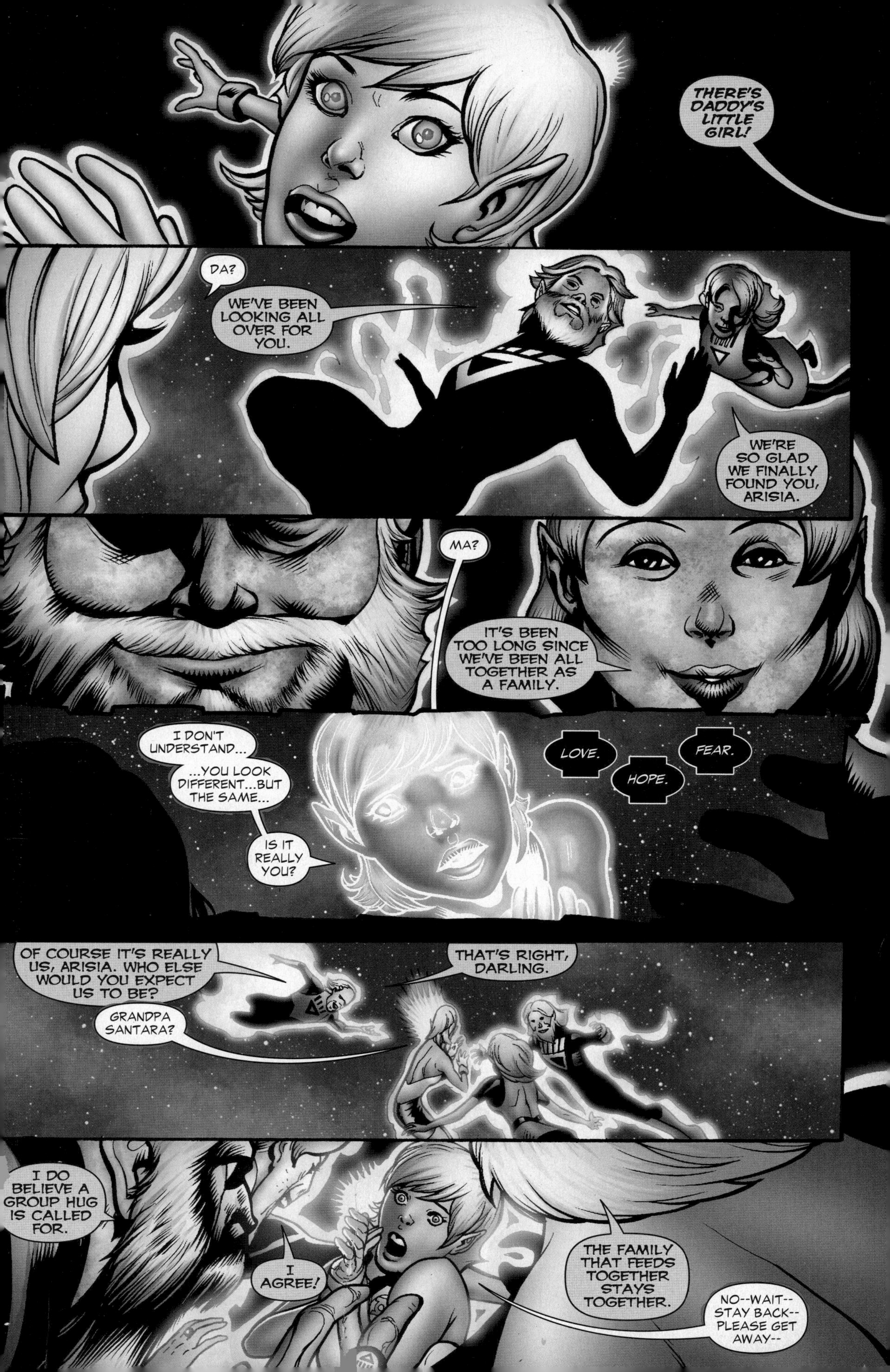
THERE'S DADDY'S LITTLE GIRL!
DA?
WE'VE BEEN LOOKING ALL OVER FOR YOU.
WE'RE SO GLAD WE FINALLY FOUND YOU, ARISIA.
MA?
IT'S BEEN TOO LONG SINCE WE'VE BEEN ALL TOGETHER AS A FAMILY.
I DON'T UNDERSTAND...
...YOU LOOK DIFFERENT...BUT THE SAME...
IS IT REALLY YOU?
LOVE.
HOPE.
FEAR.
OF COURSE IT'S REALLY US, ARISIA. WHO ELSE WOULD YOU EXPECT US TO BE?
THAT'S RIGHT, DARLING.
GRANDPA SANTARA?
I DO BELIEVE A GROUP HUG IS CALLED FOR.
I AGREE!
THE FAMILY THAT FEEDS TOGETHER STAYS TOGETHER.
NO--WAIT--STAY BACK--PLEASE GET AWAY--

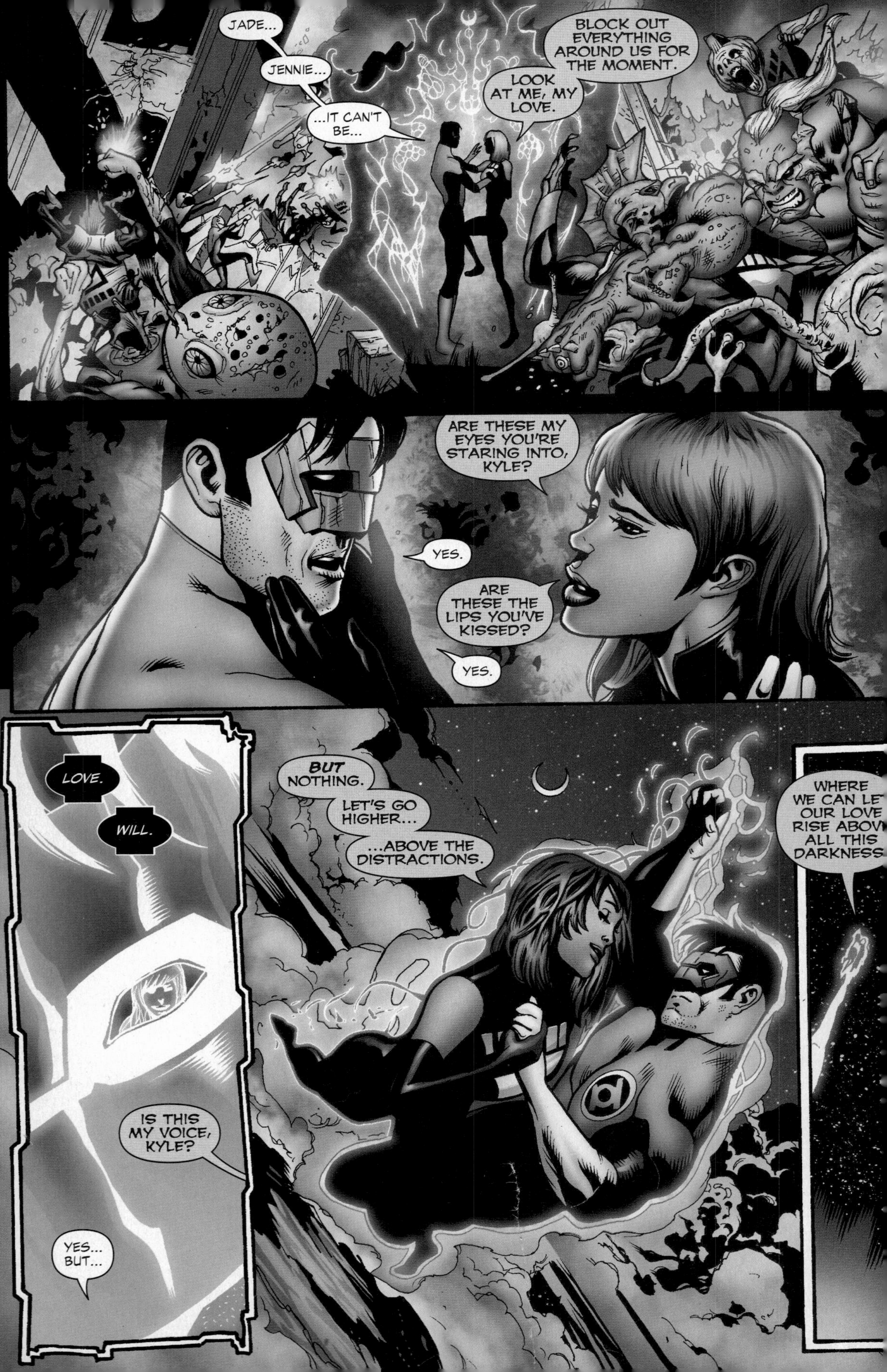
JADE...
JENNIE...
...IT CAN'T BE...
BLOCK OUT EVERYTHING AROUND US FOR THE MOMENT.
LOOK AT ME, MY LOVE.
ARE THESE MY EYES YOU'RE STARING INTO, KYLE?
YES.
ARE THESE THE LIPS YOU'VE KISSED?
YES.
LOVE.
WILL.
IS THIS MY VOICE, KYLE?
YES... BUT...
BUT NOTHING.
LET'S GO HIGHER...
...ABOVE THE DISTRACTIONS.
WHERE WE CAN LE OUR LOVE RISE ABOV ALL THIS DARKNESS

KYLE, I UNDERSTAND HOW STRANGE THIS ALL SEEMS...

...BUT I'M HERE *BECAUSE* OF YOU.

YOU BROUGHT ME HERE.

HOW DID I BRING YOU HERE?

YOUR UNDYING LOVE FOR ME.

IT'S ANCHORED ME.

KEPT ME WARM.

WANTING...

...*NEEDING*...

...YOUR TOUCH HAS KEPT ME WARMER.

JEN...

EVERYTHING WE SHARED TOGETHER.

OUR LIVES.

OUR HEARTS.

OUR SOULS.

LOVE NEVER DIES.

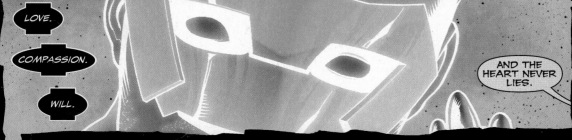

LOVE.

COMPASSION.

WILL.

AND THE HEART NEVER LIES.

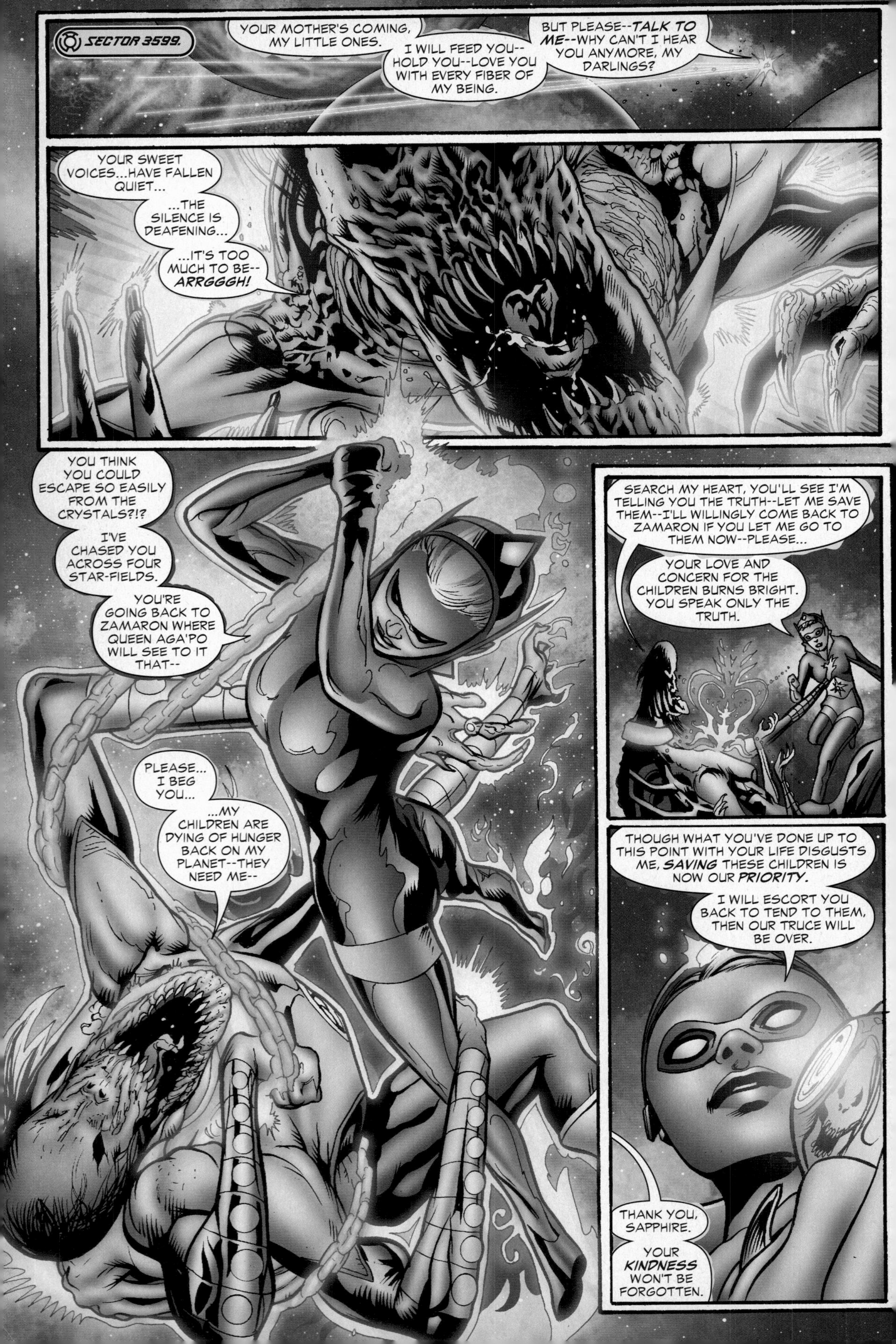
SECTOR 3599.
YOUR MOTHER'S COMING, MY LITTLE ONES.
I WILL FEED YOU--HOLD YOU--LOVE YOU WITH EVERY FIBER OF MY BEING.
BUT PLEASE--TALK TO ME--WHY CAN'T I HEAR YOU ANYMORE, MY DARLINGS?
YOUR SWEET VOICES...HAVE FALLEN QUIET...
...THE SILENCE IS DEAFENING...
...IT'S TOO MUCH TO BE--ARRGGGH!
YOU THINK YOU COULD ESCAPE SO EASILY FROM THE CRYSTALS?!?
I'VE CHASED YOU ACROSS FOUR STAR-FIELDS.
YOU'RE GOING BACK TO ZAMARON WHERE QUEEN AGA'PO WILL SEE TO IT THAT--
PLEASE... I BEG YOU...
...MY CHILDREN ARE DYING OF HUNGER BACK ON MY PLANET--THEY NEED ME--
SEARCH MY HEART, YOU'LL SEE I'M TELLING YOU THE TRUTH--LET ME SAVE THEM--I'LL WILLINGLY COME BACK TO ZAMARON IF YOU LET ME GO TO THEM NOW--PLEASE...
YOUR LOVE AND CONCERN FOR THE CHILDREN BURNS BRIGHT. YOU SPEAK ONLY THE TRUTH.
THOUGH WHAT YOU'VE DONE UP TO THIS POINT WITH YOUR LIFE DISGUSTS ME, SAVING THESE CHILDREN IS NOW OUR PRIORITY.
I WILL ESCORT YOU BACK TO TEND TO THEM, THEN OUR TRUCE WILL BE OVER.
THANK YOU, SAPPHIRE.
YOUR KINDNESS WON'T BE FORGOTTEN.

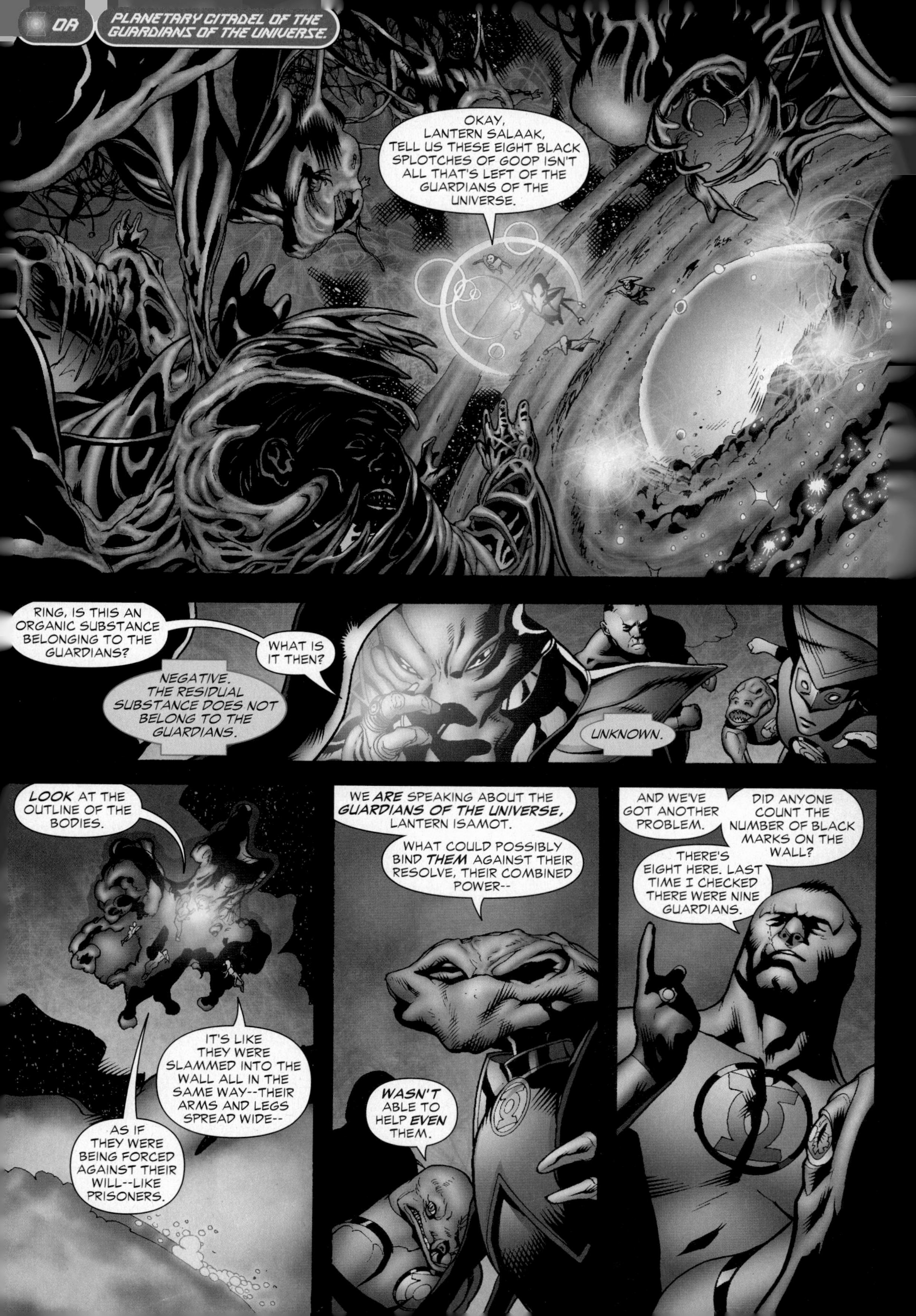
OA
PLANETARY CITADEL OF THE GUARDIANS OF THE UNIVERSE.
OKAY, LANTERN SALAAK, TELL US THESE EIGHT BLACK SPLOTCHES OF GOOP ISN'T ALL THAT'S LEFT OF THE GUARDIANS OF THE UNIVERSE.
RING, IS THIS AN ORGANIC SUBSTANCE BELONGING TO THE GUARDIANS?
NEGATIVE. THE RESIDUAL SUBSTANCE DOES NOT BELONG TO THE GUARDIANS.
WHAT IS IT THEN?
UNKNOWN.
LOOK AT THE OUTLINE OF THE BODIES.
IT'S LIKE THEY WERE SLAMMED INTO THE WALL ALL IN THE SAME WAY--THEIR ARMS AND LEGS SPREAD WIDE--
AS IF THEY WERE BEING FORCED AGAINST THEIR WILL--LIKE PRISONERS.
WE ARE SPEAKING ABOUT THE GUARDIANS OF THE UNIVERSE, LANTERN ISAMOT.
WHAT COULD POSSIBLY BIND THEM AGAINST THEIR RESOLVE, THEIR COMBINED POWER--
WASN'T ABLE TO HELP EVEN THEM.
AND WE'VE GOT ANOTHER PROBLEM.
DID ANYONE COUNT THE NUMBER OF BLACK MARKS ON THE WALL?
THERE'S EIGHT HERE. LAST TIME I CHECKED THERE WERE NINE GUARDIANS.

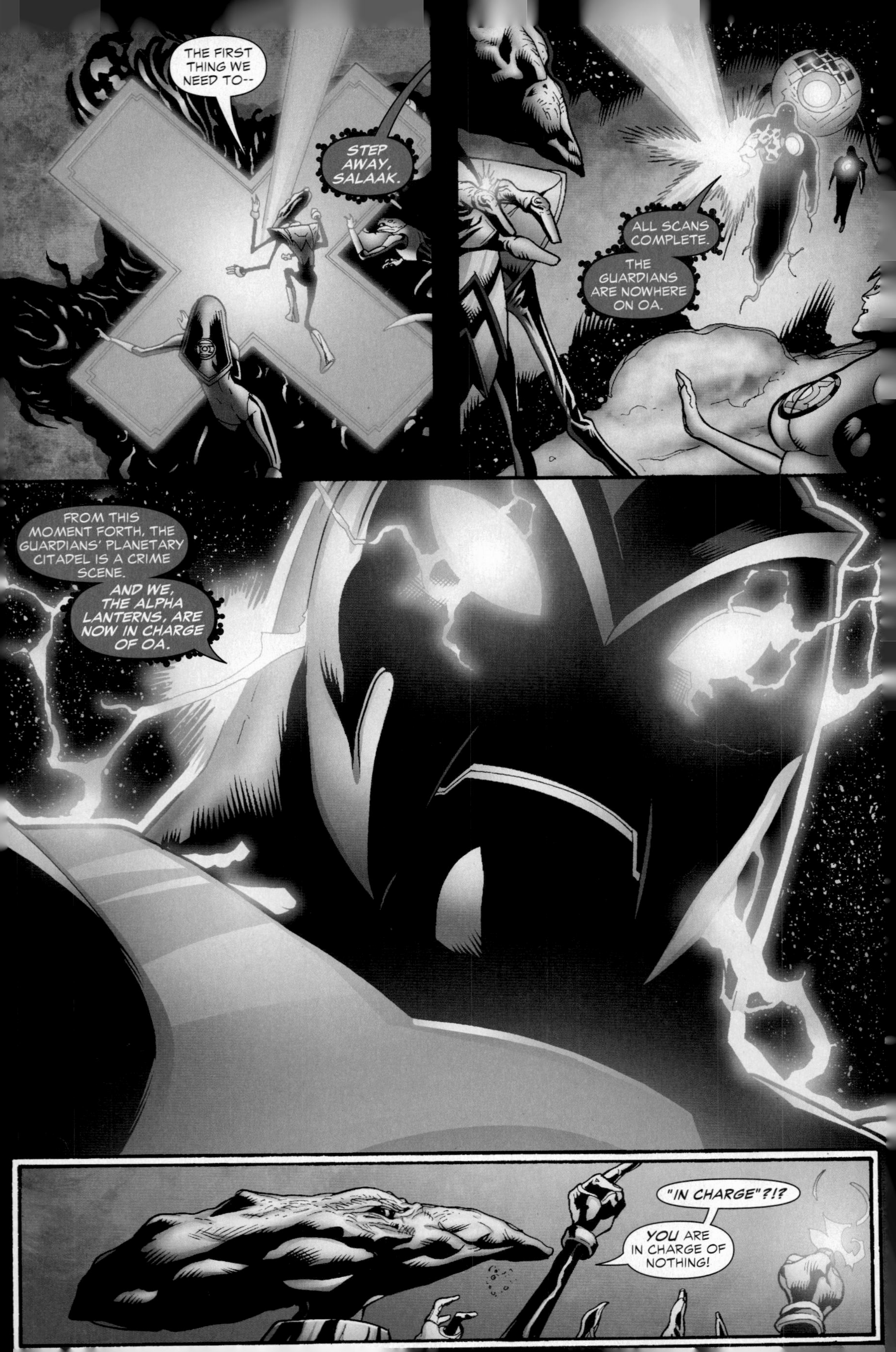
THE FIRST THING WE NEED TO--
STEP AWAY, SALAAK.
ALL SCANS COMPLETE.
THE GUARDIANS ARE NOWHERE ON OA.
FROM THIS MOMENT FORTH, THE GUARDIANS' PLANETARY CITADEL IS A CRIME SCENE.
AND WE, THE ALPHA LANTERNS, ARE NOW IN CHARGE OF OA.
"IN CHARGE"?!?
YOU ARE IN CHARGE OF NOTHING!

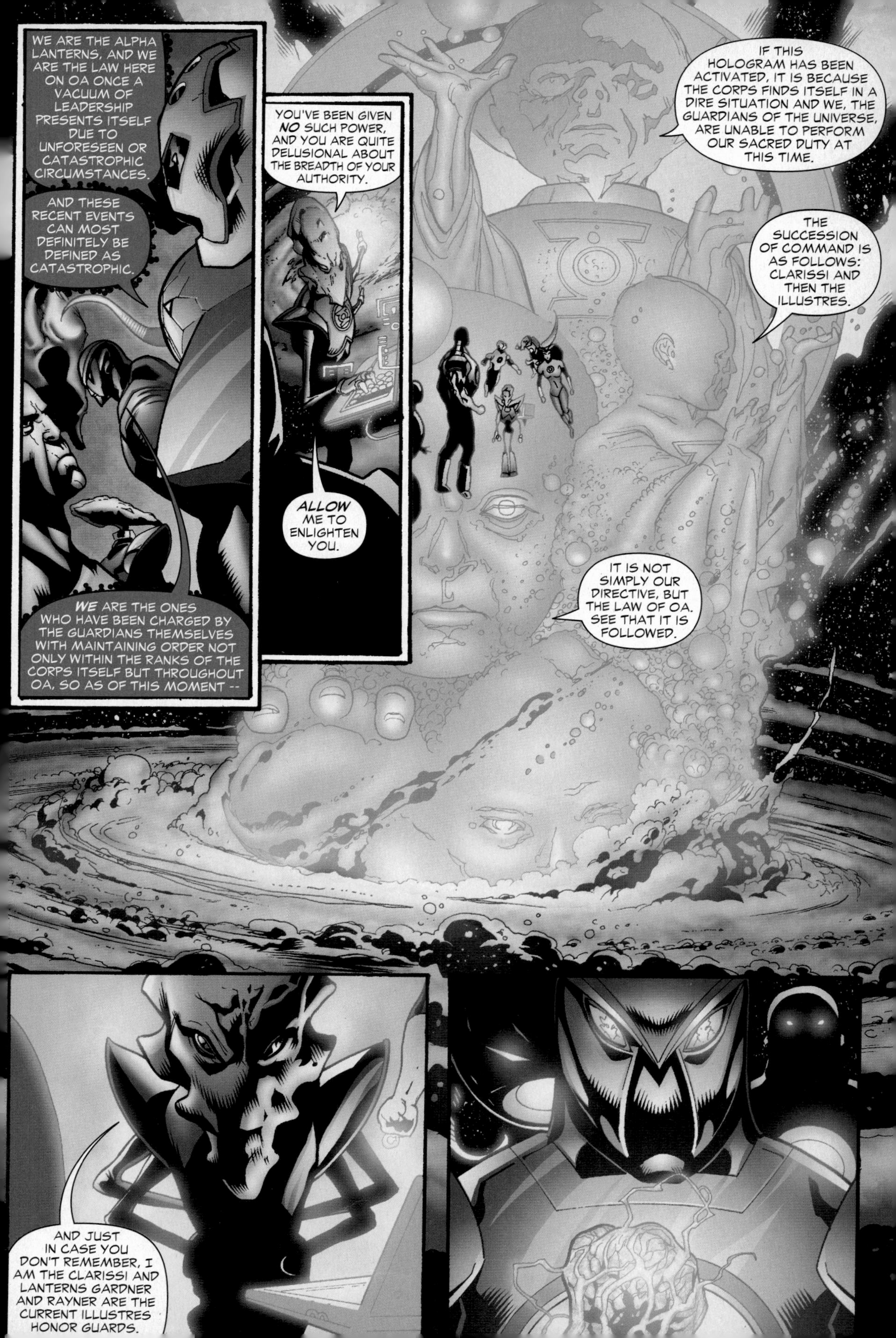
WE ARE THE ALPHA LANTERNS, AND WE ARE THE LAW HERE ON OA ONCE A VACUUM OF LEADERSHIP PRESENTS ITSELF DUE TO UNFORESEEN OR CATASTROPHIC CIRCUMSTANCES.
AND THESE RECENT EVENTS CAN MOST DEFINITELY BE DEFINED AS CATASTROPHIC.
WE ARE THE ONES WHO HAVE BEEN CHARGED BY THE GUARDIANS THEMSELVES WITH MAINTAINING ORDER NOT ONLY WITHIN THE RANKS OF THE CORPS ITSELF BUT THROUGHOUT OA, SO AS OF THIS MOMENT --
YOU'VE BEEN GIVEN NO SUCH POWER, AND YOU ARE QUITE DELUSIONAL ABOUT THE BREADTH OF YOUR AUTHORITY.
ALLOW ME TO ENLIGHTEN YOU.
IF THIS HOLOGRAM HAS BEEN ACTIVATED, IT IS BECAUSE THE CORPS FINDS ITSELF IN A DIRE SITUATION AND WE, THE GUARDIANS OF THE UNIVERSE, ARE UNABLE TO PERFORM OUR SACRED DUTY AT THIS TIME.
THE SUCCESSION OF COMMAND IS AS FOLLOWS: CLARISSI AND THEN THE ILLUSTRES.
IT IS NOT SIMPLY OUR DIRECTIVE, BUT THE LAW OF OA. SEE THAT IT IS FOLLOWED.
AND JUST IN CASE YOU DON'T REMEMBER, I AM THE CLARISSI AND LANTERNS GARDNER AND RAYNER ARE THE CURRENT ILLUSTRES HONOR GUARDS.

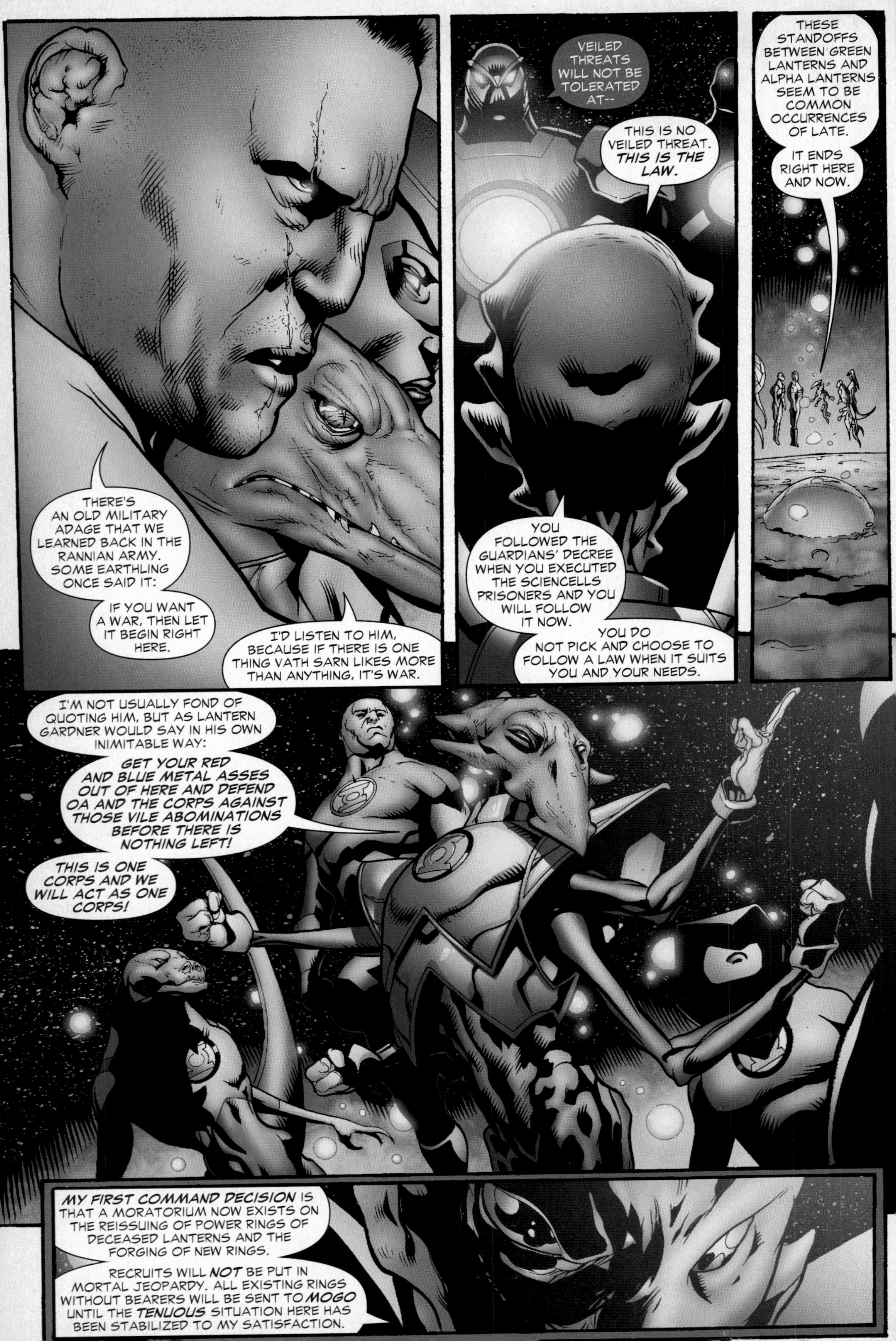

THERE'S AN OLD MILITARY ADAGE THAT WE LEARNED BACK IN THE RANNIAN ARMY. SOME EARTHLING ONCE SAID IT:
IF YOU WANT A WAR, THEN LET IT BEGIN RIGHT HERE.
I'D LISTEN TO HIM, BECAUSE IF THERE IS ONE THING VATH SARN LIKES MORE THAN ANYTHING, IT'S WAR.
VEILED THREATS WILL NOT BE TOLERATED AT--
THIS IS NO VEILED THREAT. ***THIS IS THE LAW.***
YOU FOLLOWED THE GUARDIANS' DECREE WHEN YOU EXECUTED THE SCIENCELLS PRISONERS AND YOU WILL FOLLOW IT NOW.
YOU DO NOT PICK AND CHOOSE TO FOLLOW A LAW WHEN IT SUITS YOU AND YOUR NEEDS.
THESE STANDOFFS BETWEEN GREEN LANTERNS AND ALPHA LANTERNS SEEM TO BE COMMON OCCURRENCES OF LATE.
IT ENDS RIGHT HERE AND NOW.
I'M NOT USUALLY FOND OF QUOTING HIM, BUT AS LANTERN GARDNER WOULD SAY IN HIS OWN INIMITABLE WAY:
GET YOUR RED AND BLUE METAL ASSES OUT OF HERE AND DEFEND OA AND THE CORPS AGAINST THOSE VILE ABOMINATIONS BEFORE THERE IS NOTHING LEFT!
THIS IS ONE CORPS AND WE WILL ACT AS ONE CORPS!
MY FIRST COMMAND DECISION IS THAT A MORATORIUM NOW EXISTS ON THE REISSUING OF POWER RINGS OF DECEASED LANTERNS AND THE FORGING OF NEW RINGS.
RECRUITS WILL ***NOT*** BE PUT IN MORTAL JEOPARDY. ALL EXISTING RINGS WITHOUT BEARERS WILL BE SENT TO ***MOGO*** UNTIL THE ***TENUOUS*** SITUATION HERE HAS BEEN STABILIZED TO MY SATISFACTION.

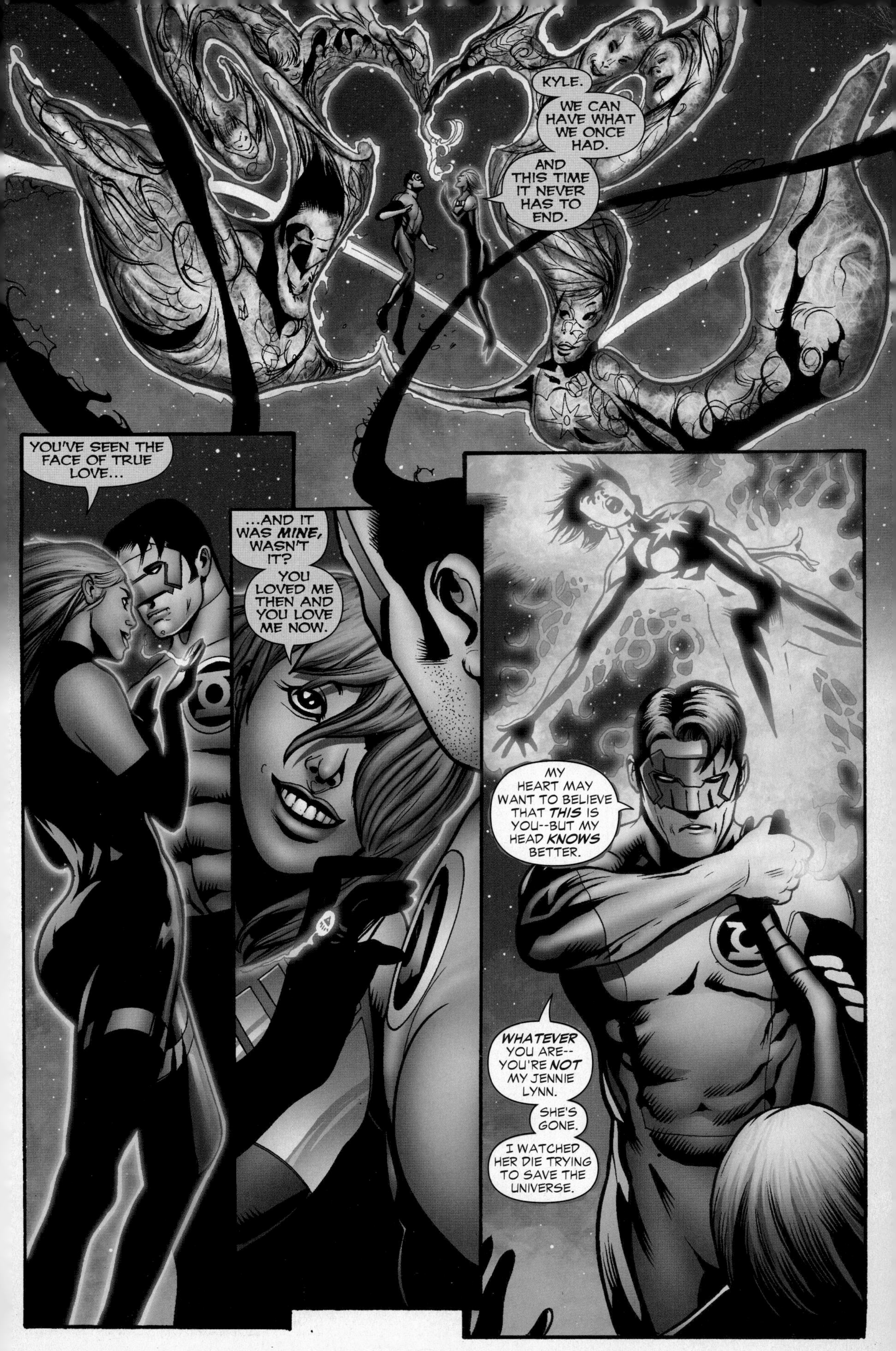

KYLE.
WE CAN HAVE WHAT WE ONCE HAD.
AND THIS TIME IT NEVER HAS TO END.
YOU'VE SEEN THE FACE OF TRUE LOVE...
...AND IT WAS *MINE,* WASN'T IT?
YOU LOVED ME THEN AND YOU LOVE ME NOW.
MY HEART MAY WANT TO BELIEVE THAT *THIS* IS YOU--BUT MY HEAD *KNOWS* BETTER.
WHATEVER YOU ARE--YOU'RE *NOT* MY JENNIE LYNN.
SHE'S GONE.
I WATCHED HER DIE TRYING TO SAVE THE UNIVERSE.

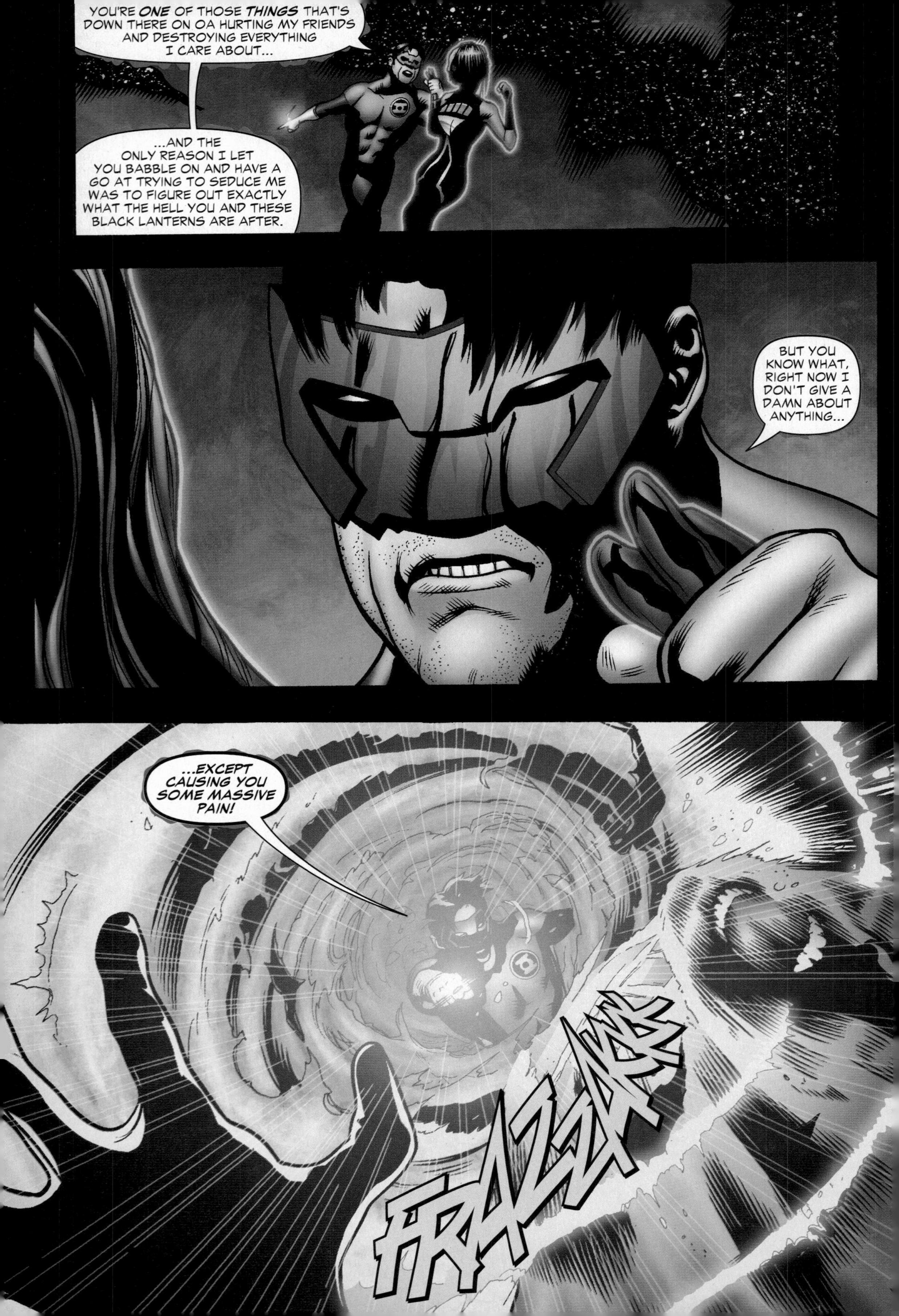
YOU'RE ONE OF THOSE THINGS THAT'S DOWN THERE ON OA HURTING MY FRIENDS AND DESTROYING EVERYTHING I CARE ABOUT...
...AND THE ONLY REASON I LET YOU BABBLE ON AND HAVE A GO AT TRYING TO SEDUCE ME WAS TO FIGURE OUT EXACTLY WHAT THE HELL YOU AND THESE BLACK LANTERNS ARE AFTER.
BUT YOU KNOW WHAT, RIGHT NOW I DON'T GIVE A DAMN ABOUT ANYTHING...
...EXCEPT CAUSING YOU SOME MASSIVE PAIN!
FRAZZAKK

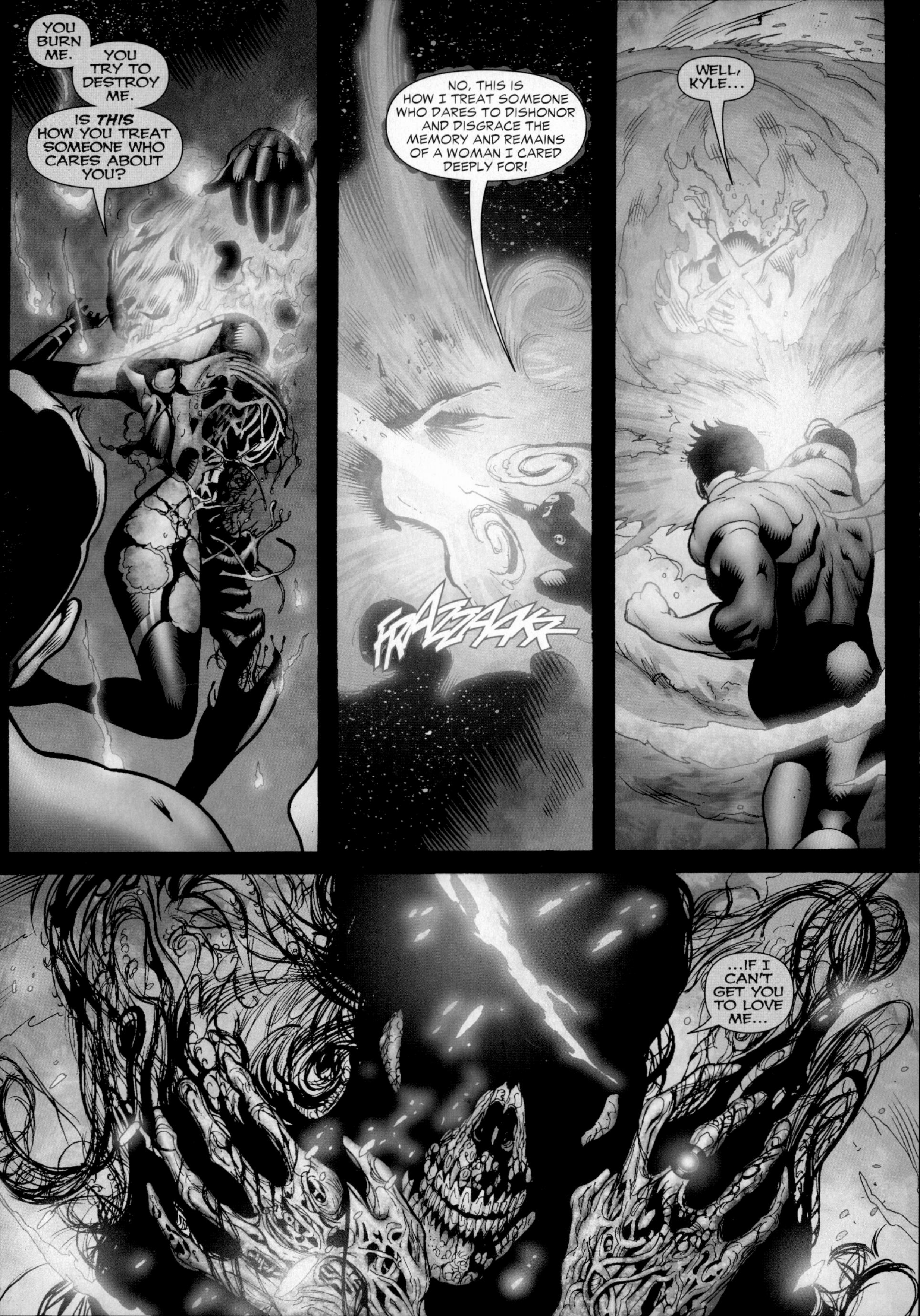
YOU BURN ME.
YOU TRY TO DESTROY ME.
IS THIS HOW YOU TREAT SOMEONE WHO CARES ABOUT YOU?
NO, THIS IS HOW I TREAT SOMEONE WHO DARES TO DISHONOR AND DISGRACE THE MEMORY AND REMAINS OF A WOMAN I CARED DEEPLY FOR!
FRAZZAAKK
WELL, KYLE...
...IF I CAN'T GET YOU TO LOVE ME...

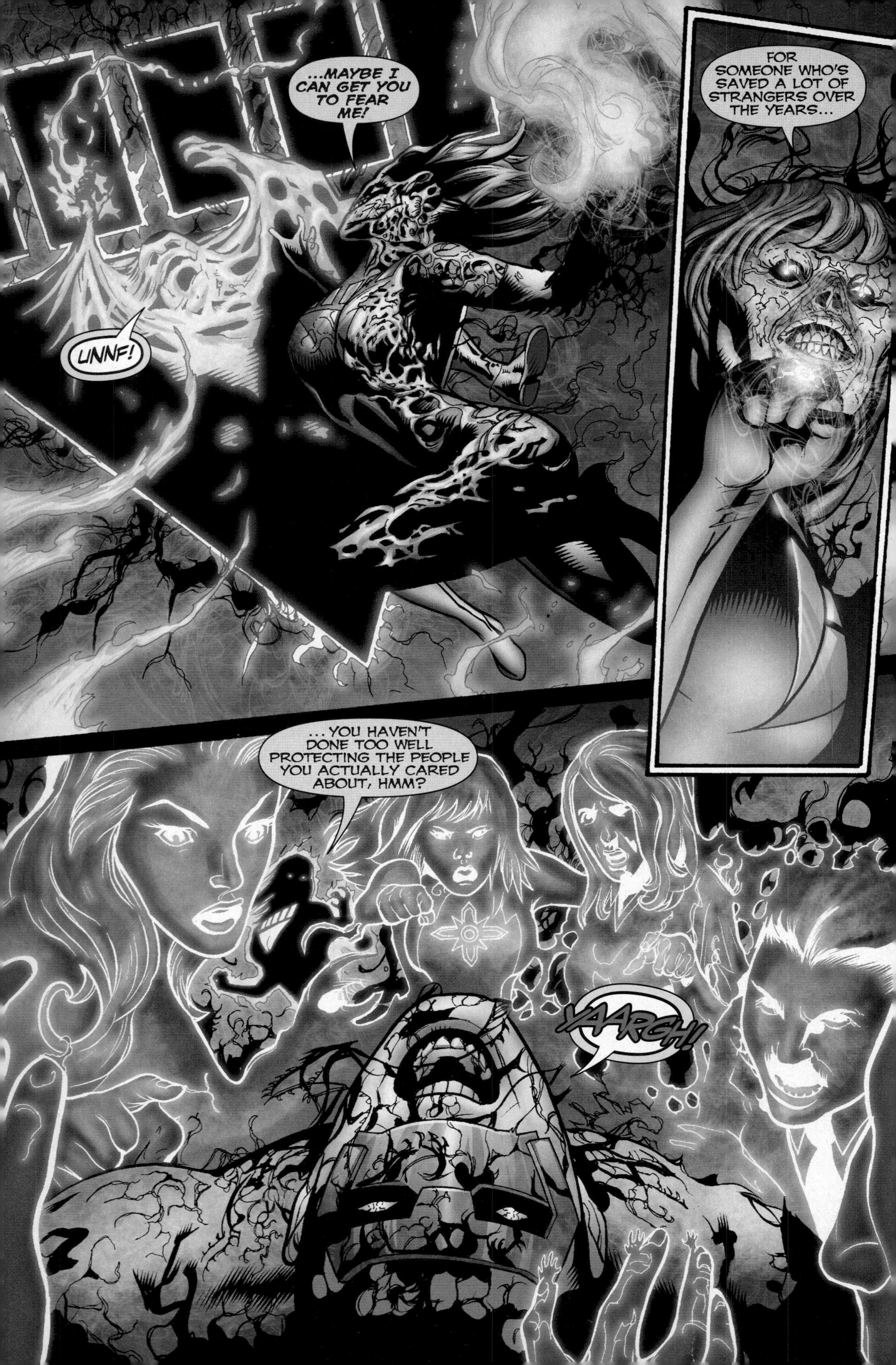
...MAYBE I CAN GET YOU TO FEAR ME!
UNNF!
FOR SOMEONE WHO'S SAVED A LOT OF STRANGERS OVER THE YEARS...
...YOU HAVEN'T DONE TOO WELL PROTECTING THE PEOPLE YOU ACTUALLY CARED ABOUT, HMM?
YAARGH!

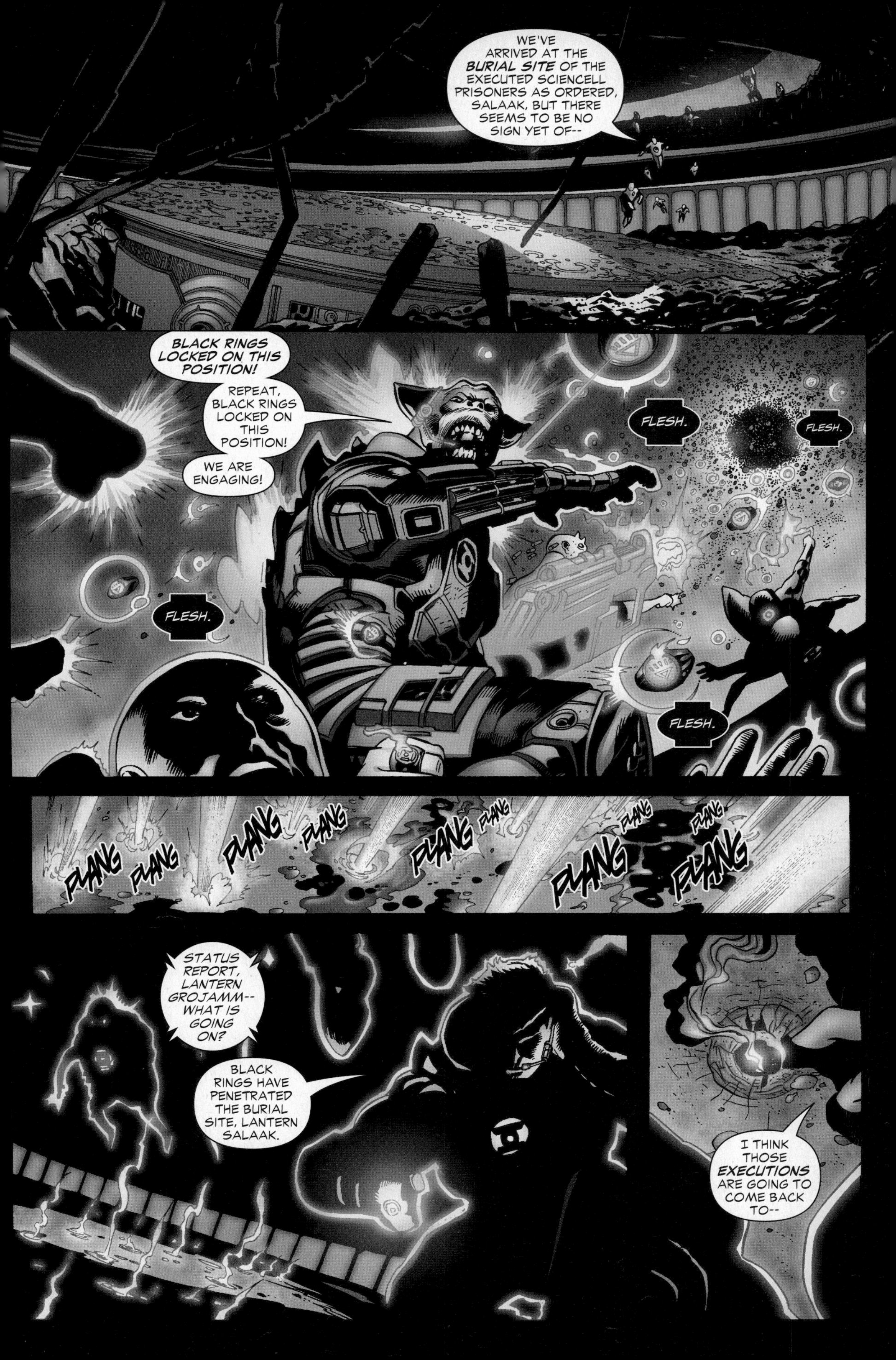
WE'VE ARRIVED AT THE BURIAL SITE OF THE EXECUTED SCIENCELL PRISONERS AS ORDERED, SALAAK, BUT THERE SEEMS TO BE NO SIGN YET OF--
BLACK RINGS LOCKED ON THIS POSITION!
REPEAT, BLACK RINGS LOCKED ON THIS POSITION!
WE ARE ENGAGING!
FLESH.
FLESH.
FLESH.
FLESH.
PLANG PLANG PLANG PLANG PLANG PLANG PLANG PLANG PLANG PLANG PLANG
STATUS REPORT, LANTERN GROJAMM-- WHAT IS GOING ON?
BLACK RINGS HAVE PENETRATED THE BURIAL SITE, LANTERN SALAAK.
I THINK THOSE EXECUTIONS ARE GOING TO COME BACK TO--

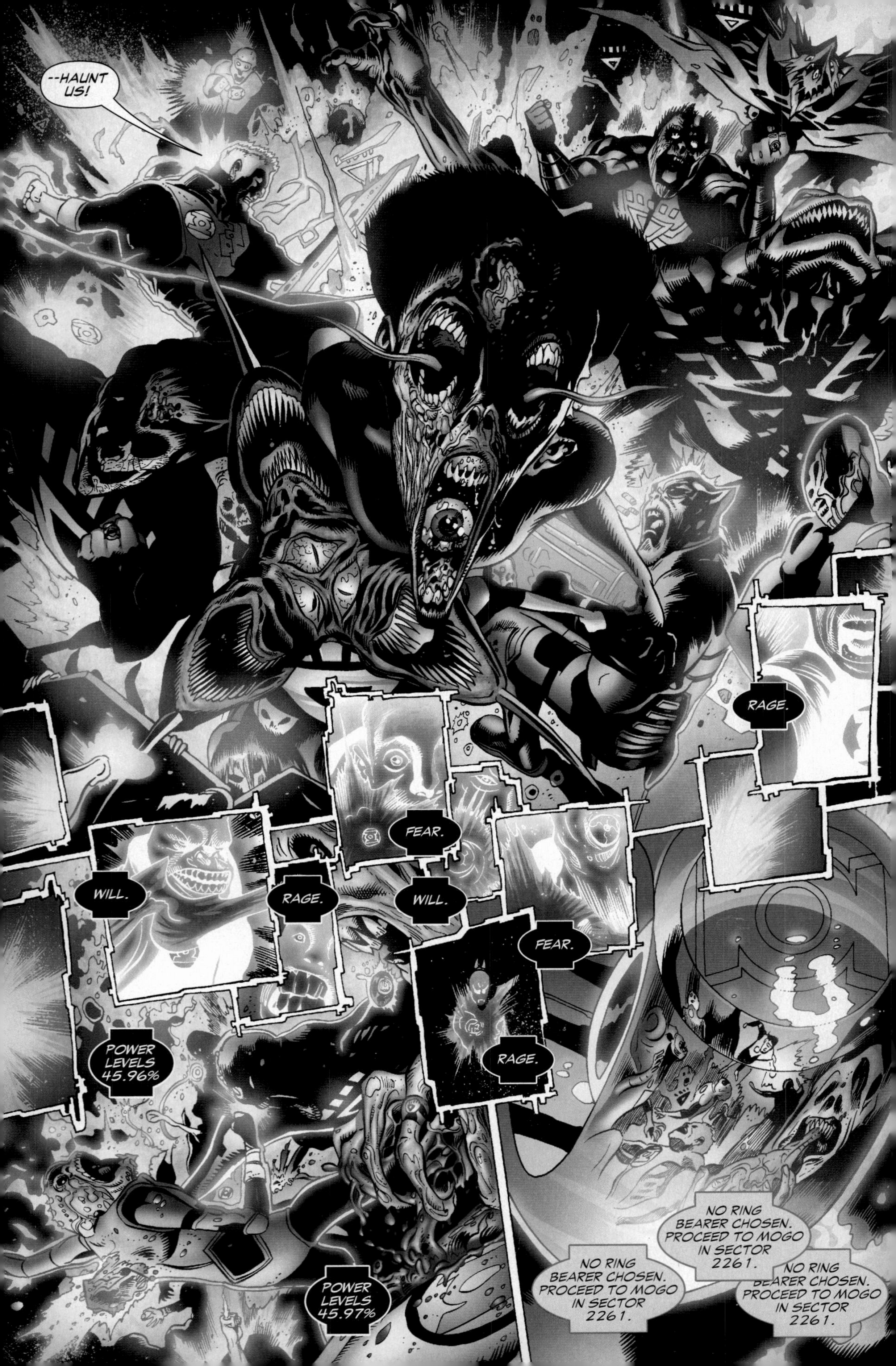
--HAUNT US!
RAGE.
FEAR.
WILL.
RAGE.
WILL.
FEAR.
RAGE.
POWER LEVELS 45.96%
POWER LEVELS 45.97%
NO RING BEARER CHOSEN. PROCEED TO MOGO IN SECTOR 2261.
NO RING BEARER CHOSEN. PROCEED TO MOGO IN SECTOR 2261.
NO RING BEARER CHOSEN. PROCEED TO MOGO IN SECTOR 2261.

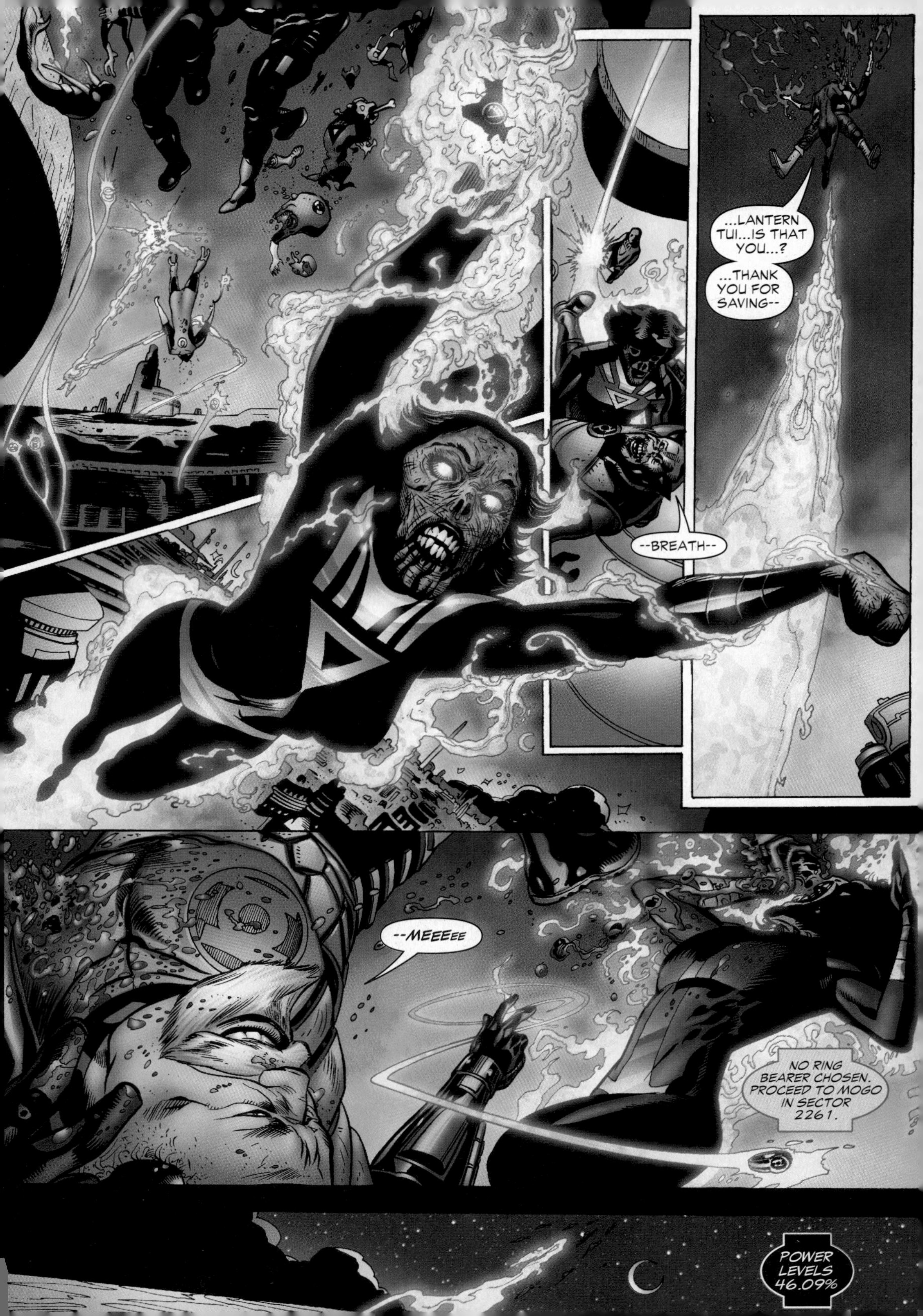
...LANTERN TUI...IS THAT YOU...?
...THANK YOU FOR SAVING--
--BREATH--
--MEEEEee
NO RING BEARER CHOSEN. PROCEED TO MOGO IN SECTOR 2261.
POWER LEVELS 46.09%

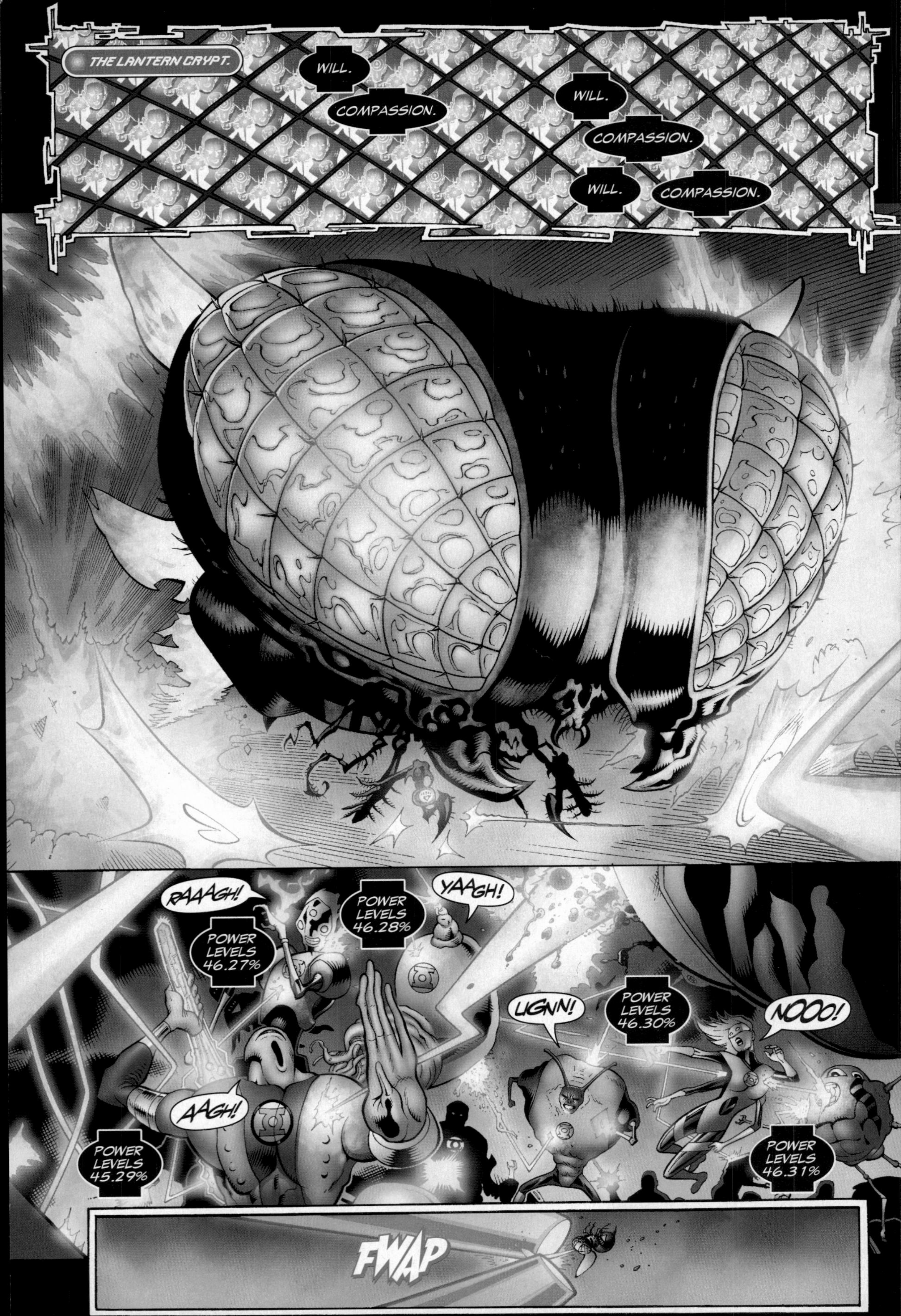
THE LANTERN CRYPT.
WILL.
COMPASSION.
WILL.
COMPASSION.
WILL.
COMPASSION.
RAAAGH!
POWER LEVELS 46.28%
YAAGH!
POWER LEVELS 46.27%
UGNN!
POWER LEVELS 46.30%
NOOO!
AAGH!
POWER LEVELS 45.29%
POWER LEVELS 46.31%
FWAP

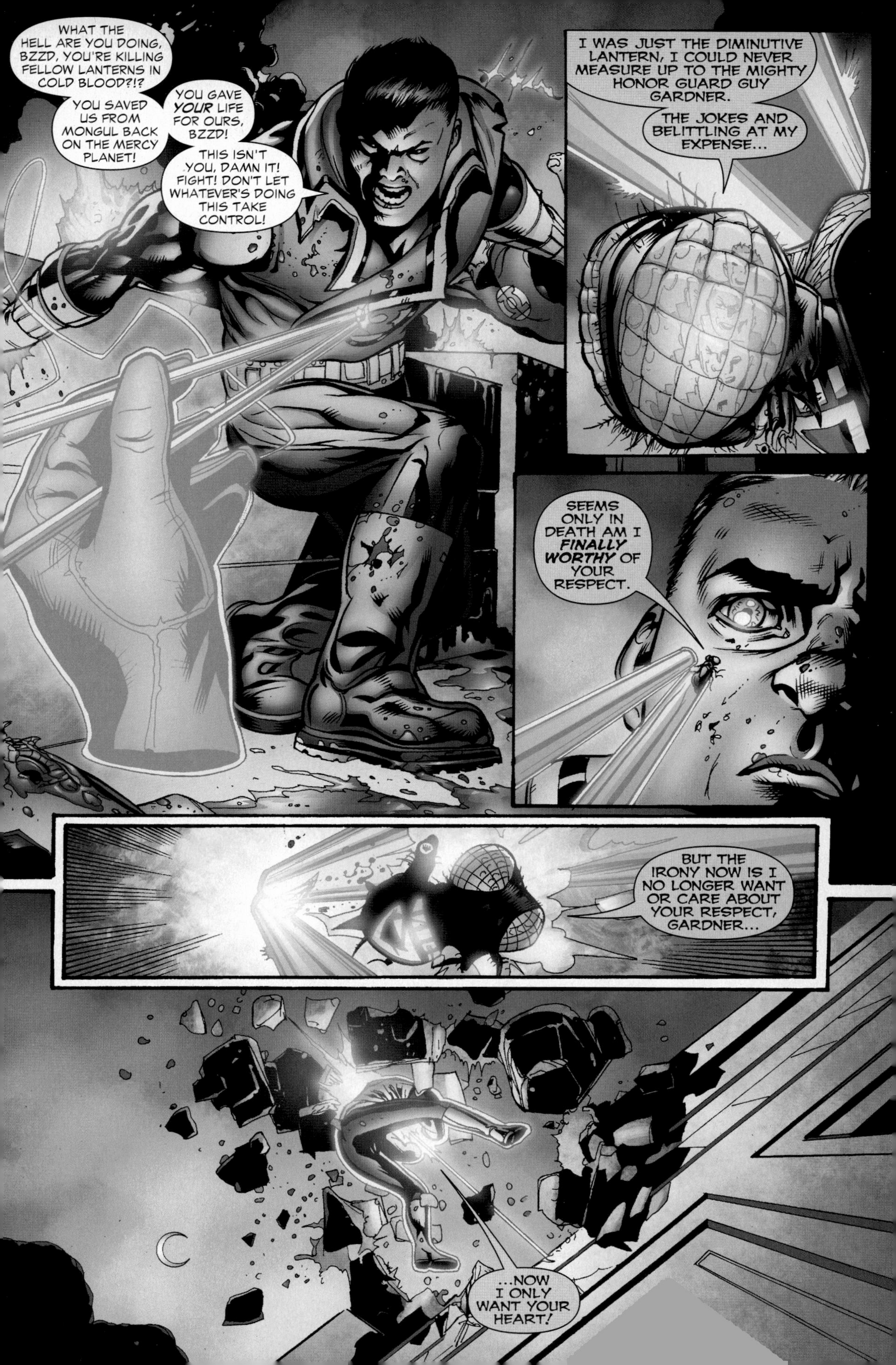
WHAT THE HELL ARE YOU DOING, BZZD, YOU'RE KILLING FELLOW LANTERNS IN COLD BLOOD?!?
YOU SAVED US FROM MONGUL BACK ON THE MERCY PLANET!
YOU GAVE YOUR LIFE FOR OURS, BZZD!
THIS ISN'T YOU, DAMN IT! FIGHT! DON'T LET WHATEVER'S DOING THIS TAKE CONTROL!
I WAS JUST THE DIMINUTIVE LANTERN, I COULD NEVER MEASURE UP TO THE MIGHTY HONOR GUARD GUY GARDNER.
THE JOKES AND BELITTLING AT MY EXPENSE...
SEEMS ONLY IN DEATH AM I FINALLY WORTHY OF YOUR RESPECT.
BUT THE IRONY NOW IS I NO LONGER WANT OR CARE ABOUT YOUR RESPECT, GARDNER...
...NOW I ONLY WANT YOUR HEART!

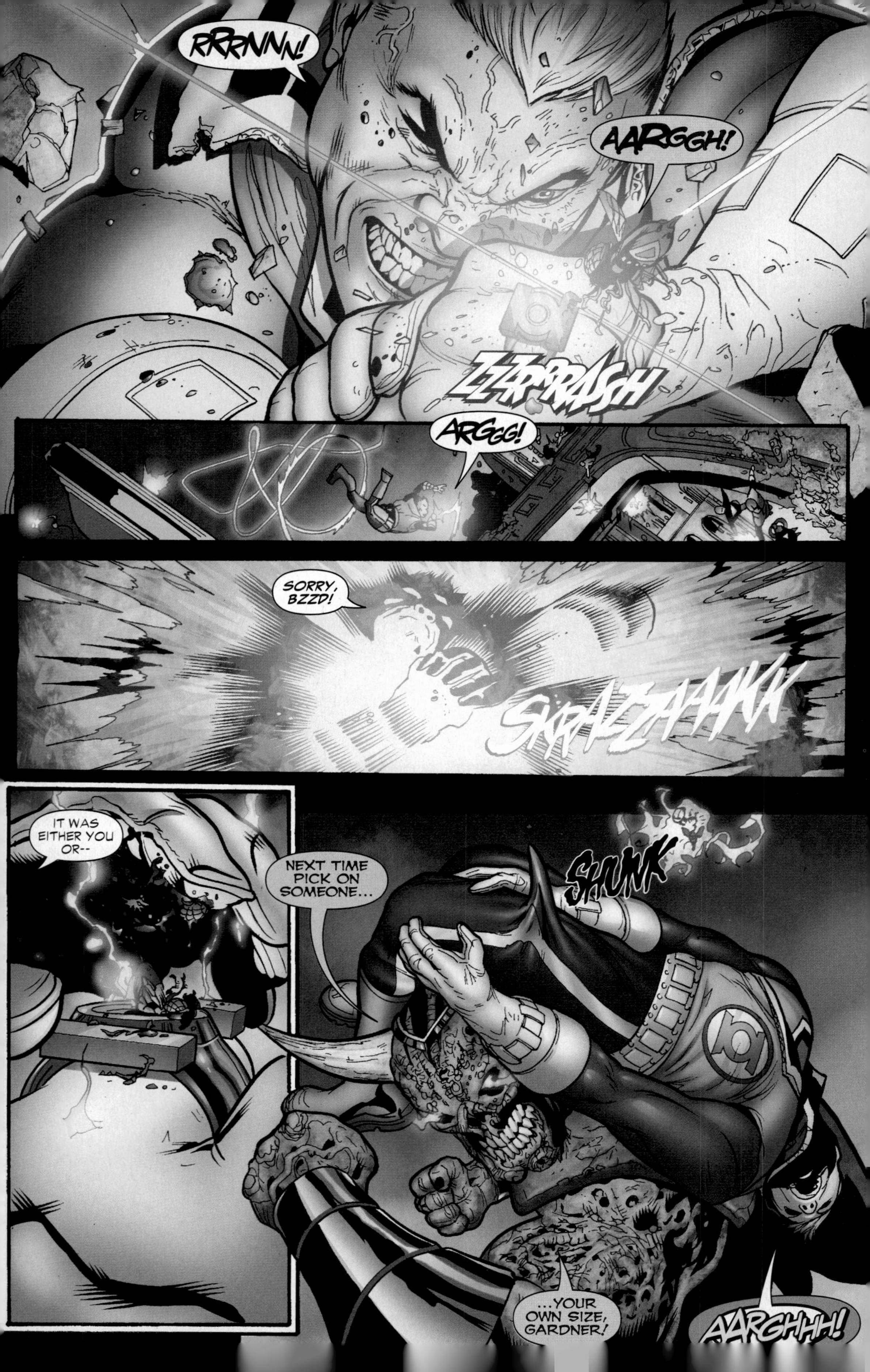
RRRNNN!
AARGGH!
ZZZRRRASH
ARGGG!
SORRY, BZZD!
SKRAKZAAAKK
IT WAS EITHER YOU OR--
NEXT TIME PICK ON SOMEONE...
SHUNK
...YOUR OWN SIZE, GARDNER!
AARGHHH!

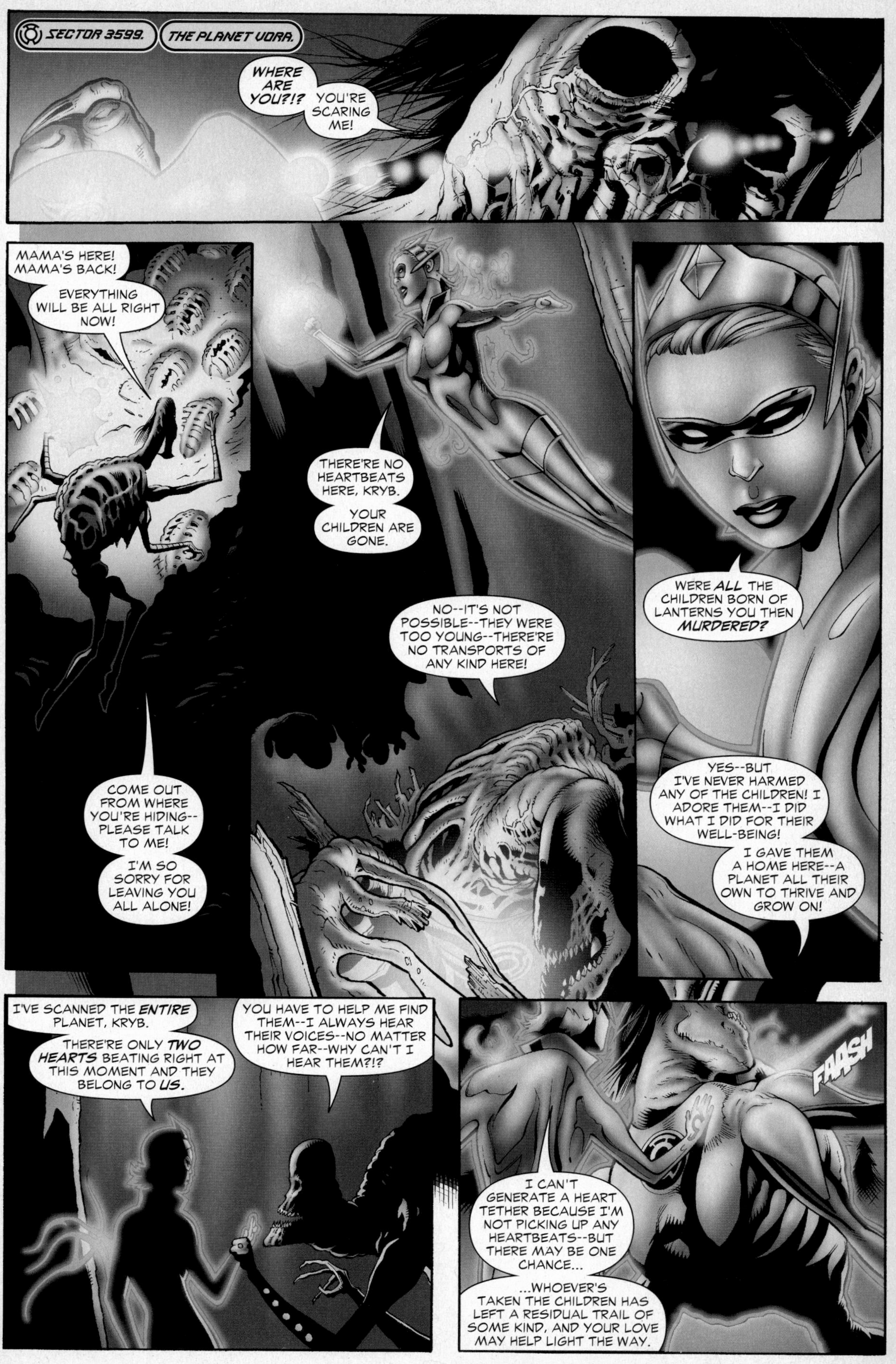
SECTOR 3599.
THE PLANET VORA.
WHERE ARE YOU?!? YOU'RE SCARING ME!
MAMA'S HERE! MAMA'S BACK!
EVERYTHING WILL BE ALL RIGHT NOW!
THERE'RE NO HEARTBEATS HERE, KRYB.
YOUR CHILDREN ARE GONE.
WERE ALL THE CHILDREN BORN OF LANTERNS YOU THEN MURDERED?
NO--IT'S NOT POSSIBLE--THEY WERE TOO YOUNG--THERE'RE NO TRANSPORTS OF ANY KIND HERE!
COME OUT FROM WHERE YOU'RE HIDING--PLEASE TALK TO ME!
I'M SO SORRY FOR LEAVING YOU ALL ALONE!
YES--BUT I'VE NEVER HARMED ANY OF THE CHILDREN! I ADORE THEM--I DID WHAT I DID FOR THEIR WELL-BEING!
I GAVE THEM A HOME HERE--A PLANET ALL THEIR OWN TO THRIVE AND GROW ON!
I'VE SCANNED THE ENTIRE PLANET, KRYB.
THERE'RE ONLY TWO HEARTS BEATING RIGHT AT THIS MOMENT AND THEY BELONG TO US.
YOU HAVE TO HELP ME FIND THEM--I ALWAYS HEAR THEIR VOICES--NO MATTER HOW FAR--WHY CAN'T I HEAR THEM?!?
FAASH
I CAN'T GENERATE A HEART TETHER BECAUSE I'M NOT PICKING UP ANY HEARTBEATS--BUT THERE MAY BE ONE CHANCE...
...WHOEVER'S TAKEN THE CHILDREN HAS LEFT A RESIDUAL TRAIL OF SOME KIND, AND YOUR LOVE MAY HELP LIGHT THE WAY.

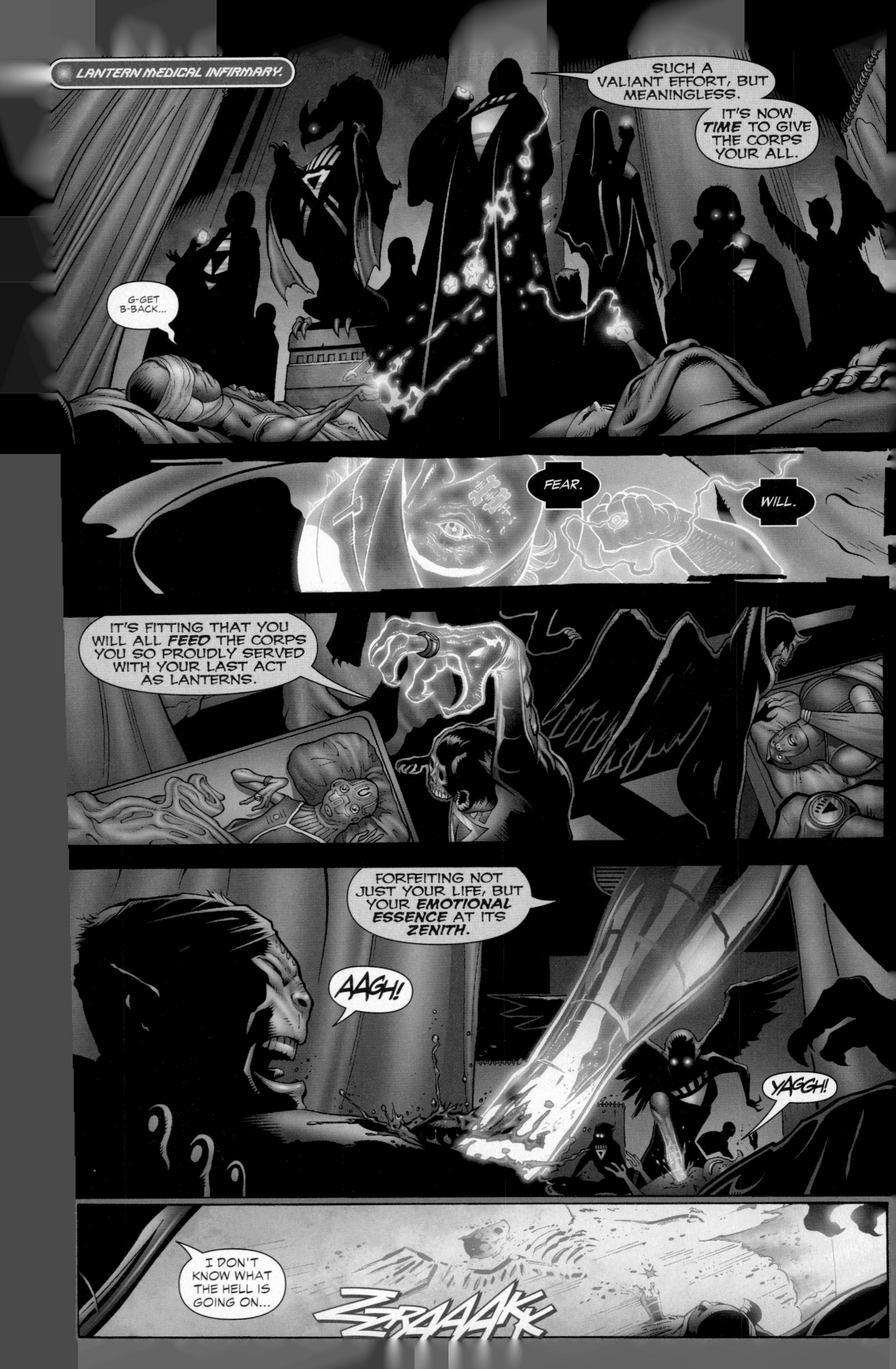
LANTERN MEDICAL INFIRMARY.
SUCH A VALIANT EFFORT, BUT MEANINGLESS.
IT'S NOW TIME TO GIVE THE CORPS YOUR ALL.
G-GET B-BACK...
FEAR.
WILL.
IT'S FITTING THAT YOU WILL ALL FEED THE CORPS YOU SO PROUDLY SERVED WITH YOUR LAST ACT AS LANTERNS.
FORFEITING NOT JUST YOUR LIFE, BUT YOUR EMOTIONAL ESSENCE AT ITS ZENITH.
AAGH!
YAGGH!
I DON'T KNOW WHAT THE HELL IS GOING ON...
ZZRAAAKK

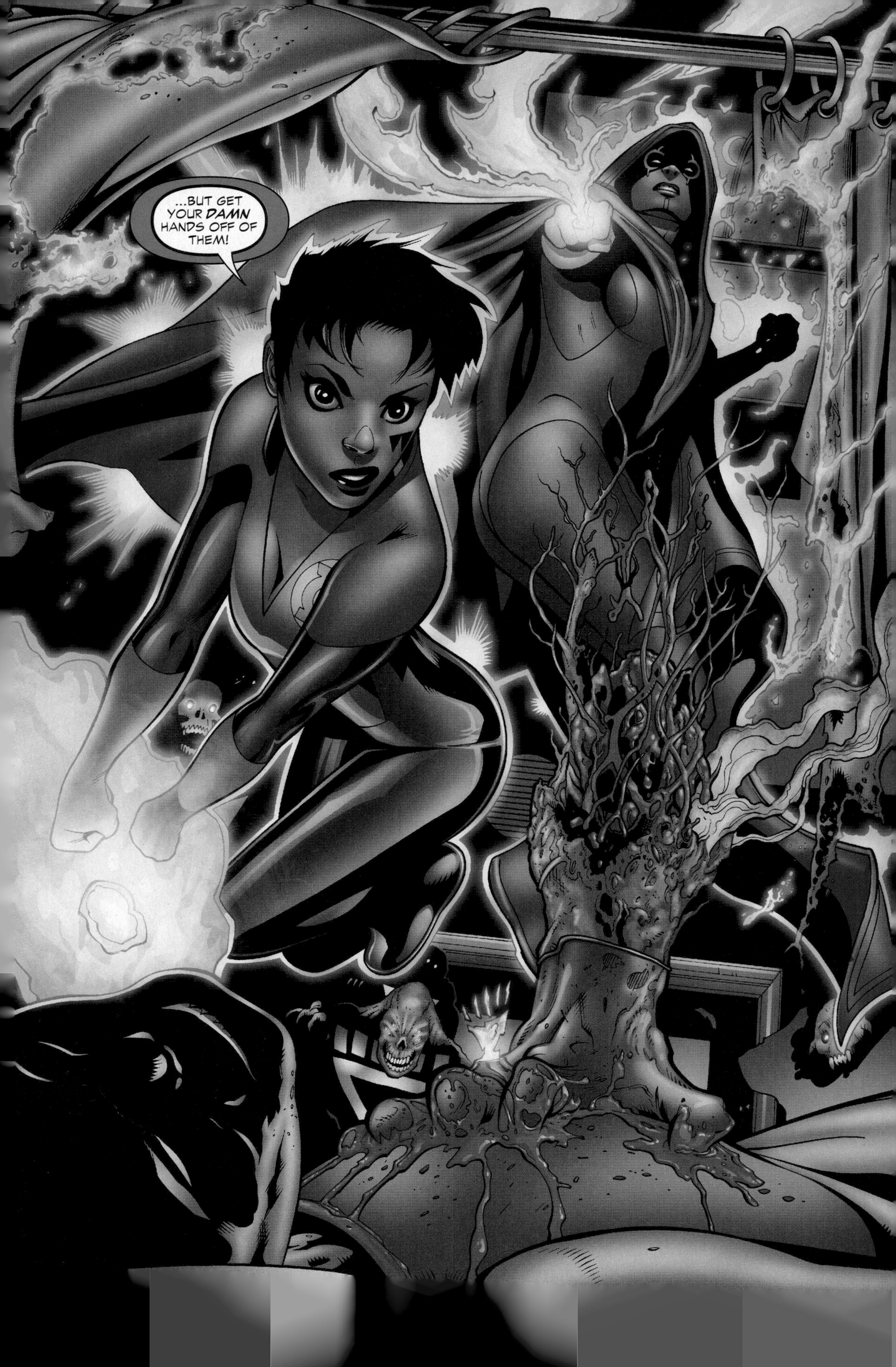
...BUT GET YOUR DAMN HANDS OFF OF THEM!

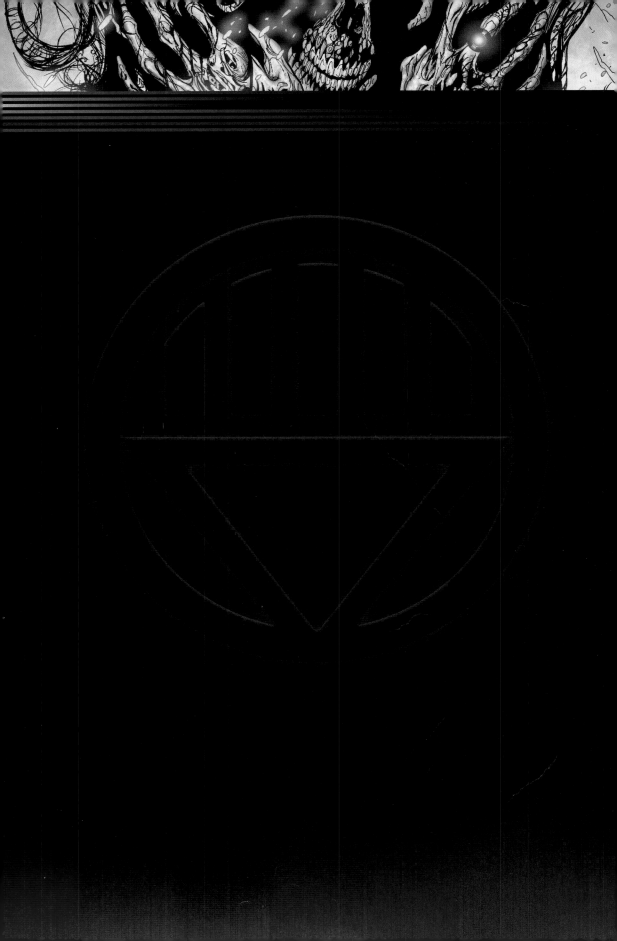

GREEN LANTERN CORPS 41

Cover by Patrick Gleason and Rebecca Buchman with Randy Mayor

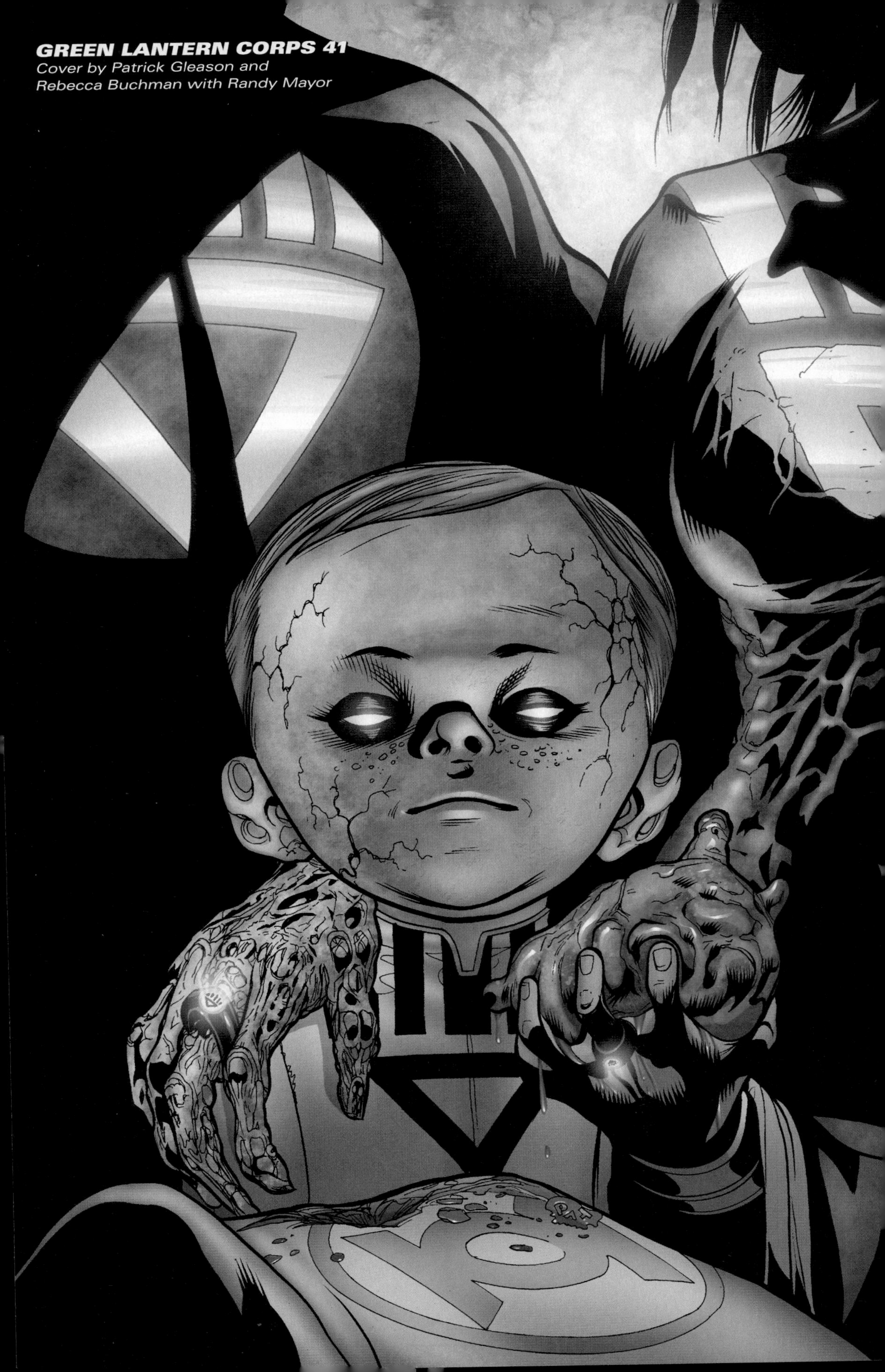

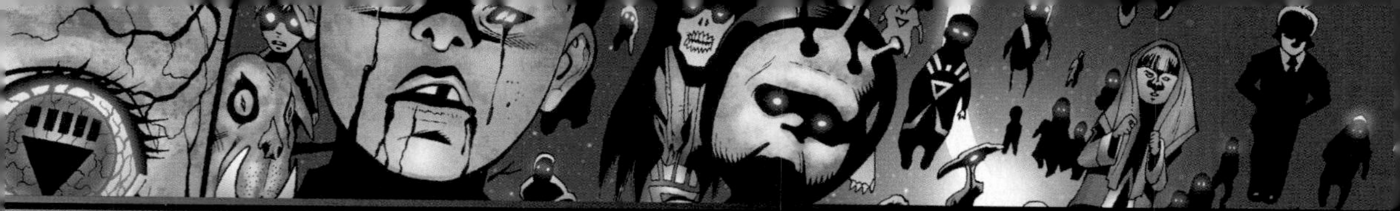

HUNGRY HEART

PATRICK GLEASON
PENCILS

REBECCA BUCHMAN
KEITH CHAMPAGNE
TOM NGUYEN
INKS

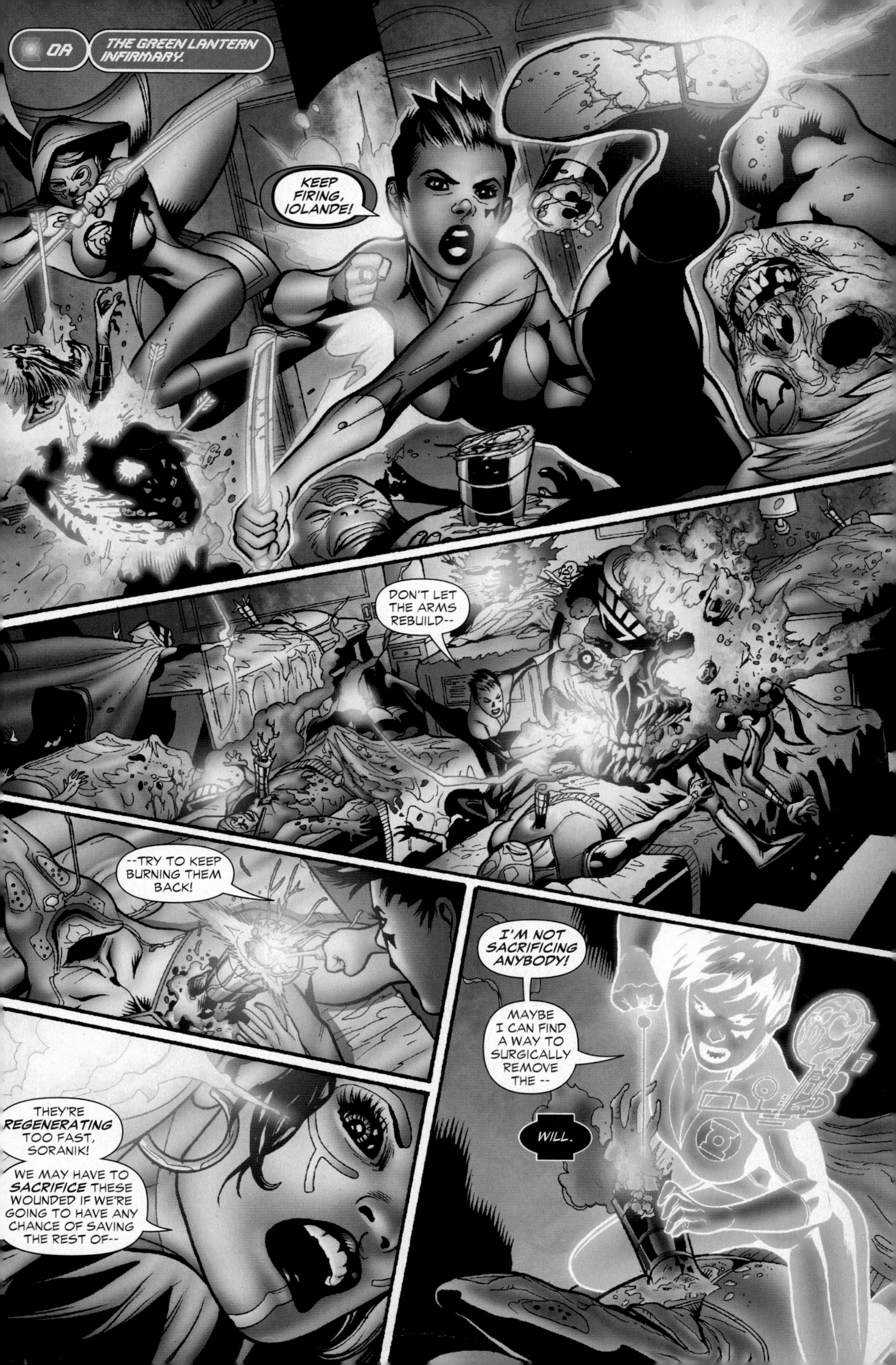
OA
THE GREEN LANTERN INFIRMARY.
KEEP FIRING, IOLANDE!
DON'T LET THE ARMS REBUILD--
--TRY TO KEEP BURNING THEM BACK!
THEY'RE REGENERATING TOO FAST, SORANIK!
WE MAY HAVE TO SACRIFICE THESE WOUNDED IF WE'RE GOING TO HAVE ANY CHANCE OF SAVING THE REST OF--
I'M NOT SACRIFICING ANYBODY!
MAYBE I CAN FIND A WAY TO SURGICALLY REMOVE THE --
WILL.

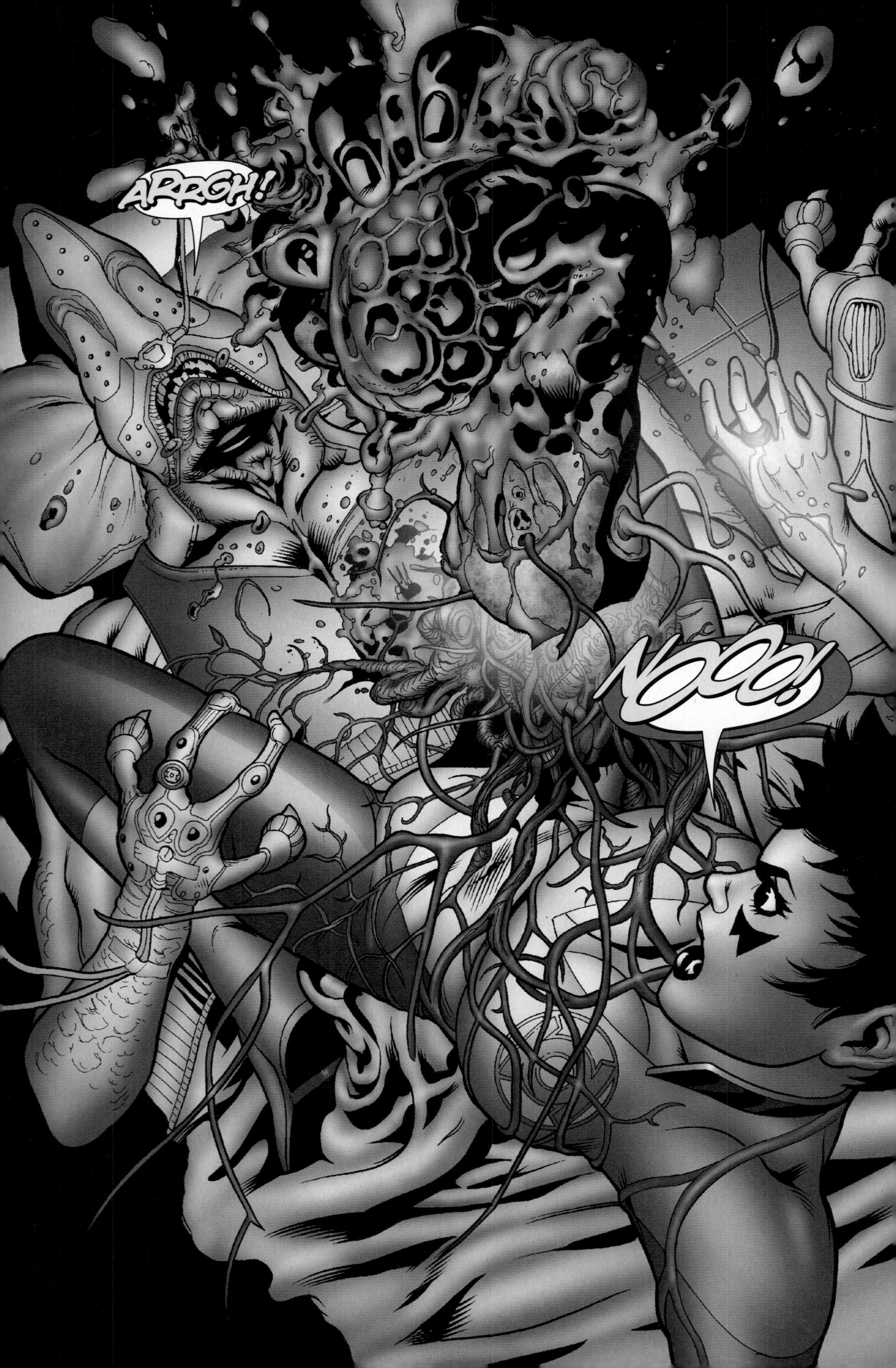
ARRGH!
NOOO!

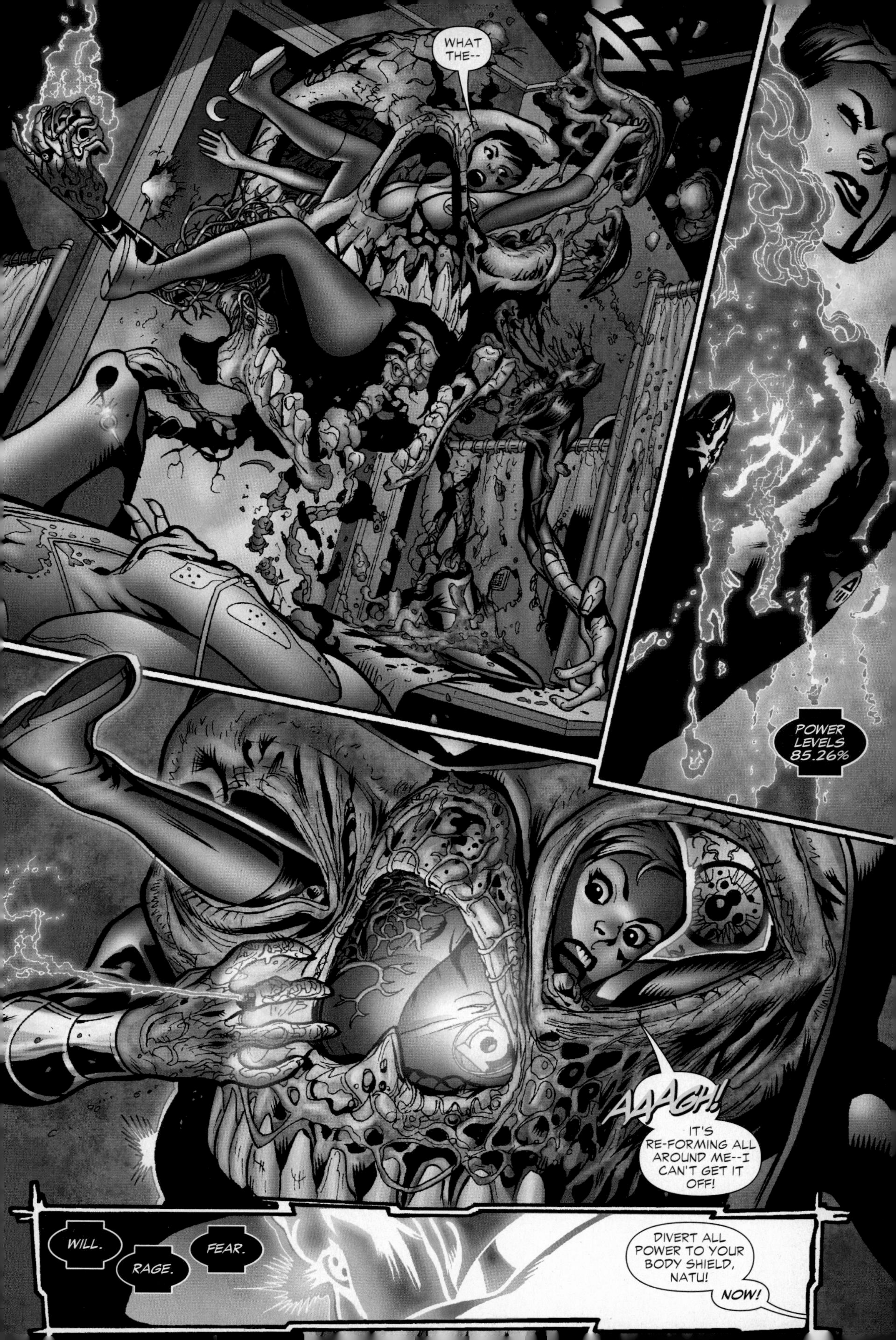
WHAT THE--
POWER LEVELS 85.26%
AAAGH!
IT'S RE-FORMING ALL AROUND ME--I CAN'T GET IT OFF!
WILL.
RAGE.
FEAR.
DIVERT ALL POWER TO YOUR BODY SHIELD, NATU!
NOW!

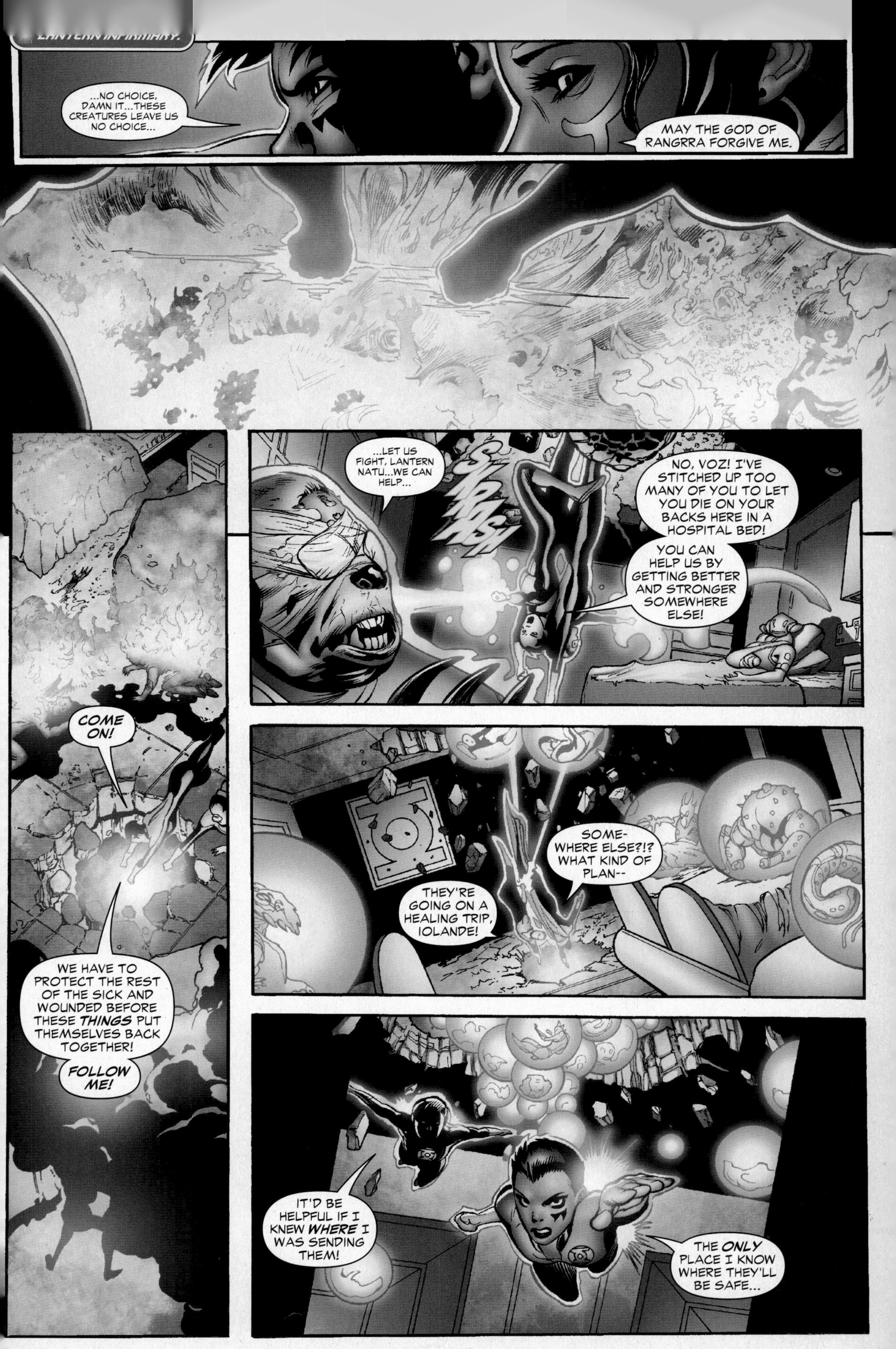

LANTERN INFIRMARY.
...NO CHOICE, DAMN IT...THESE CREATURES LEAVE US NO CHOICE...
MAY THE GOD OF RANGRRA FORGIVE ME.
...LET US FIGHT, LANTERN NATU...WE CAN HELP...
SKRASH
NO, VOZ! I'VE STITCHED UP TOO MANY OF YOU TO LET YOU DIE ON YOUR BACKS HERE IN A HOSPITAL BED!
YOU CAN HELP US BY GETTING BETTER AND STRONGER SOMEWHERE ELSE!
COME ON!
WE HAVE TO PROTECT THE REST OF THE SICK AND WOUNDED BEFORE THESE THINGS PUT THEMSELVES BACK TOGETHER!
FOLLOW ME!
SOME-WHERE ELSE?!? WHAT KIND OF PLAN--
THEY'RE GOING ON A HEALING TRIP, IOLANDE!
IT'D BE HELPFUL IF I KNEW WHERE I WAS SENDING THEM!
THE ONLY PLACE I KNOW WHERE THEY'LL BE SAFE...

...MOGO.

WE'LL ESCORT THEM TO THE EDGE OF THE SECTOR AND--

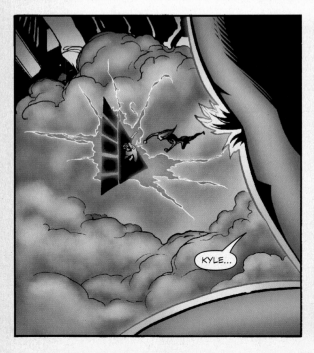

KYLE...

...NO...

I'LL ESCORT THE WOUNDED. YOU GET DOWN--

I CAN'T LEAVE YOU ALONE TO--

GO. NOW!

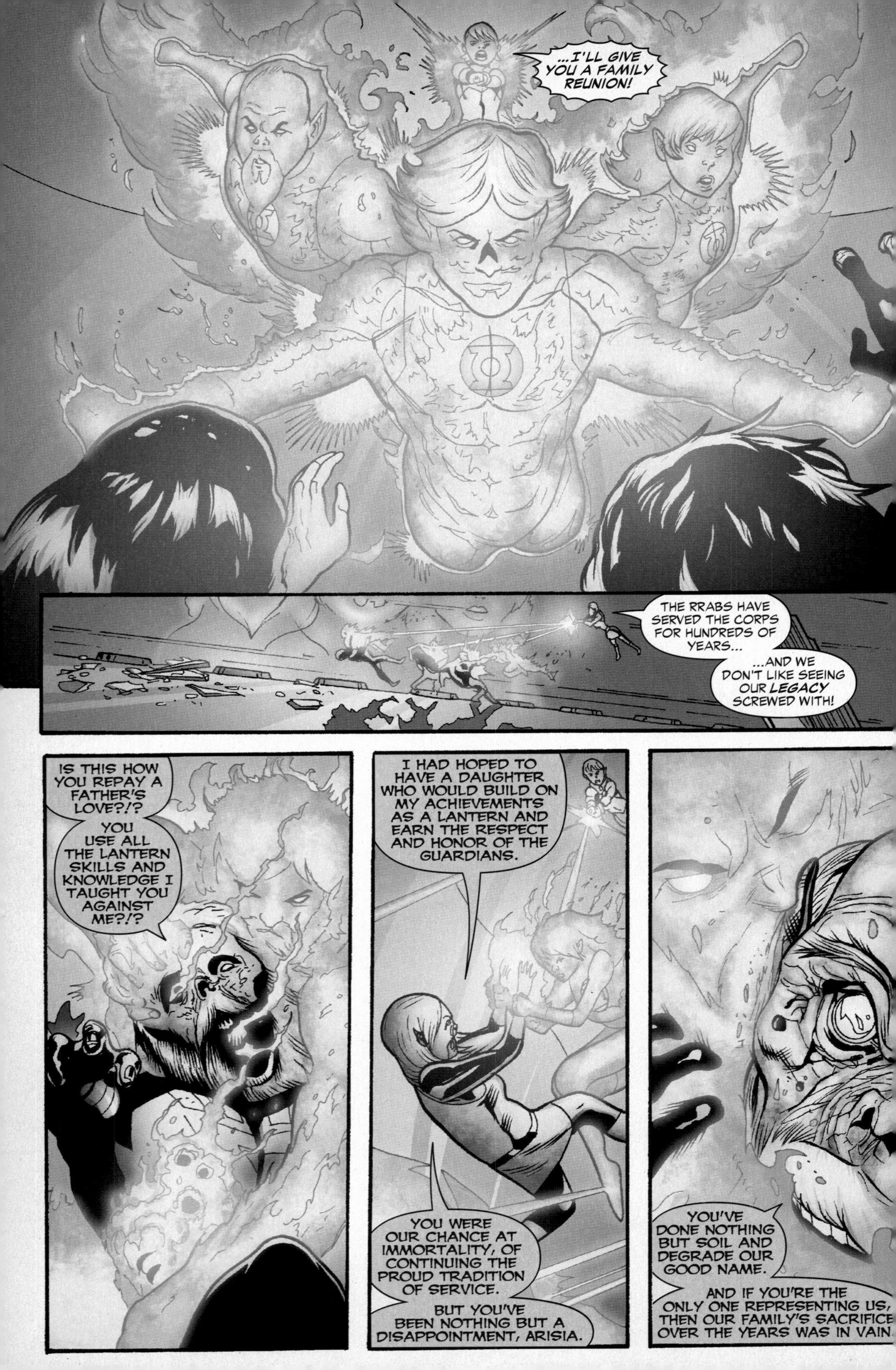
...I'LL GIVE YOU A FAMILY REUNION!
THE RRABS HAVE SERVED THE CORPS FOR HUNDREDS OF YEARS...
...AND WE DON'T LIKE SEEING OUR LEGACY SCREWED WITH!
IS THIS HOW YOU REPAY A FATHER'S LOVE?!?
YOU USE ALL THE LANTERN SKILLS AND KNOWLEDGE I TAUGHT YOU AGAINST ME?!?
I HAD HOPED TO HAVE A DAUGHTER WHO WOULD BUILD ON MY ACHIEVEMENTS AS A LANTERN AND EARN THE RESPECT AND HONOR OF THE GUARDIANS.
YOU WERE OUR CHANCE AT IMMORTALITY, OF CONTINUING THE PROUD TRADITION OF SERVICE.
BUT YOU'VE BEEN NOTHING BUT A DISAPPOINTMENT, ARISIA.
YOU'VE DONE NOTHING BUT SOIL AND DEGRADE OUR GOOD NAME.
AND IF YOU'RE THE ONLY ONE REPRESENTING US, THEN OUR FAMILY'S SACRIFICE OVER THE YEARS WAS IN VAIN.

KEEP THE FORMATION TIGHT!

FULL POWER, POOZERS!

THESE THINGS ARE US! HOW CAN WE FIRE AT OUR OWN--

SCRAP THAT OUT OF YOUR HEADS *NOW!* THESE THINGS ARE *NOT* OUR HONORED DEAD!

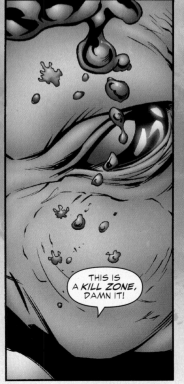

THIS IS A *KILL ZONE,* DAMN IT!

THAT MEANS KILL OR BE KILL*AAAARGH!*

GREEN LANTERN CORPS 42

Cover by Patrick Gleason and
Rebecca Buchman with Randy Mayor

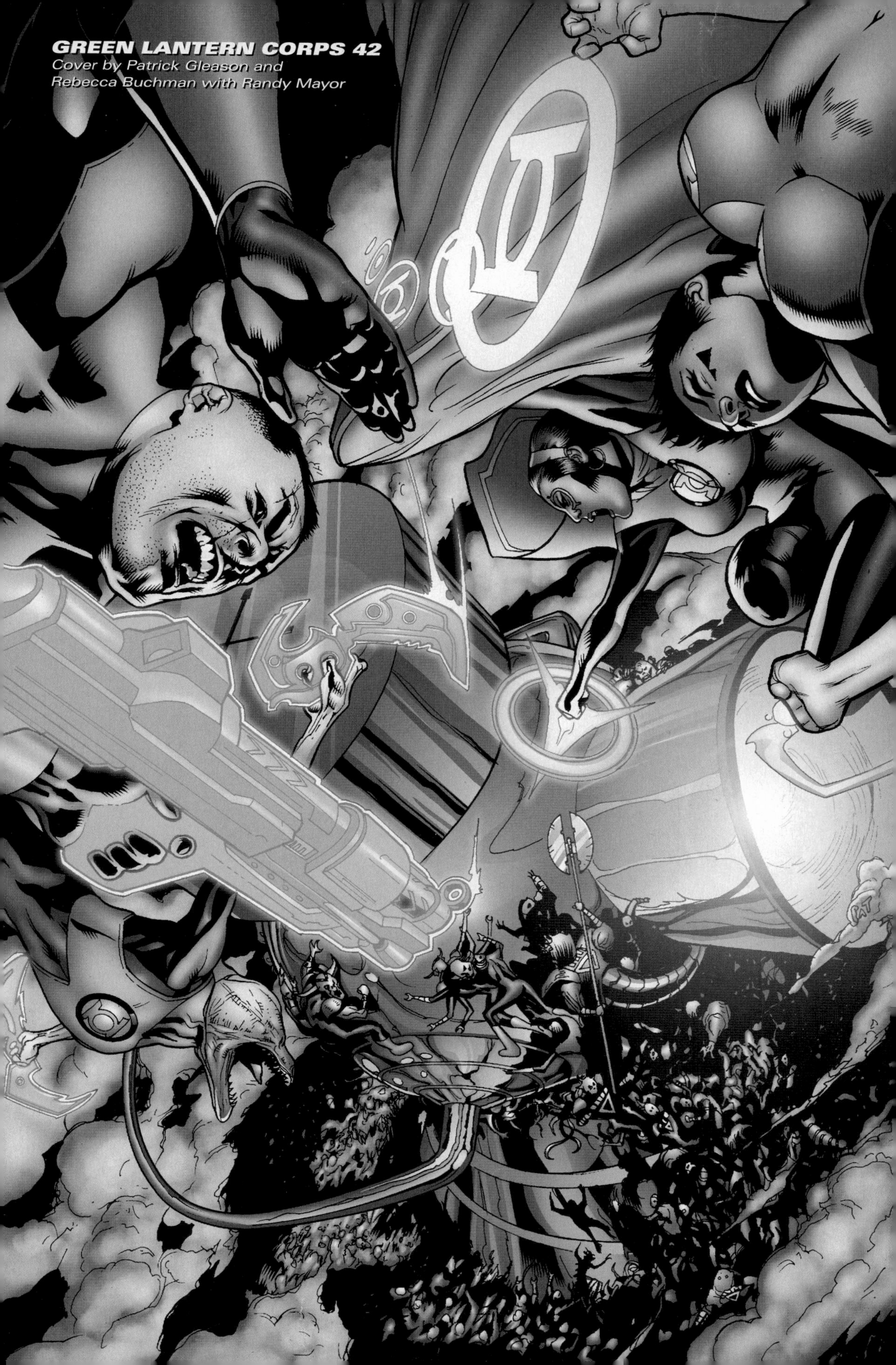

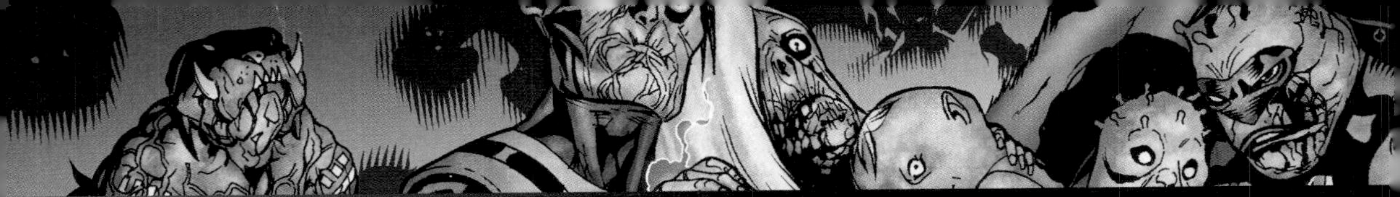

SACRIFICE OF WILL

PATRICK GLEASON
PENCILS

REBECCA BUCHMAN
TOM NGUYEN
INKS

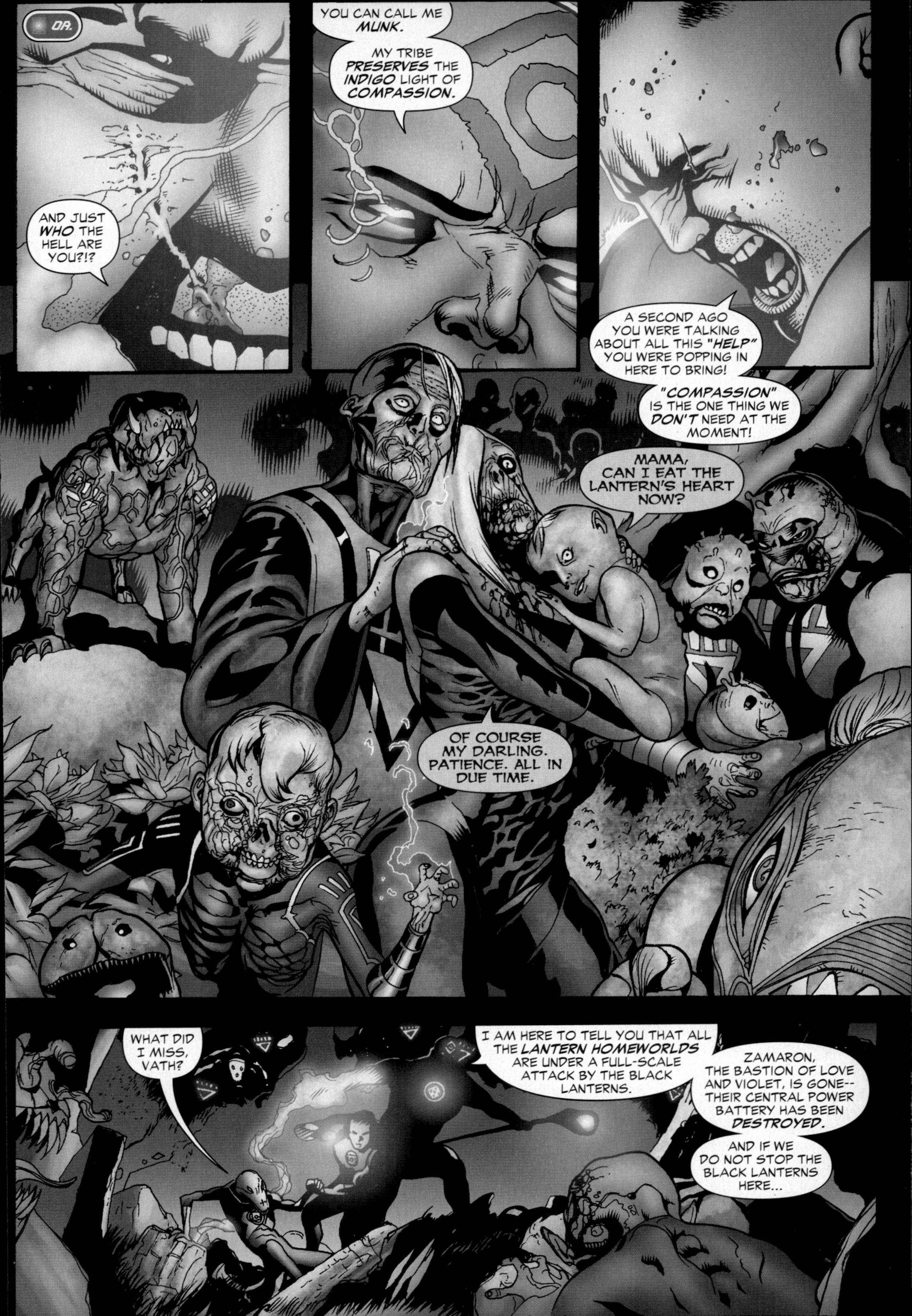

AND JUST WHO THE HELL ARE YOU?!?
YOU CAN CALL ME MUNK.
MY TRIBE PRESERVES THE INDIGO LIGHT OF COMPASSION.
A SECOND AGO YOU WERE TALKING ABOUT ALL THIS "HELP" YOU WERE POPPING IN HERE TO BRING!
"COMPASSION" IS THE ONE THING WE DON'T NEED AT THE MOMENT!
MAMA, CAN I EAT THE LANTERN'S HEART NOW?
OF COURSE MY DARLING. PATIENCE. ALL IN DUE TIME.
WHAT DID I MISS, VATH?
I AM HERE TO TELL YOU THAT ALL THE LANTERN HOMEWORLDS ARE UNDER A FULL-SCALE ATTACK BY THE BLACK LANTERNS.
ZAMARON, THE BASTION OF LOVE AND VIOLET, IS GONE-- THEIR CENTRAL POWER BATTERY HAS BEEN DESTROYED.
AND IF WE DO NOT STOP THE BLACK LANTERNS HERE...

AARRGH!

WHAT ARE YOU SCREAMING FOR, BRILLOLOG?

IF I WERE YOU I'D BE LOOKING FORWARD TO THE BLACKNESS.

YOU'VE FAILED EVERYONE.

YOUR PEOPLE.

YOUR CORPS.

THE ROOKIES.

YOURSELF.

AARRGH!

NOW YOU WON'T BE ABLE TO DESTROY ANY--

100% POWER LEVEL EXCEEDED.

RRNNN.

DEVOUR WILL.

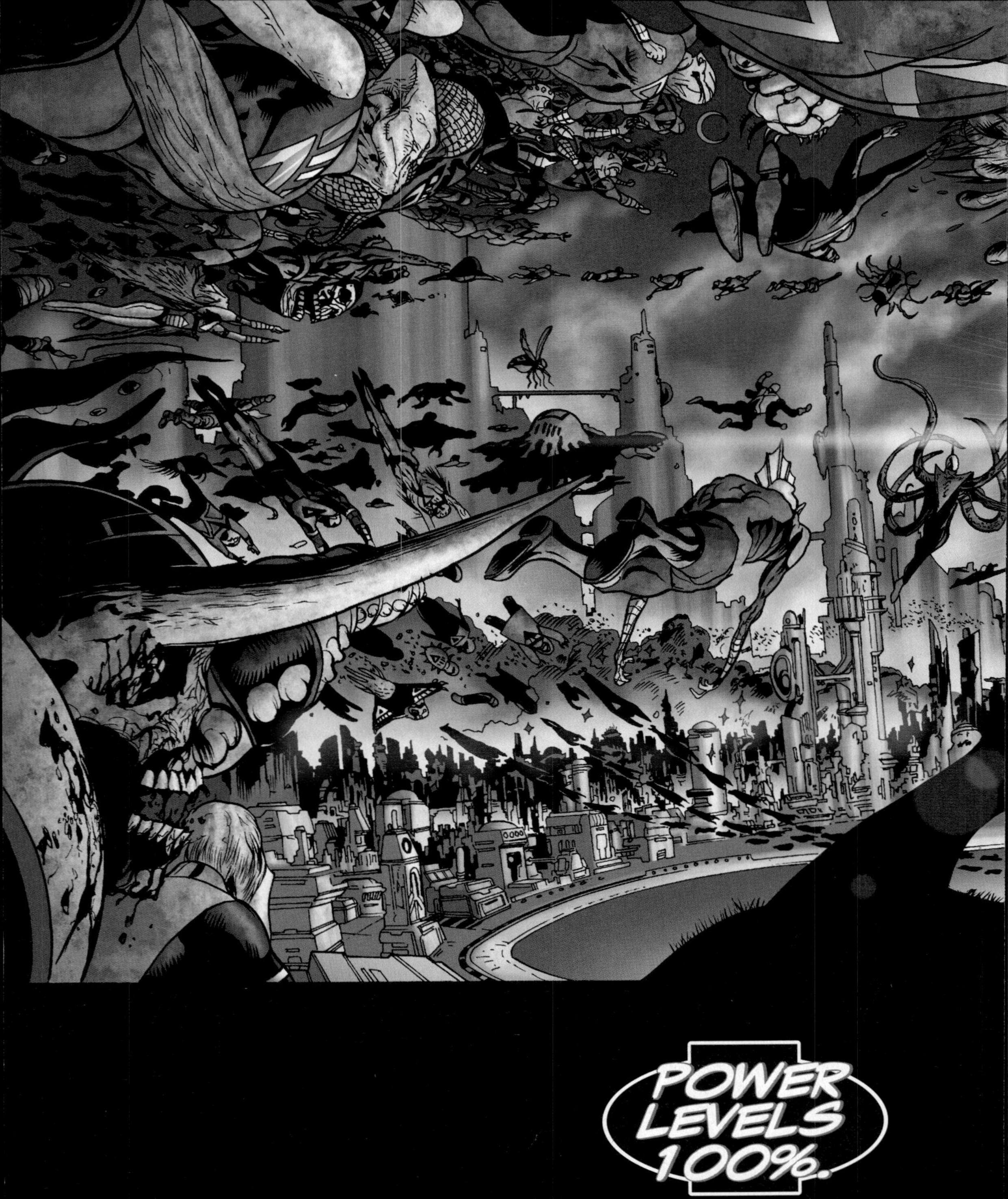
POWER LEVELS 100%.

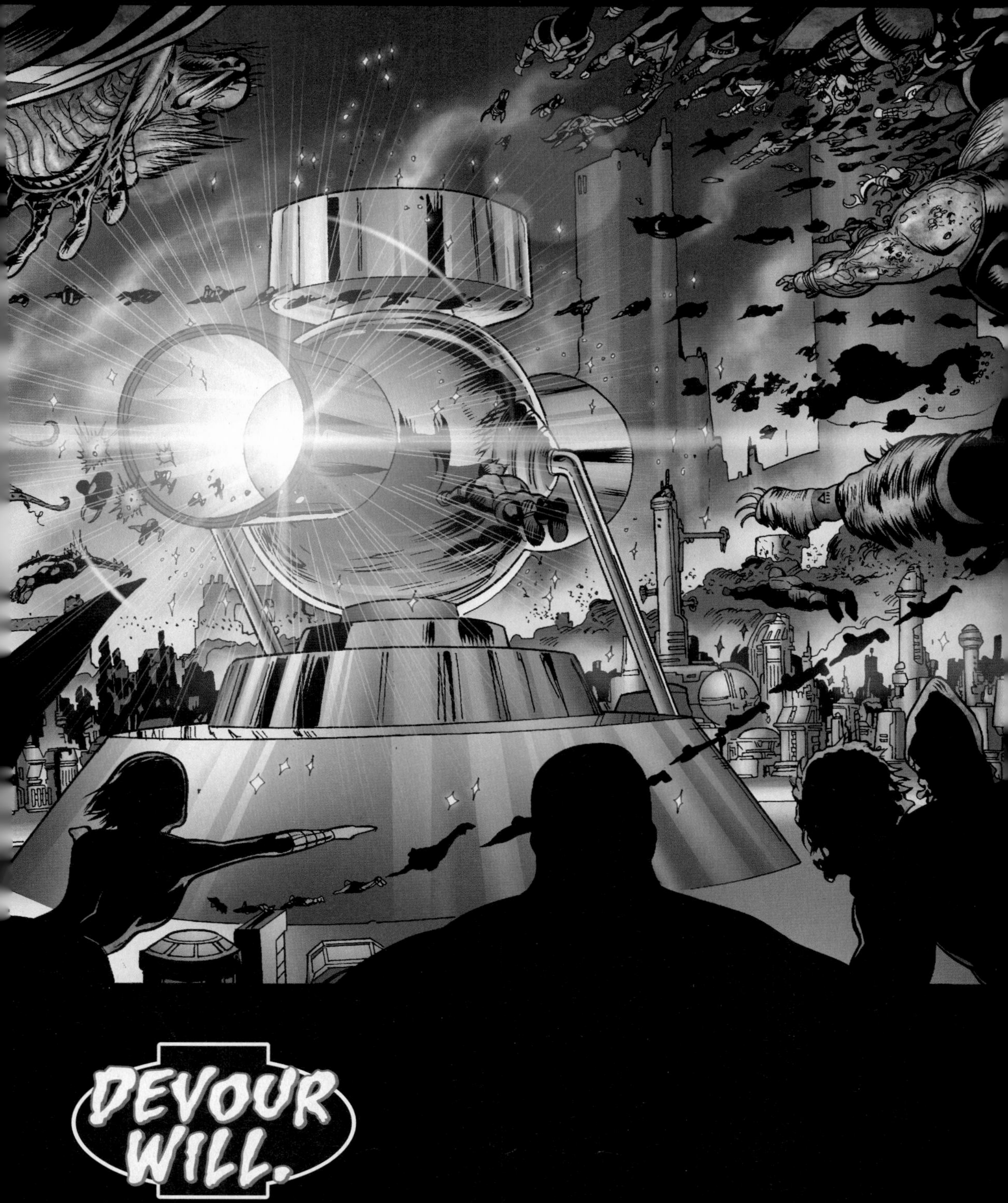
DEVOUR WILL.

DEVOUR WILL.

DEVOUR WILL.

DEVOUR WILL.

DEVOUR WILL.

THE OBJECTIVE OF THE BLACK LANTERNS HAS CHANGED!

THEY ARE SEEKING TO DESTROY THE BATTERY AND EXTINGUISH ITS LIGHT!

CEASE AND DESIST FROM ALL CURRENT BATTLE STATIONS AND REPORT TO THE CENTRAL POWER BATTERY FOR DEFENSIVE ACTION!

REPEAT, ALL LANTERNS REPORT TO THE CENTRAL POWER BATTERY FOR DEFENSIVE ACTION!

SO WHAT COLORED *CRAYOLA LANTERN* ARE YOU, BUDDY--DEEP PURPLE?!?

I AM FROM THE *INDIGO* TRIBE, GREEN LANTERN, AND IF WE CAN--

YEAH, WHATEVER-- WORKS FOR ME--I AIN'T LOOKING NO GIFT HORSE IN THE MOUTH!

CONNECTION SEVERED.

CONNECTION SEVERED.

AAIIEEEE!

AAIIEEEE!

CONSTRUCT DARK MATTER.

WITH YOUR HELP, INDIGO MAN, WE CAN FINALLY PUT SOME HURT ON THESE COCKROACHES AND STOP 'EM FROM PUTTIN' THEMSELVES--

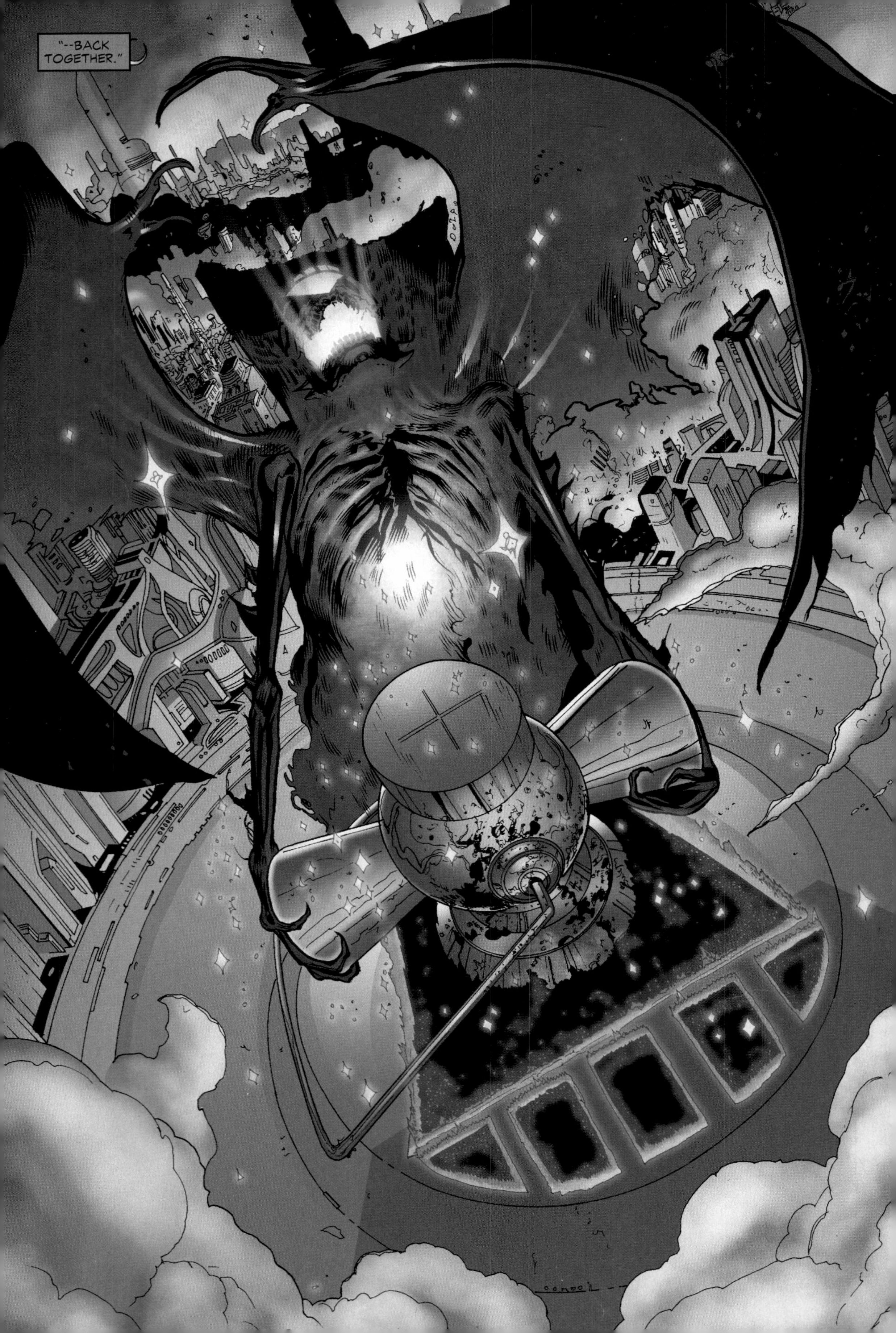
"--BACK TOGETHER."

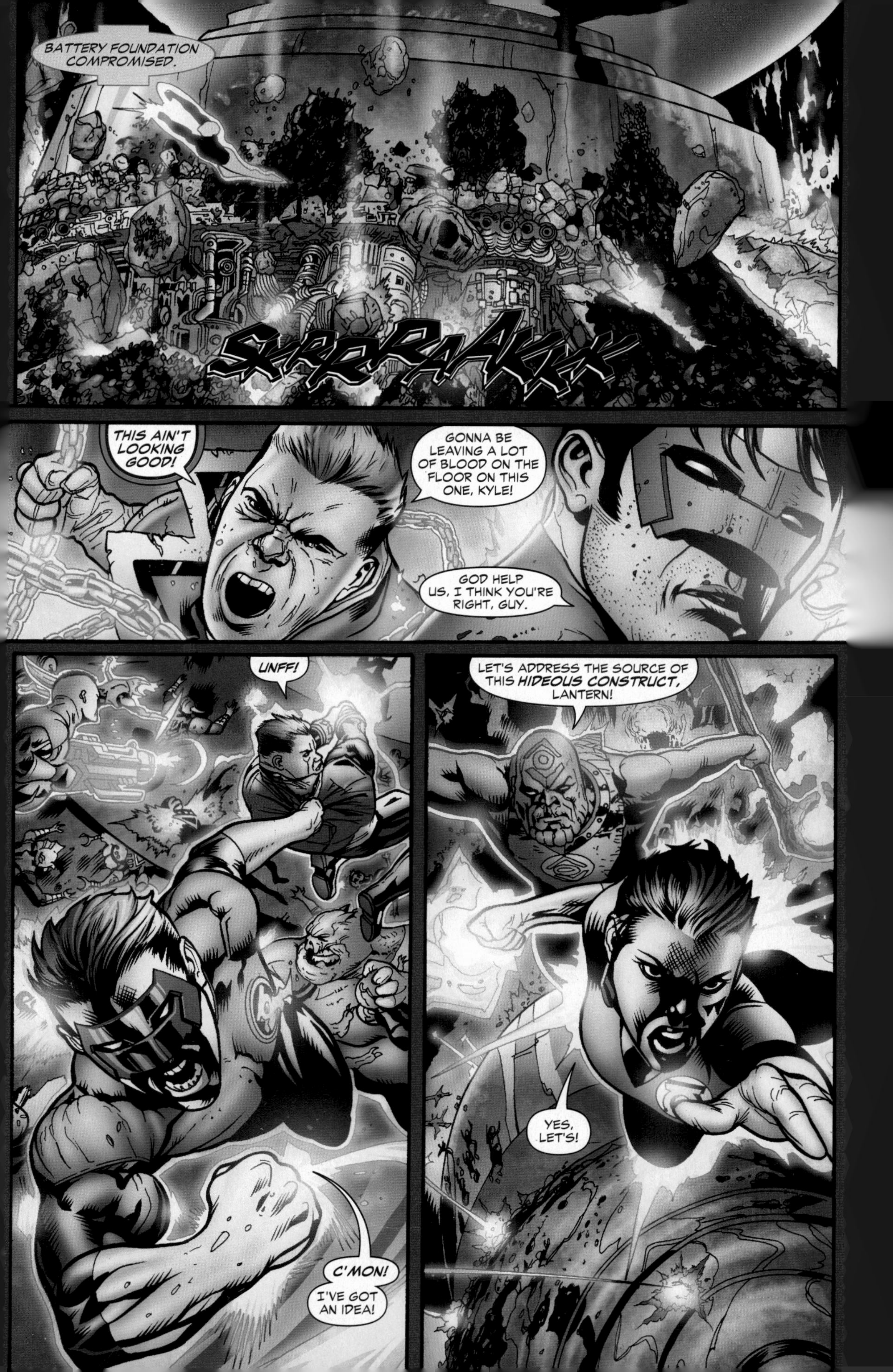
BATTERY FOUNDATION COMPROMISED.
SKRRRAAKKK
THIS AIN'T LOOKING GOOD!
GONNA BE LEAVING A LOT OF BLOOD ON THE FLOOR ON THIS ONE, KYLE!
GOD HELP US, I THINK YOU'RE RIGHT, GUY.
UNFF!
C'MON!
I'VE GOT AN IDEA!
LET'S ADDRESS THE SOURCE OF THIS HIDEOUS CONSTRUCT, LANTERN!
YES, LET'S!

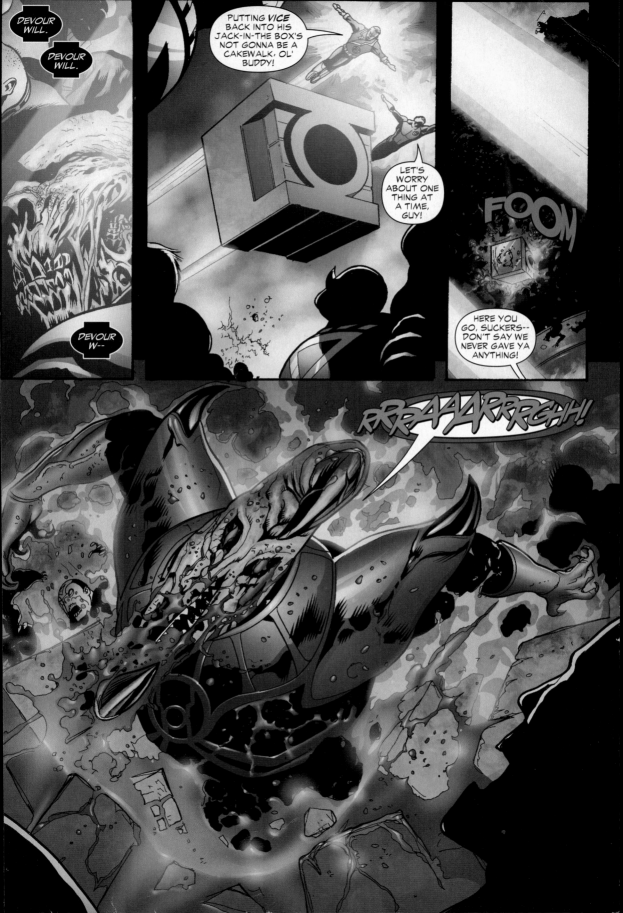

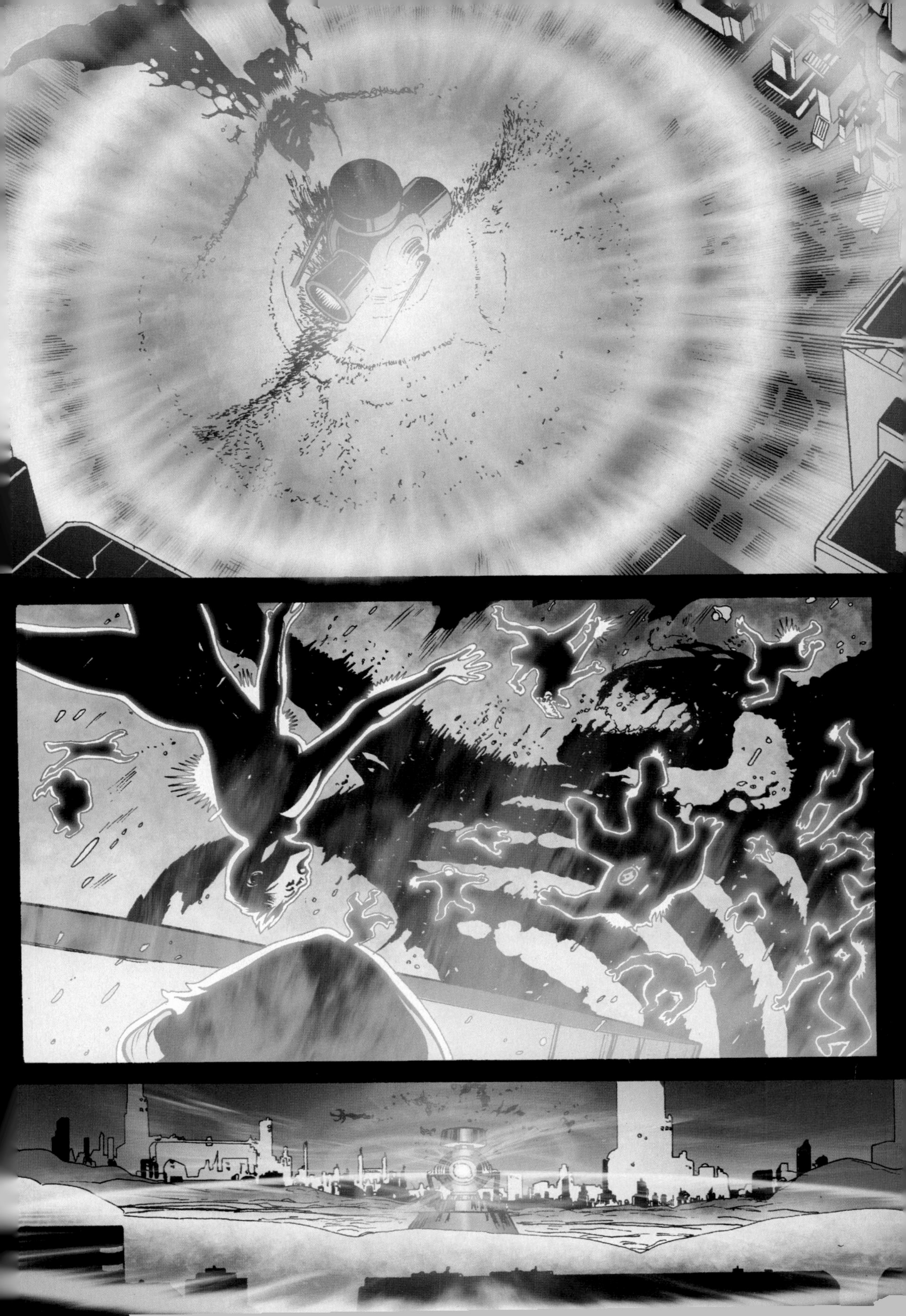

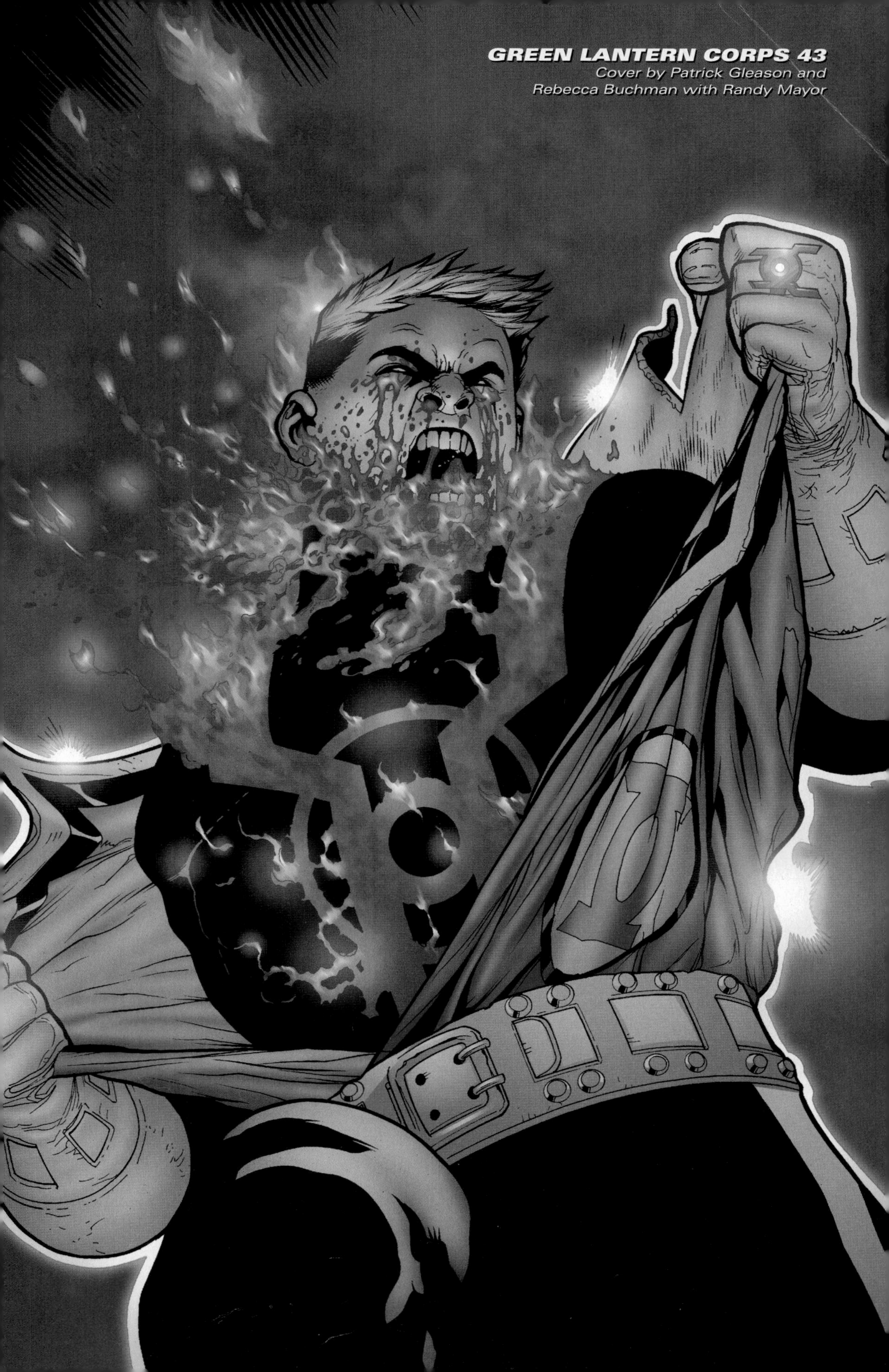

GREEN LANTERN CORPS 43
Cover by Patrick Gleason and
Rebecca Buchman with Randy Mayor

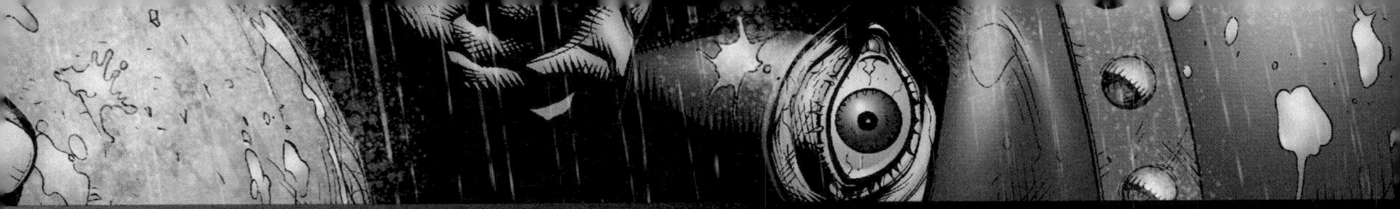

RED BADGE OF RAGE
PART ONE

PATRICK GLEASON
PENCILS

REBECCA BUCHMAN
TOM NGUYEN
PATRICK GLEASON
INKS

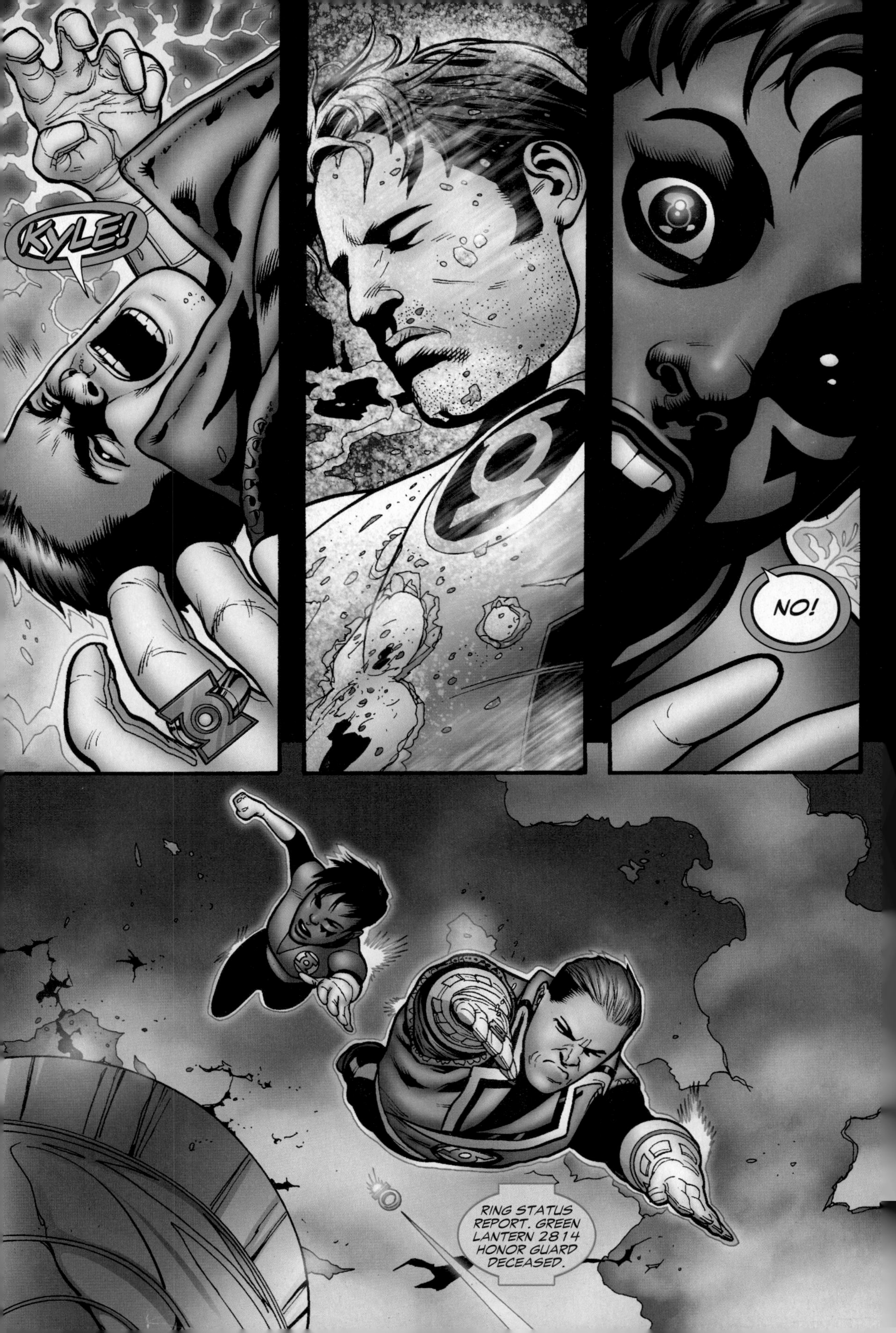
KYLE!
NO!
RING STATUS REPORT. GREEN LANTERN 2814 HONOR GUARD DECEASED.

KYLE
RAYNER OF--

YOU
CAN'T HAVE
HIM!

YOU
WON'T
HAVE
HIM!

KYLE
RAYNER--

NO!

--OF
EARTH.

OFF!
GET
OFF!

IT'S
NOT HIS
TIME!

RIS--

FAAOSH

CONNECTION
SEVERED.

IT IS EVERYONE'S
TIME, LANTERN...

...AND
IT IS NO
ONE'S TIME.

BUT YOU DO
NOT HAVE
MUCH TIME
TO BRING
THIS LANTERN
BACK BEFORE
ANOTHER
BLACK RING
SEEKS TO--
HRRM?

NO...

I TOLD YOU BEFORE, THERE WERE *NO HEARTBEATS* TO FOLLOW, KRYB.

THERE'S NO SIGN OF LIFE COMING FROM THOSE POOR CHILDREN--WE WERE LUCKY TO FIND THEM AT ALL HERE IN THE MIDDLE OF ALL *THIS*.

EAT THE GREEN.

EAT THE GREEN.

EAT THE GREEN.

THEY'RE *MOVING*-- THEY'RE *FLYING*--

...THIS *MUST* BE A MISTAKE, SAPPHIRE.

THEY *CAN'T* BE DEAD.

THEY'RE *UNDEAD*.

THEY'RE NOT THE CHILDREN YOU STOLE-- NOT THE CHILDREN *YOU* LEFT TO DIE ON YOUR DESOLATE PLANET.

GAKK!

I WAS STOLEN FROM *THEM!*

YOU AND YOUR KIND KEPT ME LOCKED IN THAT *DAMNED CRYSTAL!*

YOU HELPED KILL MY BABIES!

FZZRAKK

YAAGH!

THEY WERE *NEVER* YOUR BABIES TO BEGIN WITH, KRYB!

AND I SHOULD'VE KNOWN YOU'D NEVER KEEP YOUR PROMISE TO RETURN TO ZAMARON!

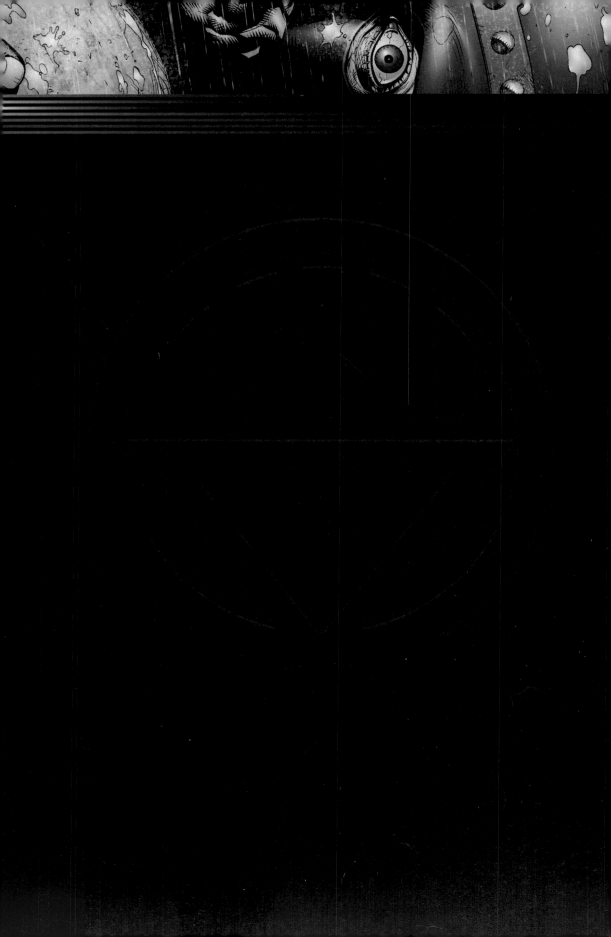

CONNECTION SEVERED.

HIS HEART'S STOPPED--WE DON'T HAVE MUCH--

I MET YOU BOTH BEFORE WHEN YOU DELIVERED THAT BEAUTIFUL BABY IN THE MIDDLE OF THAT BATTLE.

YES--BUT WE--

THE AFFECTION AND PASSION FOR THIS LANTERN WAS IN YOUR EYES EVEN THEN.

SAPPHIRE, PLEASE, HE'S--

YOUR HEART...

...IS *HIS* HEART.

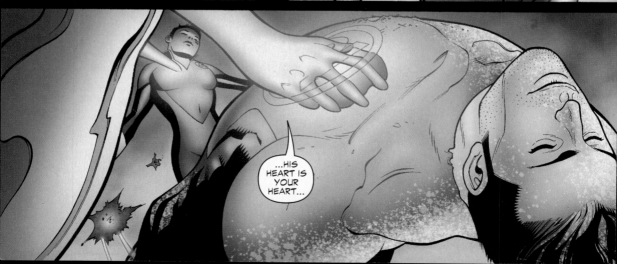

...HIS HEART IS YOUR HEART...

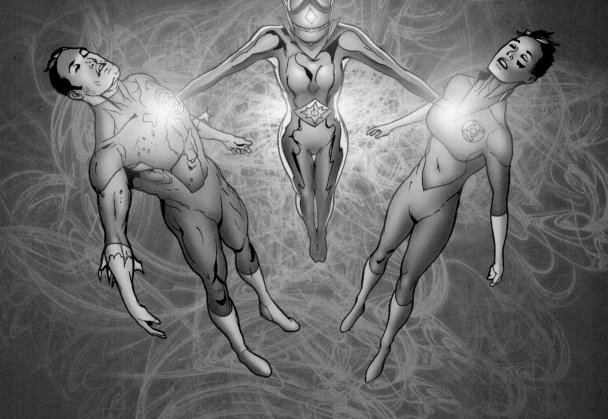

...AND WITH AN INFUSION OF LOVE AND WILL...

...TWO HEARTS ARE ONE!

AAGGHH!

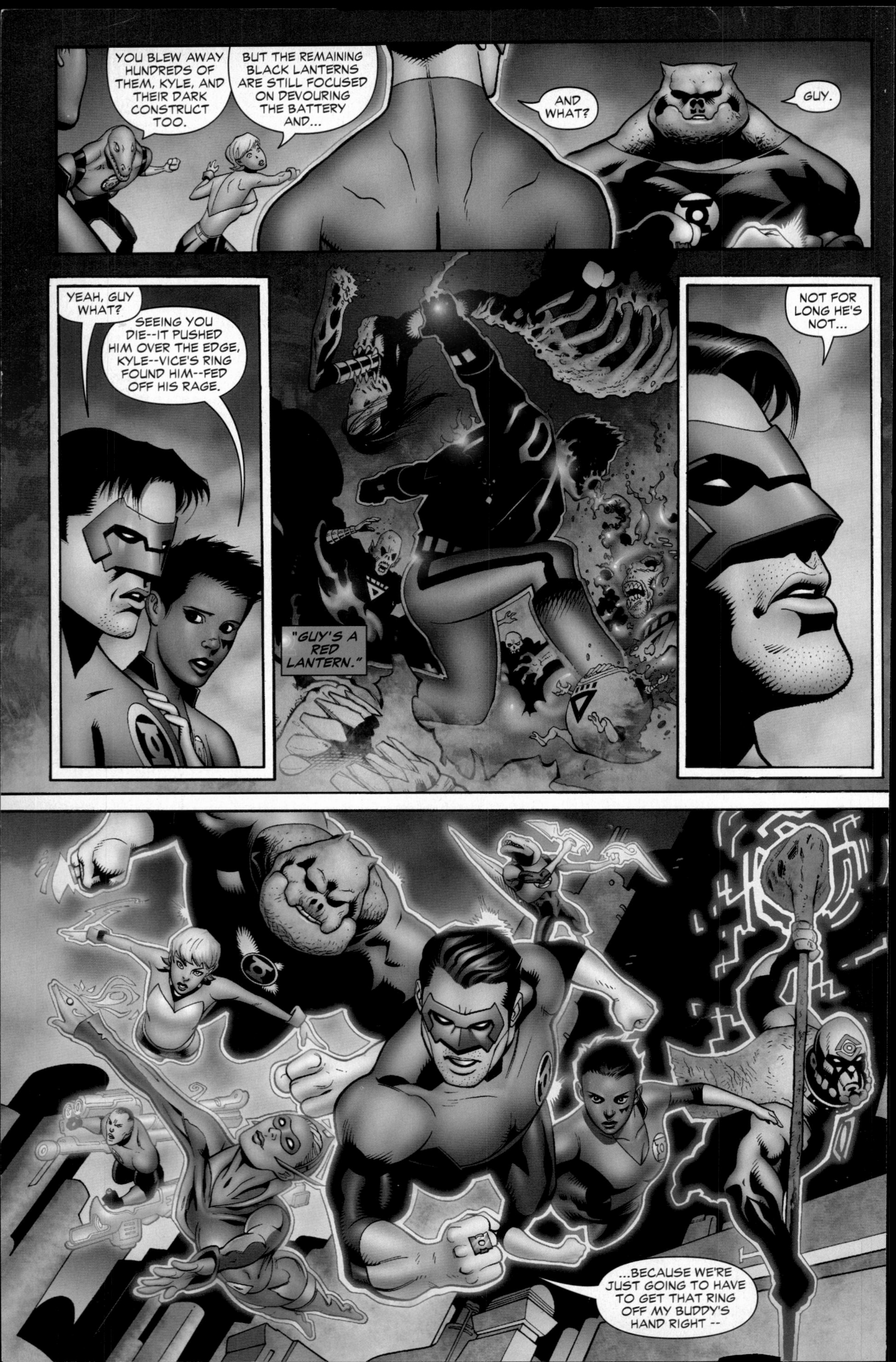
YOU BLEW AWAY HUNDREDS OF THEM, KYLE, AND THEIR DARK CONSTRUCT TOO.
BUT THE REMAINING BLACK LANTERNS ARE STILL FOCUSED ON DEVOURING THE BATTERY AND...
AND WHAT?
GUY.
YEAH, GUY WHAT?
SEEING YOU DIE--IT PUSHED HIM OVER THE EDGE, KYLE--VICE'S RING FOUND HIM--FED OFF HIS RAGE.
"GUY'S A RED LANTERN."
NOT FOR LONG HE'S NOT...
...BECAUSE WE'RE JUST GOING TO HAVE TO GET THAT RING OFF MY BUDDY'S HAND RIGHT --

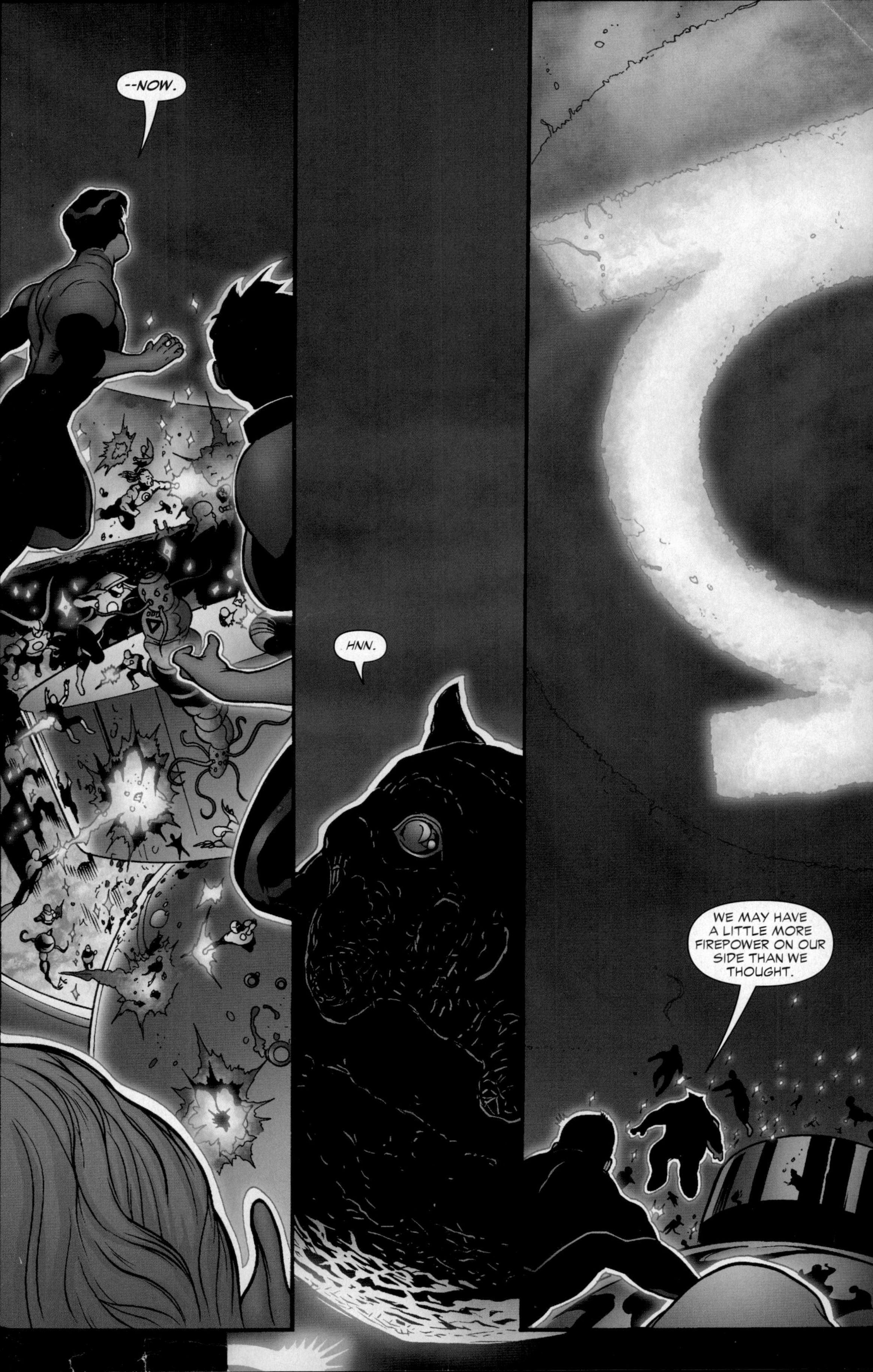
--NOW.
HNN.
WE MAY HAVE A LITTLE MORE FIREPOWER ON OUR SIDE THAN WE THOUGHT.

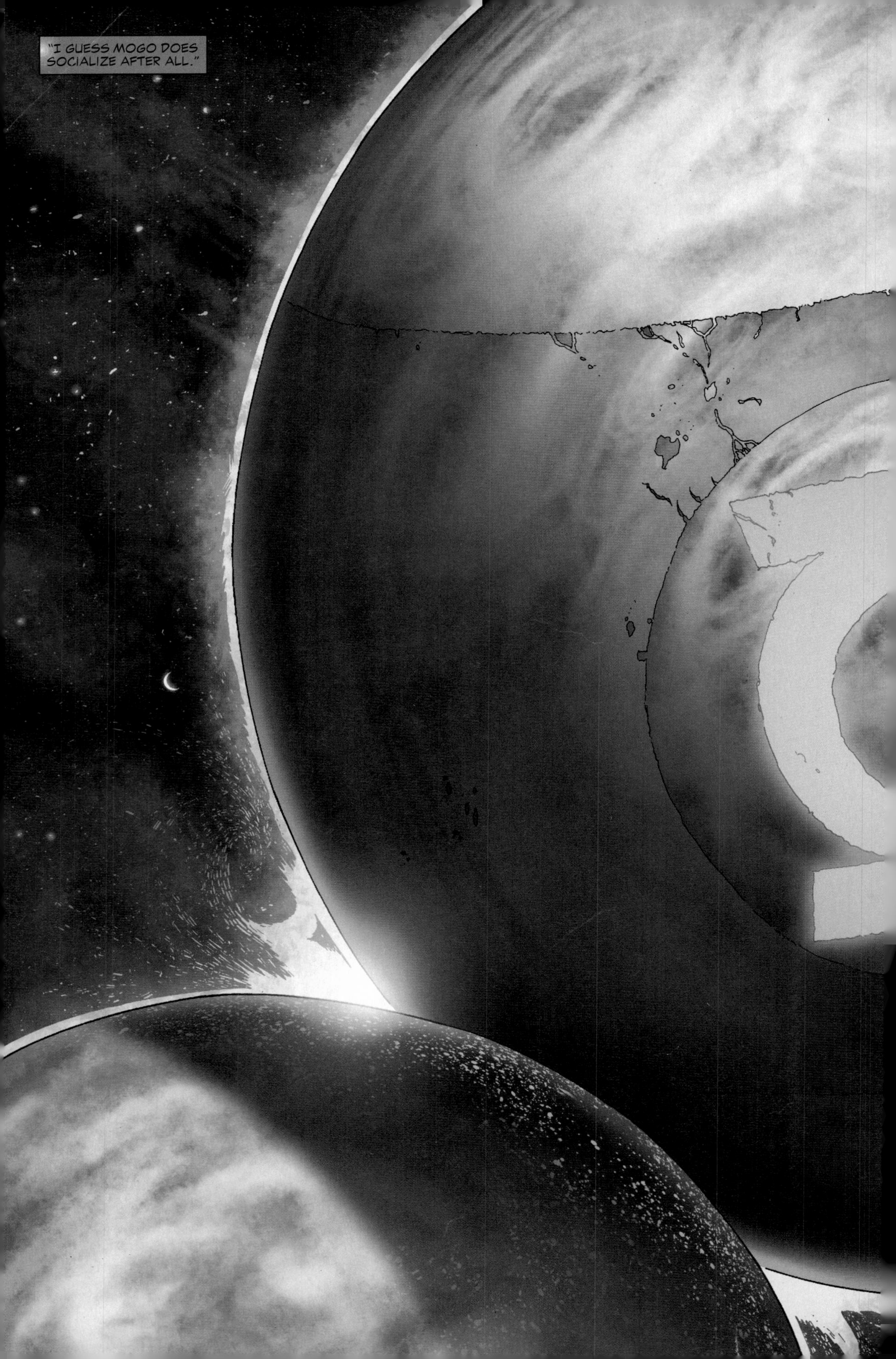
"I GUESS MOGO DOES SOCIALIZE AFTER ALL."

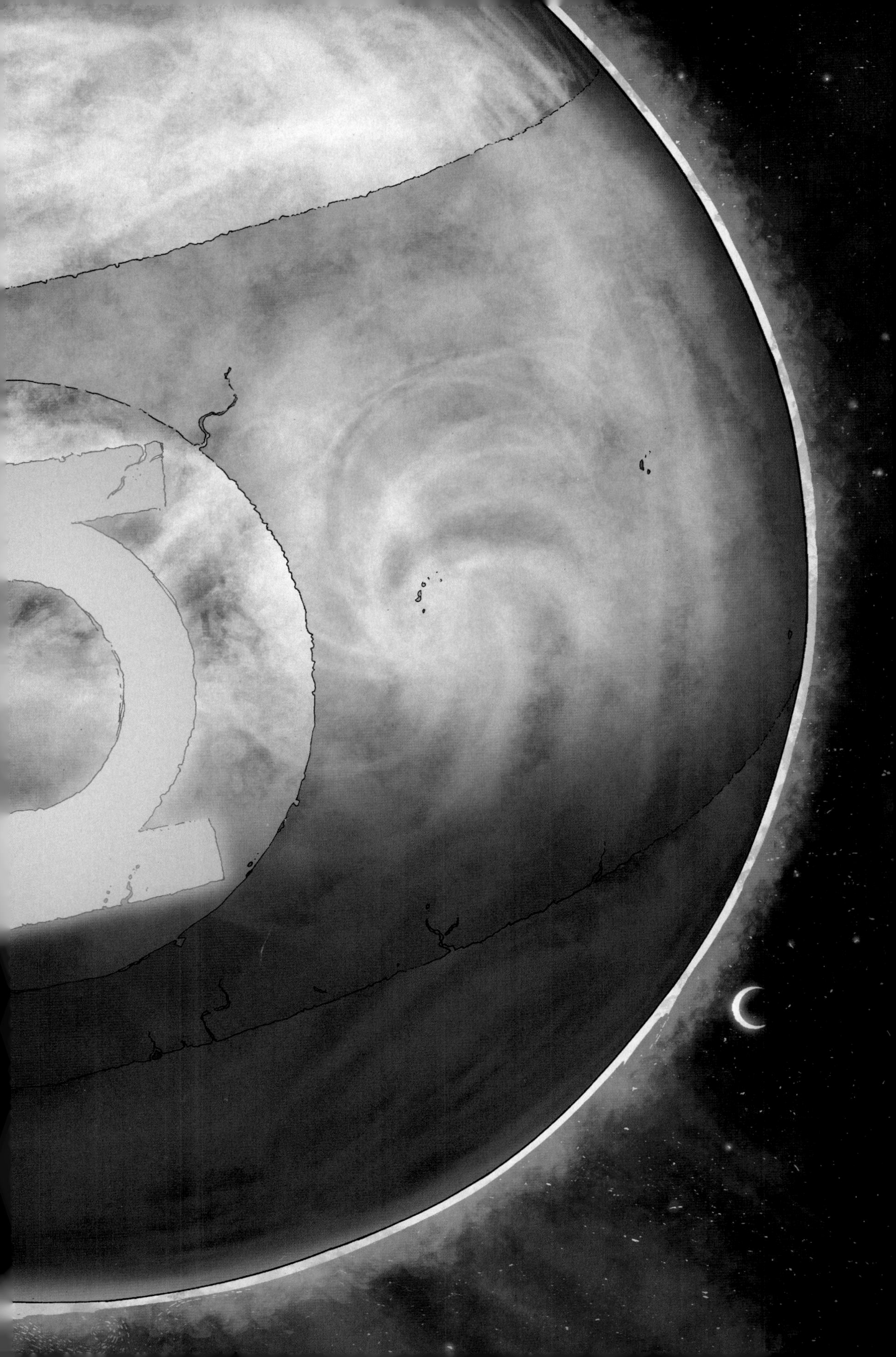

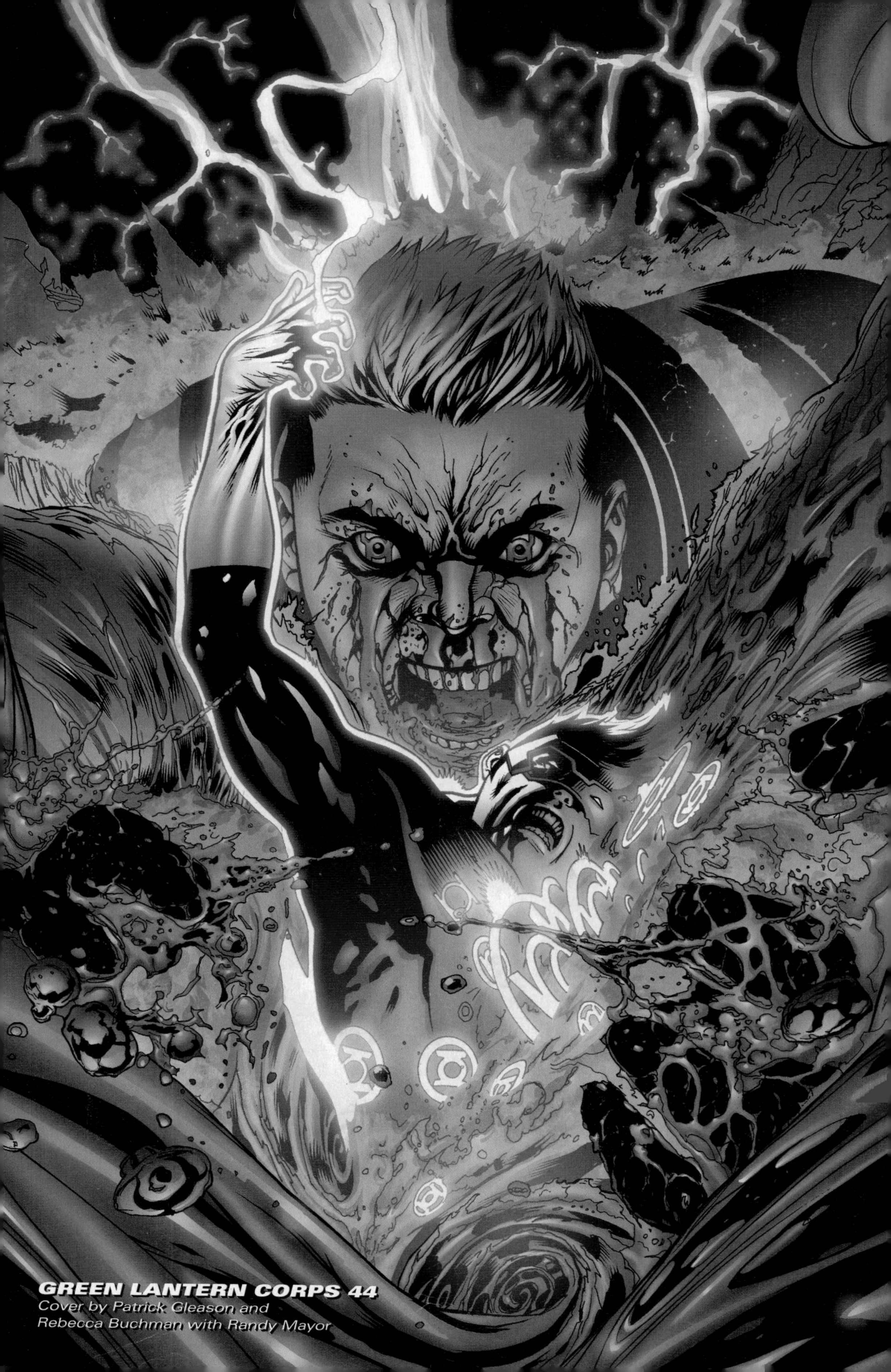

GREEN LANTERN CORPS 44
Cover by Patrick Gleason and
Rebecca Buchman with Randy Mayor

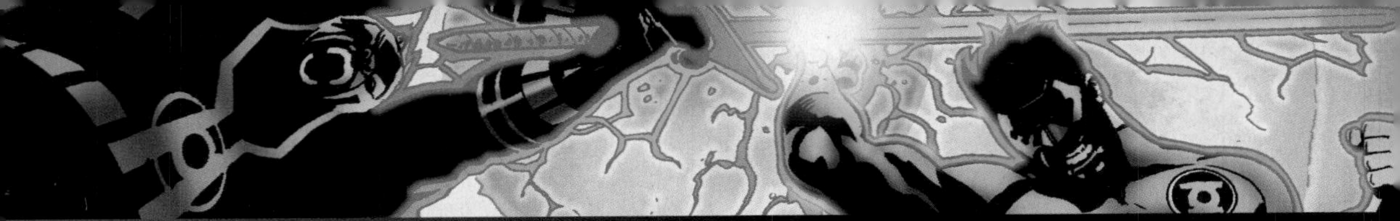

RED BADGE OF RAGE PART TWO

PATRICK GLEASON
PENCILS

REBECCA BUCHMAN
TOM NGUYEN
KEITH CHAMPAGNE
PATRICK GLEASON
INKS

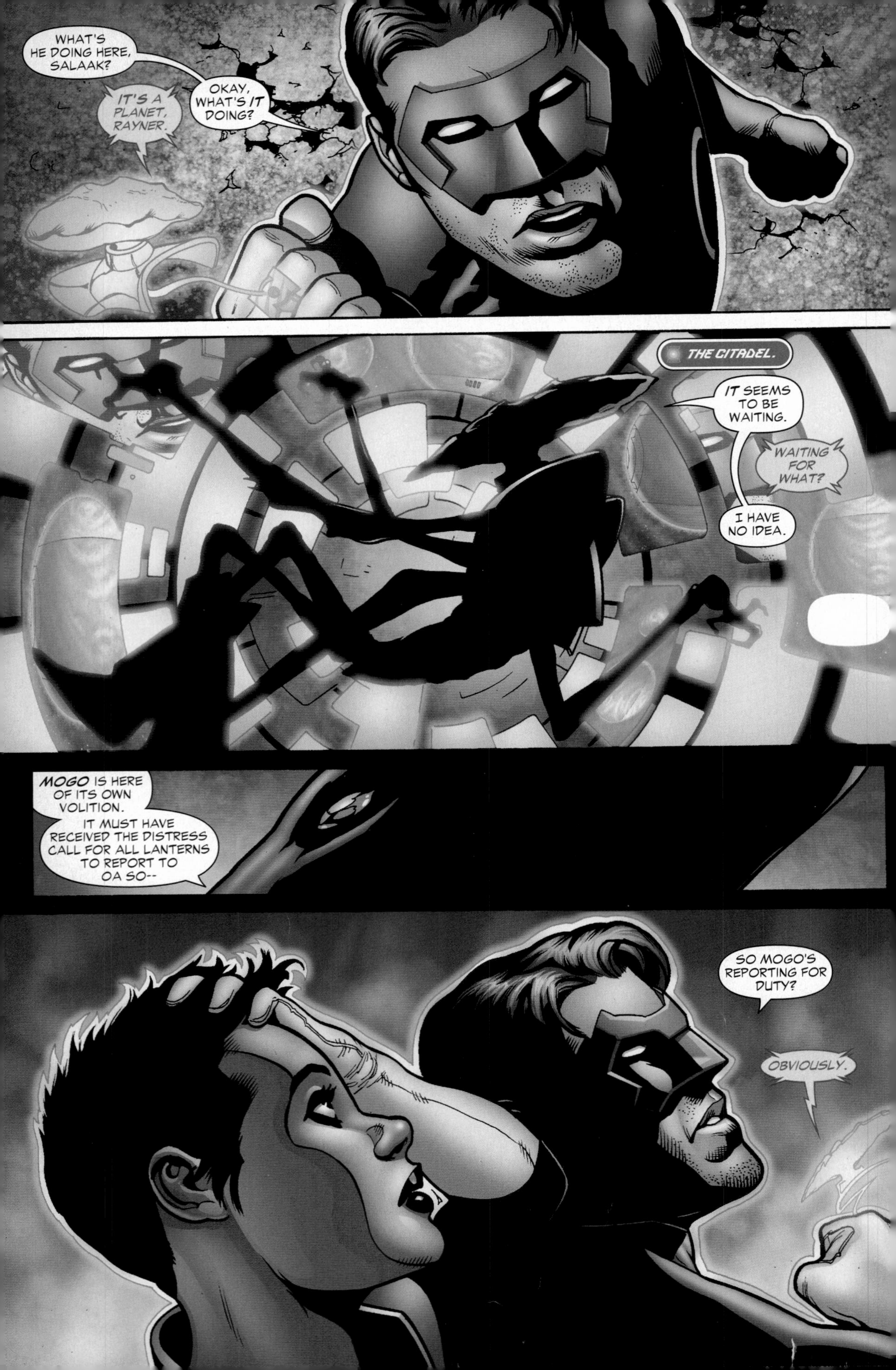
WHAT'S HE DOING HERE, SALAAK?
IT'S A PLANET, RAYNER.
OKAY, WHAT'S IT DOING?
THE CITADEL.
IT SEEMS TO BE WAITING.
WAITING FOR WHAT?
I HAVE NO IDEA.
MOGO IS HERE OF ITS OWN VOLITION.
IT MUST HAVE RECEIVED THE DISTRESS CALL FOR ALL LANTERNS TO REPORT TO OA SO--
SO MOGO'S REPORTING FOR DUTY?
OBVIOUSLY.

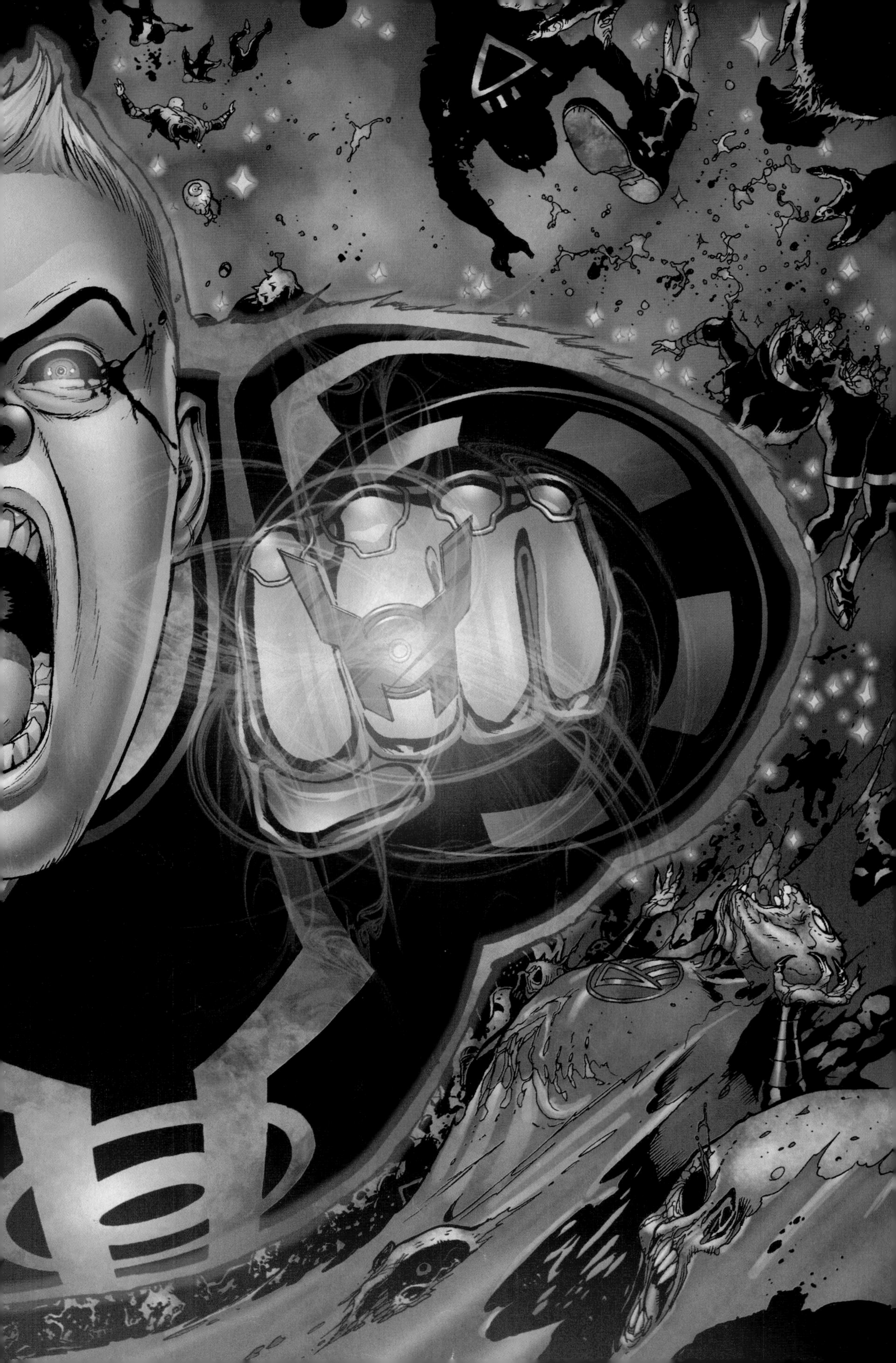

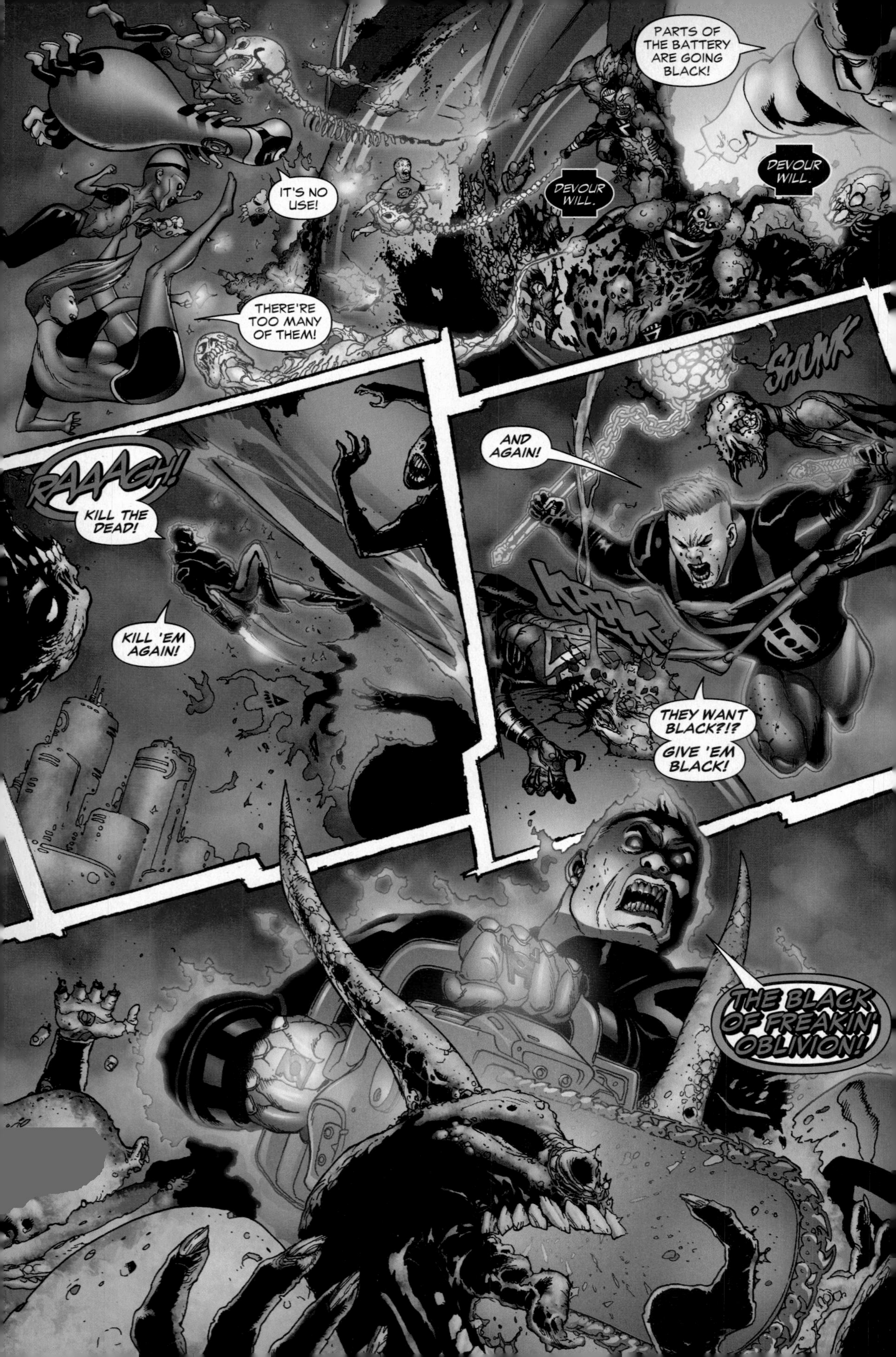
PARTS OF THE BATTERY ARE GOING BLACK!
IT'S NO USE!
DEVOUR WILL.
DEVOUR WILL.
THERE'RE TOO MANY OF THEM!
RAAAGH!
KILL THE DEAD!
KILL 'EM AGAIN!
SHUNK
AND AGAIN!
KRAK
THEY WANT BLACK?!?
GIVE 'EM BLACK!
THE BLACK OF FREAKIN' OBLIVION!

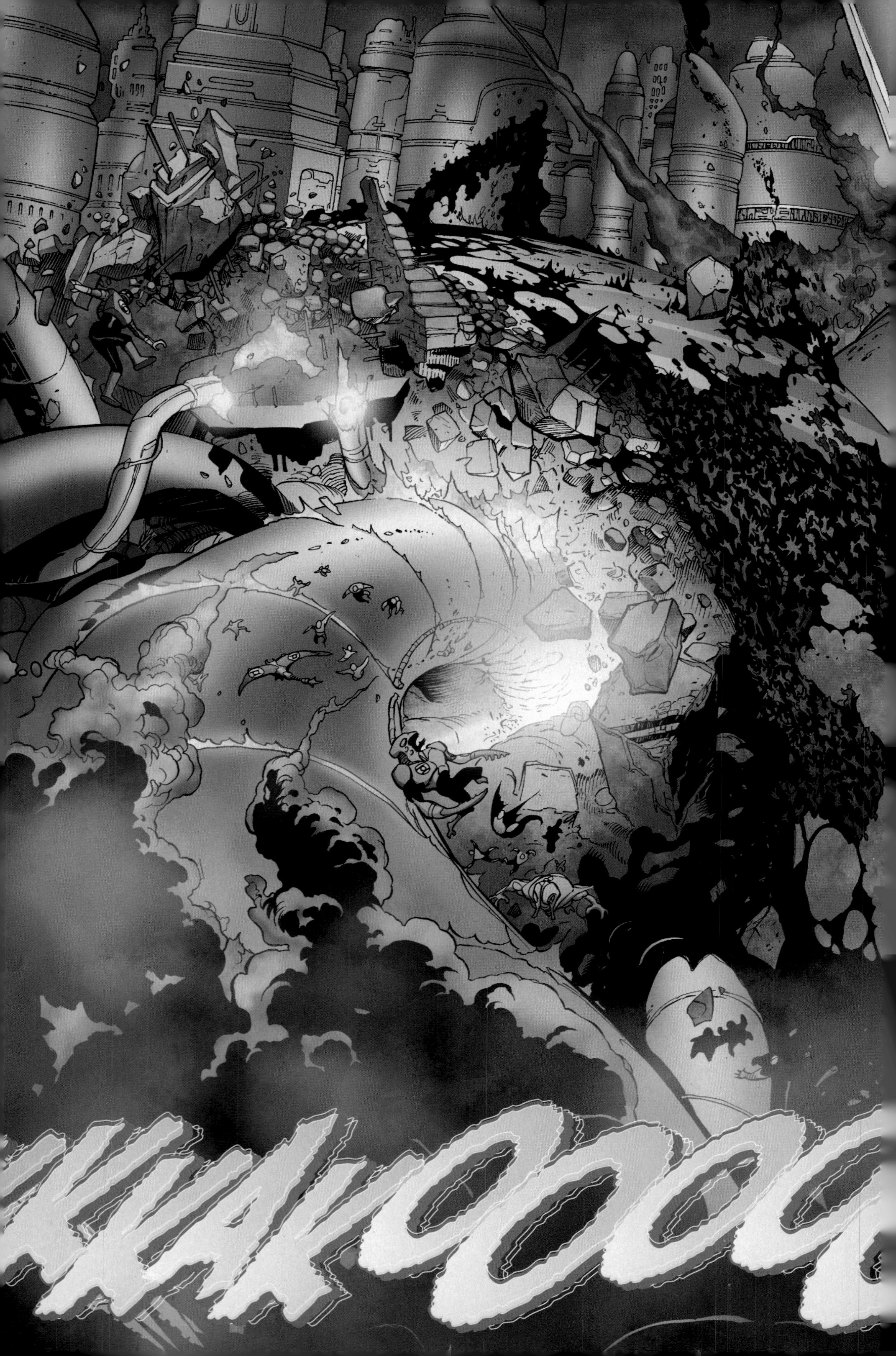

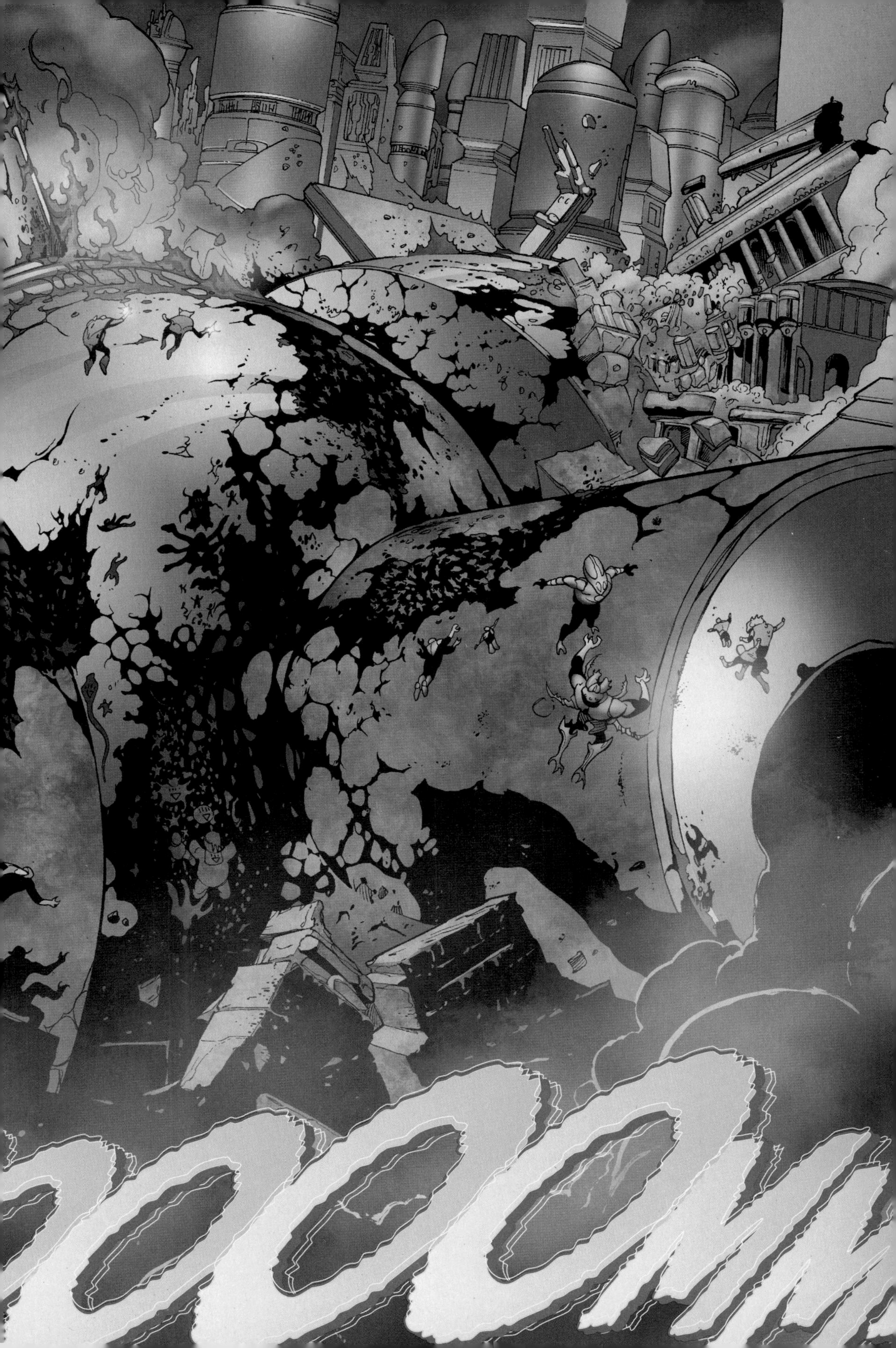

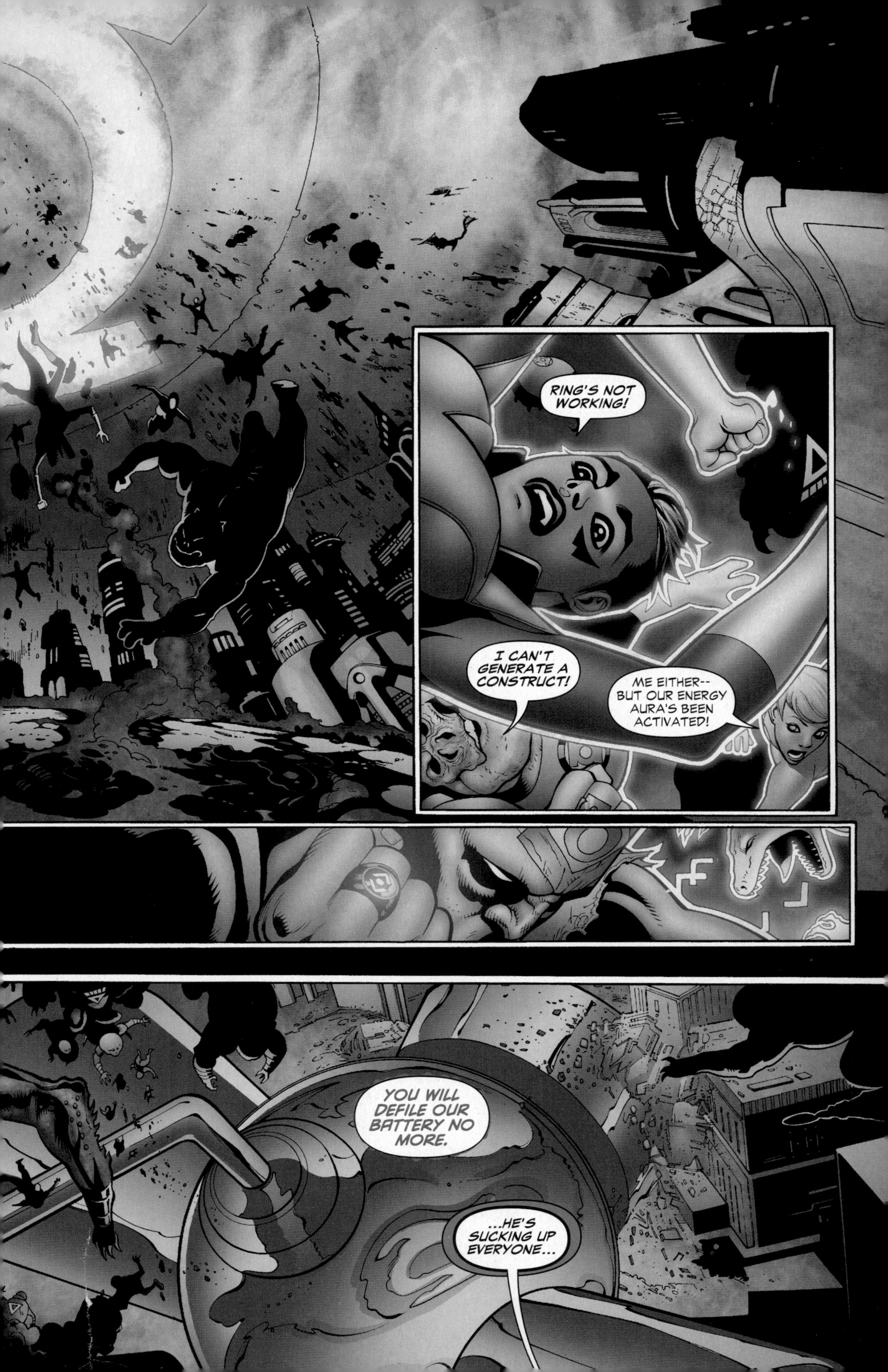
RING'S NOT WORKING!
I CAN'T GENERATE A CONSTRUCT!
ME EITHER-- BUT OUR ENERGY AURA'S BEEN ACTIVATED!
YOU WILL DEFILE OUR BATTERY NO MORE.
...HE'S SUCKING UP EVERYONE...

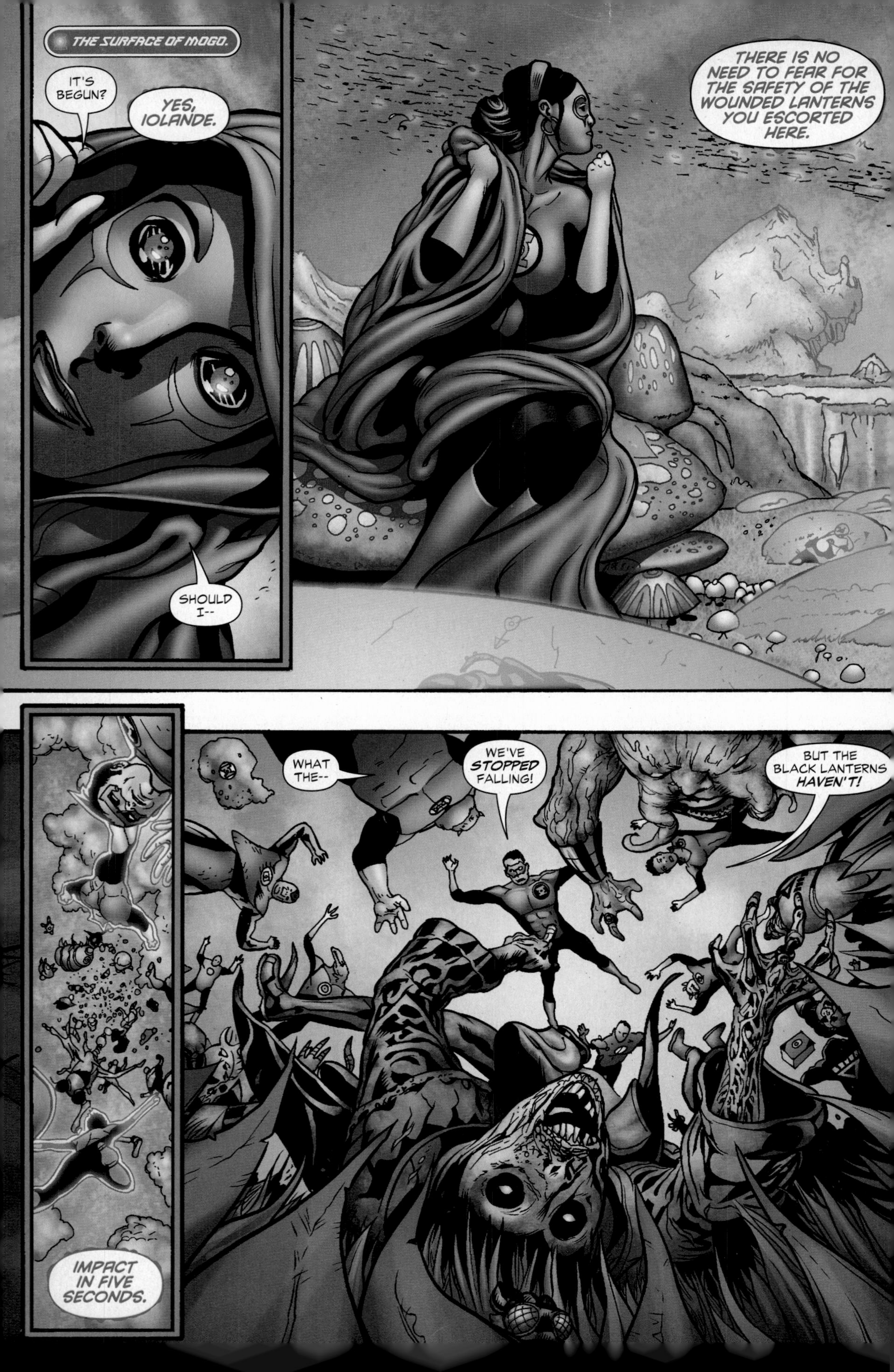
THE SURFACE OF MOGO.
IT'S BEGUN?
YES, IOLANDE.
SHOULD I--
THERE IS NO NEED TO FEAR FOR THE SAFETY OF THE WOUNDED LANTERNS YOU ESCORTED HERE.
WHAT THE--
WE'VE STOPPED FALLING!
BUT THE BLACK LANTERNS HAVEN'T!
IMPACT IN FIVE SECONDS.

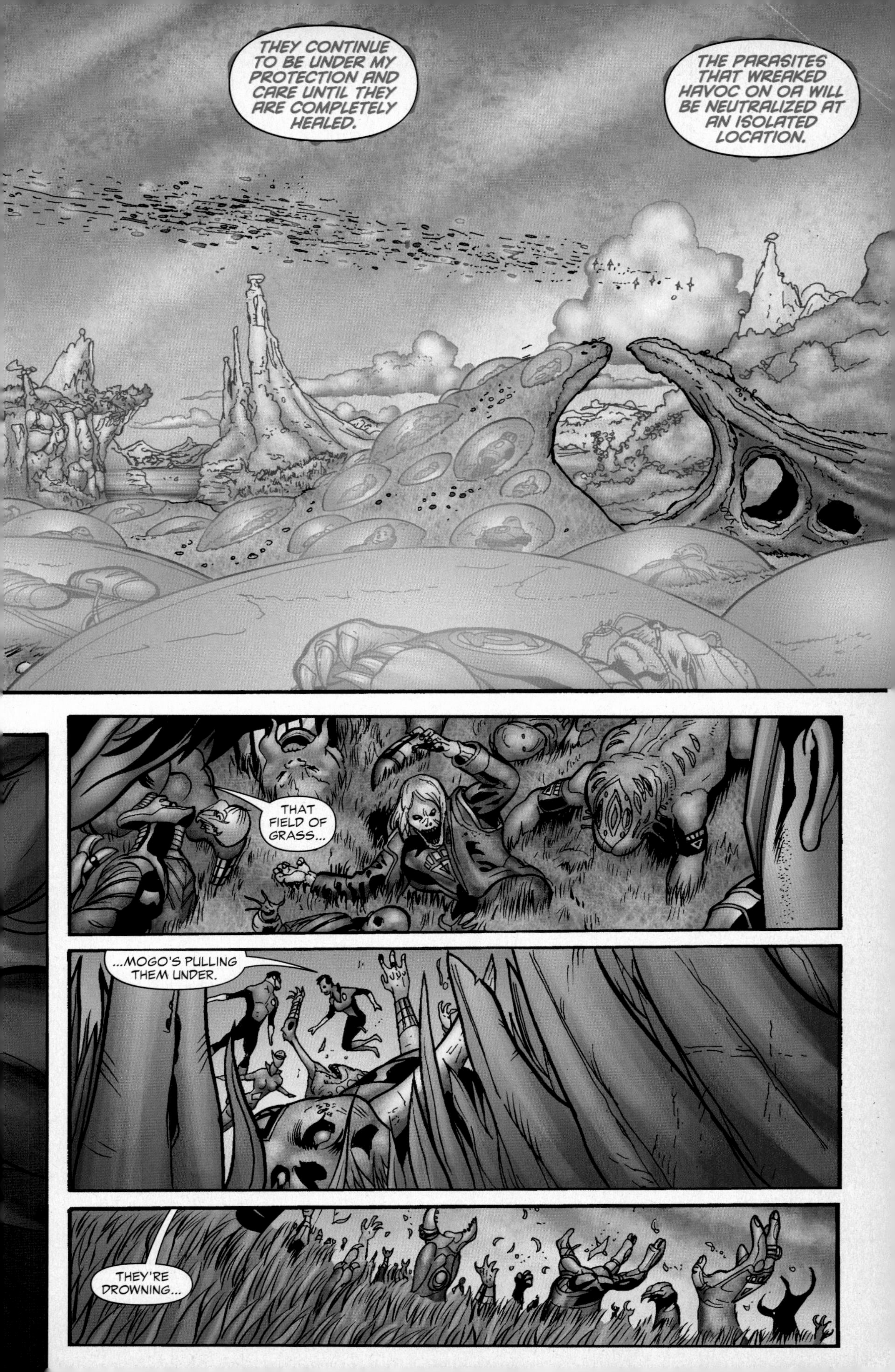
THEY CONTINUE TO BE UNDER MY PROTECTION AND CARE UNTIL THEY ARE COMPLETELY HEALED.
THE PARASITES THAT WREAKED HAVOC ON OA WILL BE NEUTRALIZED AT AN ISOLATED LOCATION.
THAT FIELD OF GRASS...
...MOGO'S PULLING THEM UNDER.
THEY'RE DROWNING...

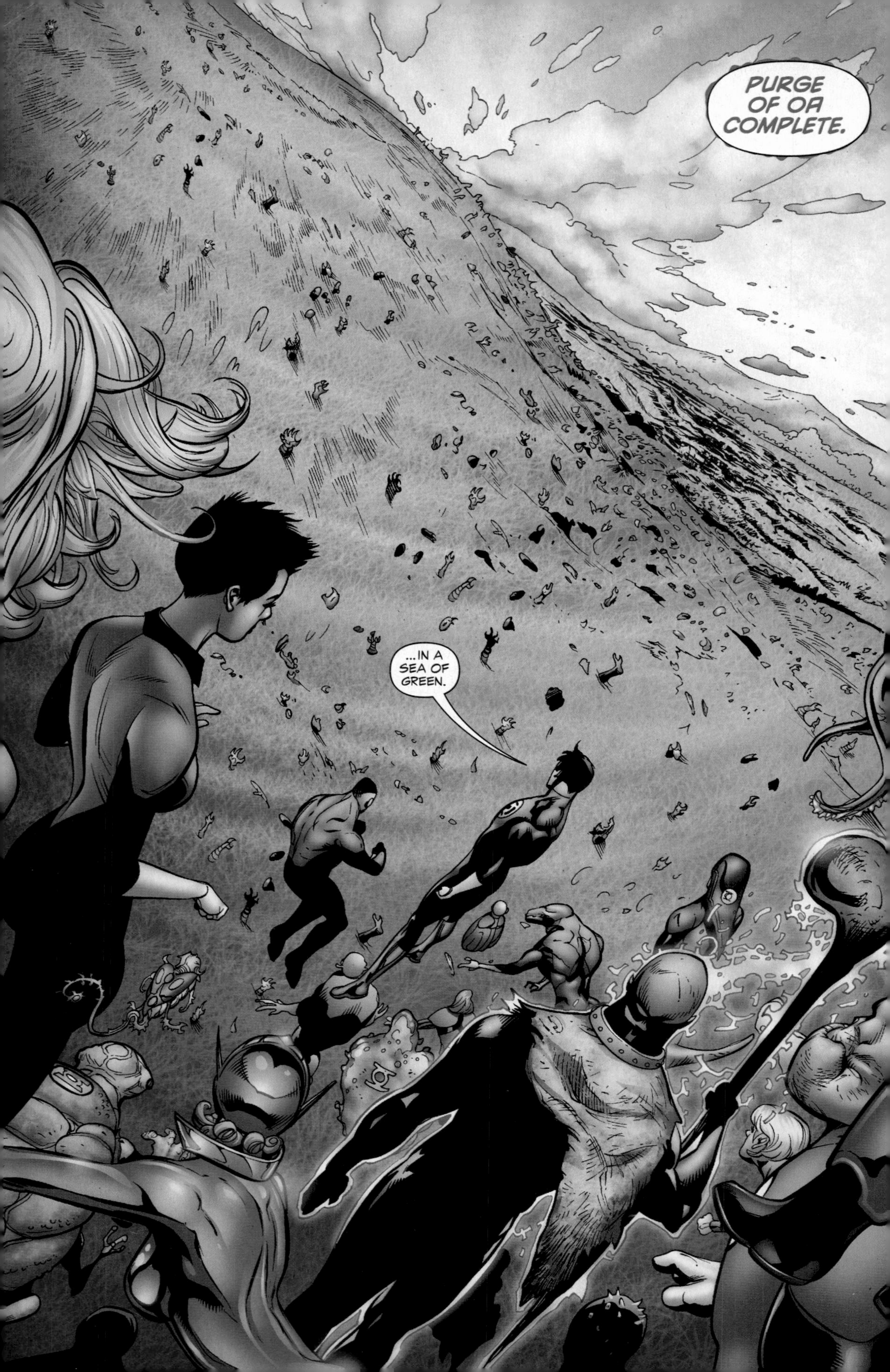
PURGE OF OA COMPLETE.
...IN A SEA OF GREEN.

GREEN LANTERN CORPS 45
Cover by Patrick Gleason and Rebecca Buchman with Randy Mayor

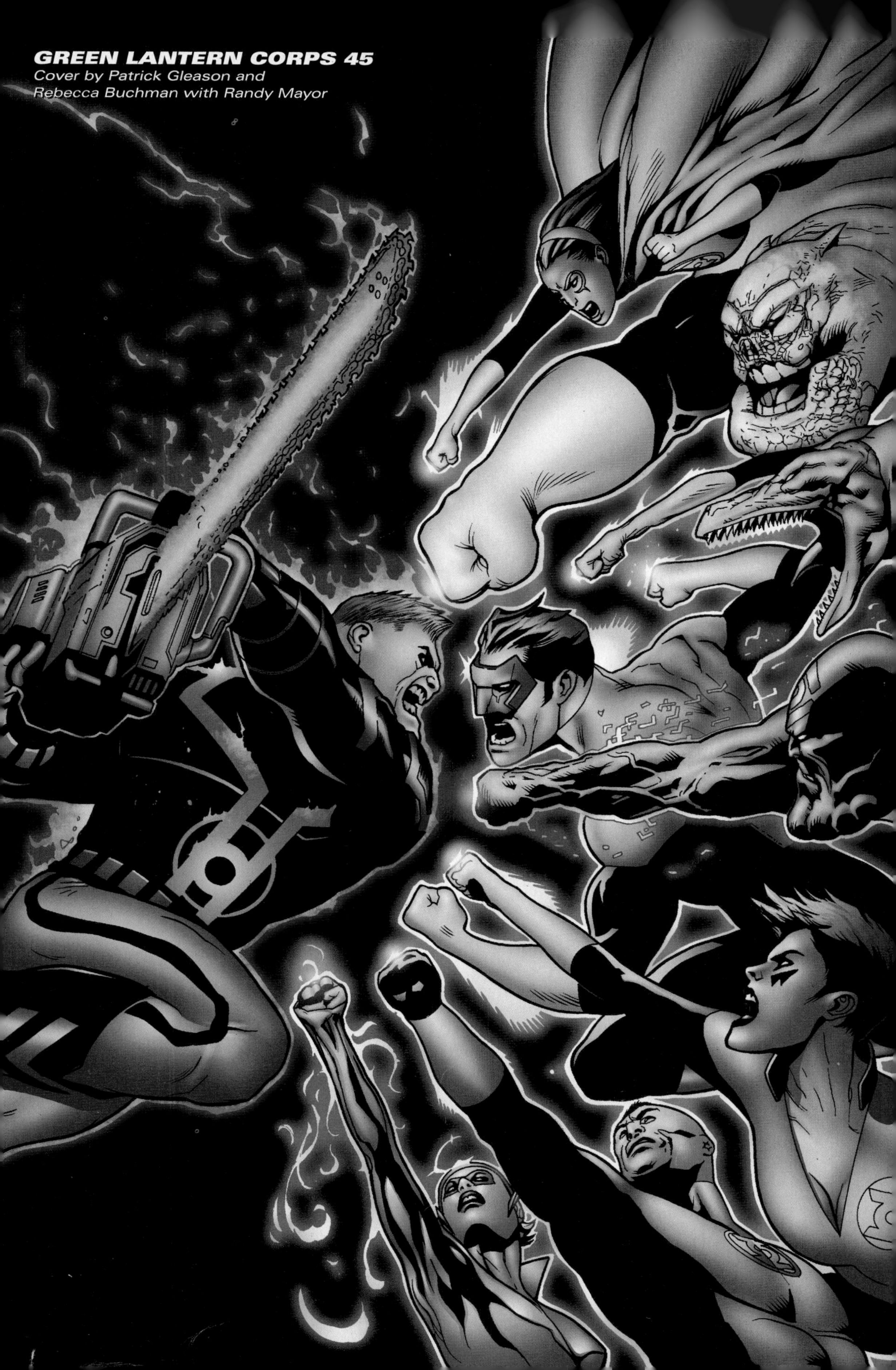

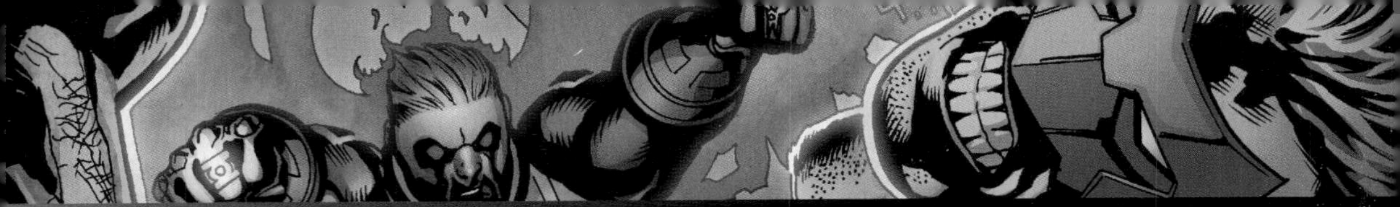

RED DAWN

PATRICK GLEASON

PENCILS

REBECCA BUCHMAN
KEITH CHAMPAGNE
TOM NGUYEN

INKS

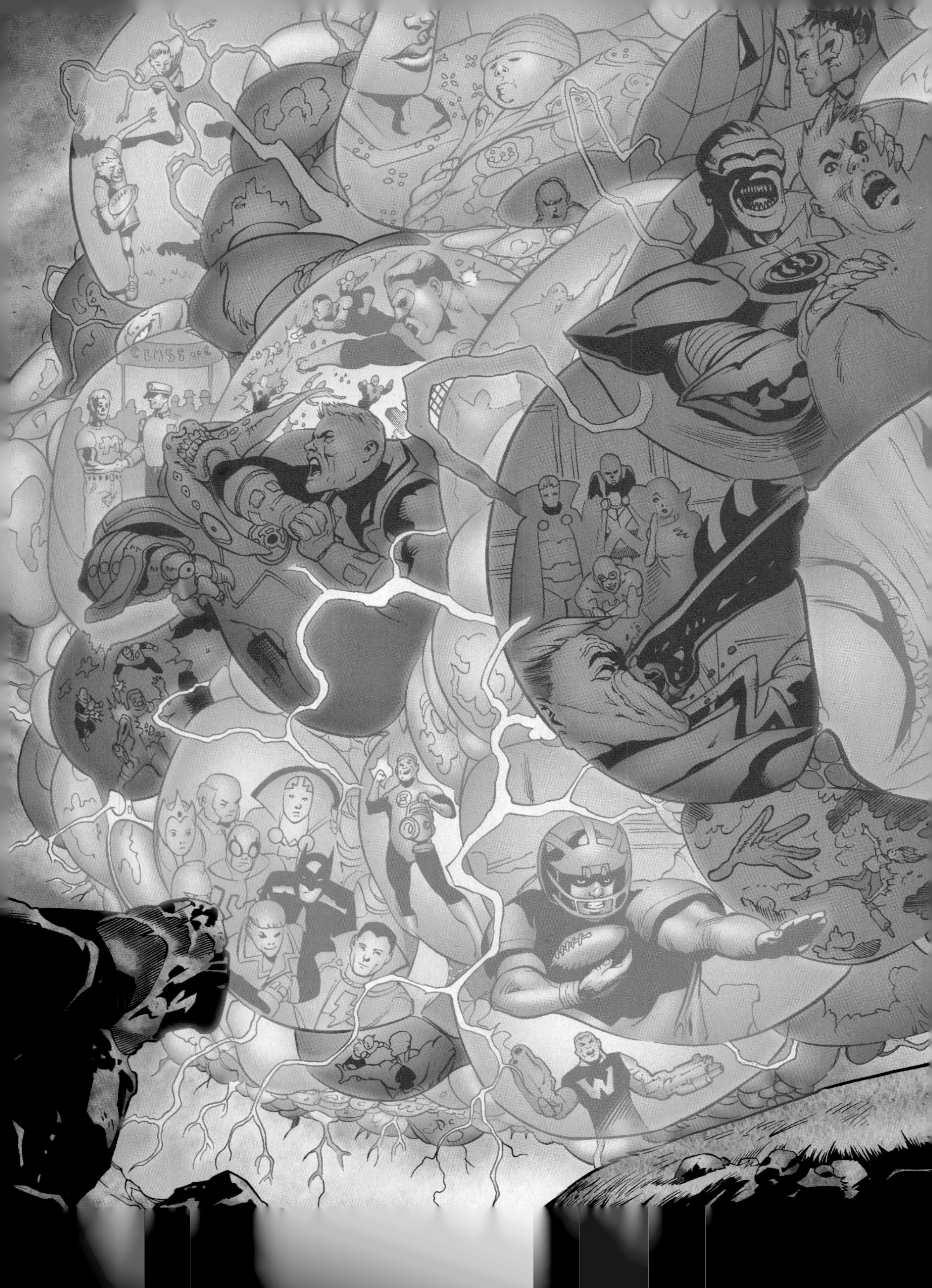
CLASS OF

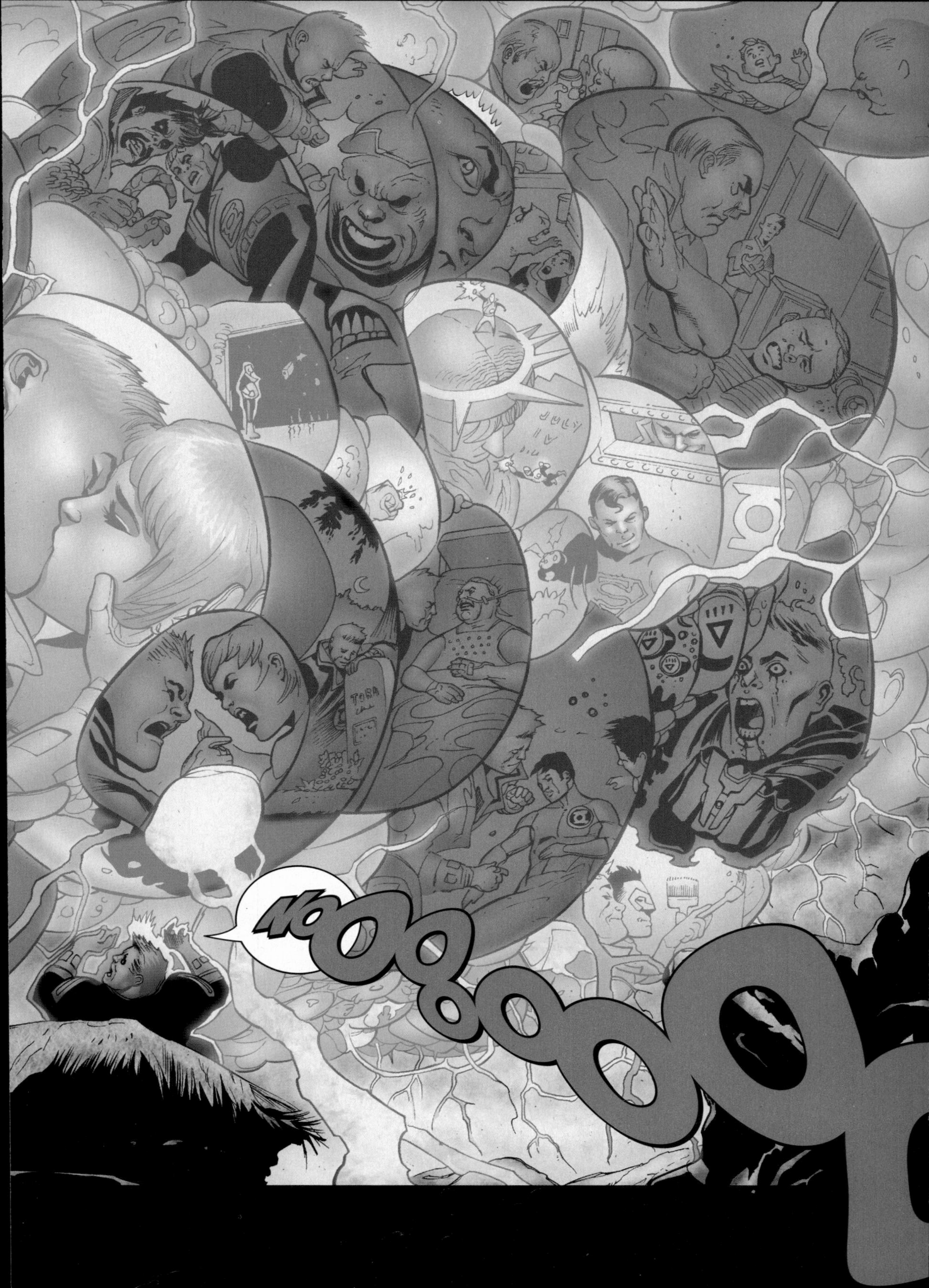
NOOOOOOOOO
TORA

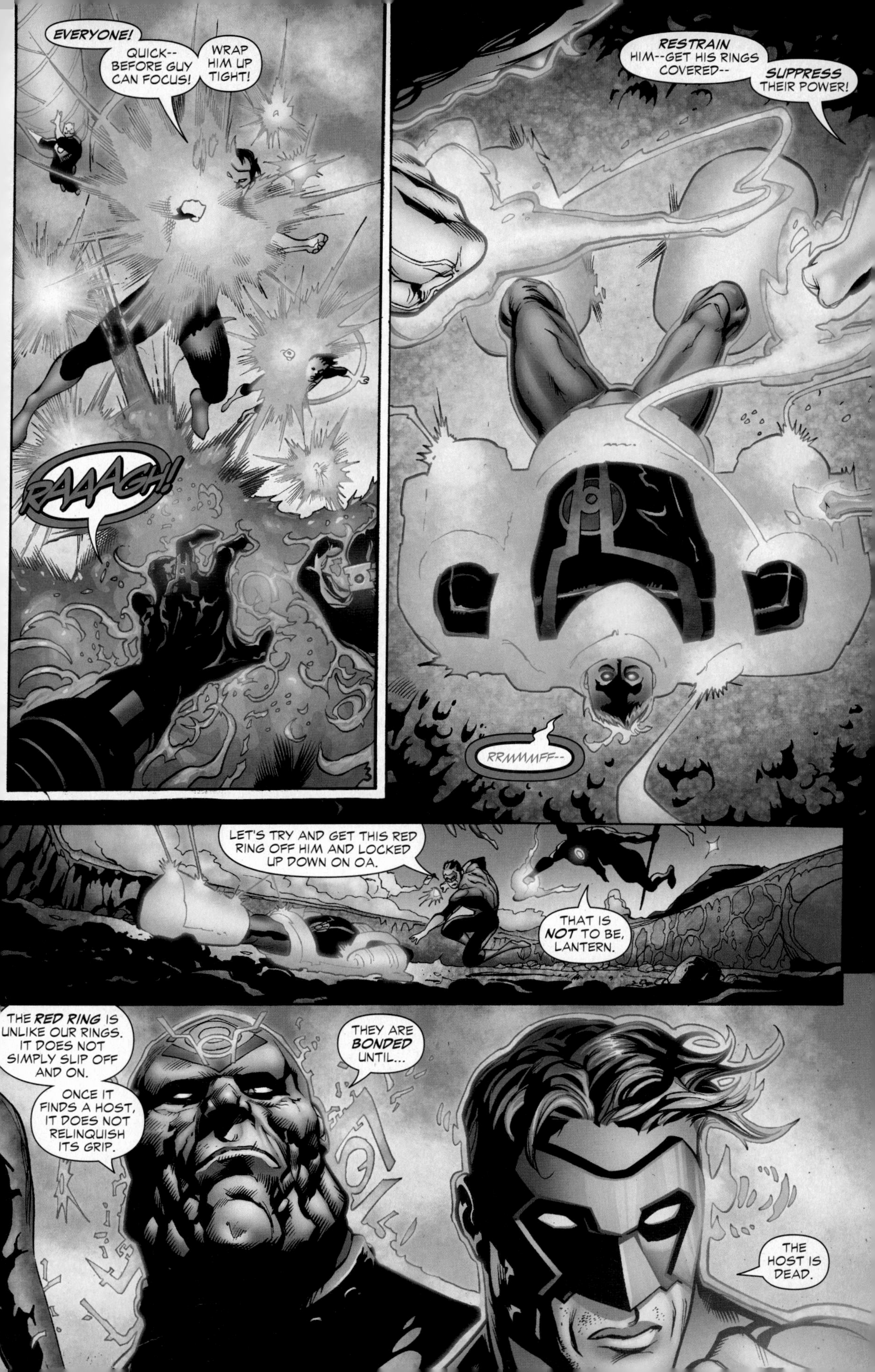
EVERYONE!
QUICK-- BEFORE GUY CAN FOCUS!
WRAP HIM UP TIGHT!
RAAAGH!
RESTRAIN HIM--GET HIS RINGS COVERED--
SUPPRESS THEIR POWER!
RRMMMFF--
LET'S TRY AND GET THIS RED RING OFF HIM AND LOCKED UP DOWN ON OA.
THAT IS NOT TO BE, LANTERN.
THE RED RING IS UNLIKE OUR RINGS. IT DOES NOT SIMPLY SLIP OFF AND ON.
ONCE IT FINDS A HOST, IT DOES NOT RELINQUISH ITS GRIP.
THEY ARE BONDED UNTIL...
THE HOST IS DEAD.

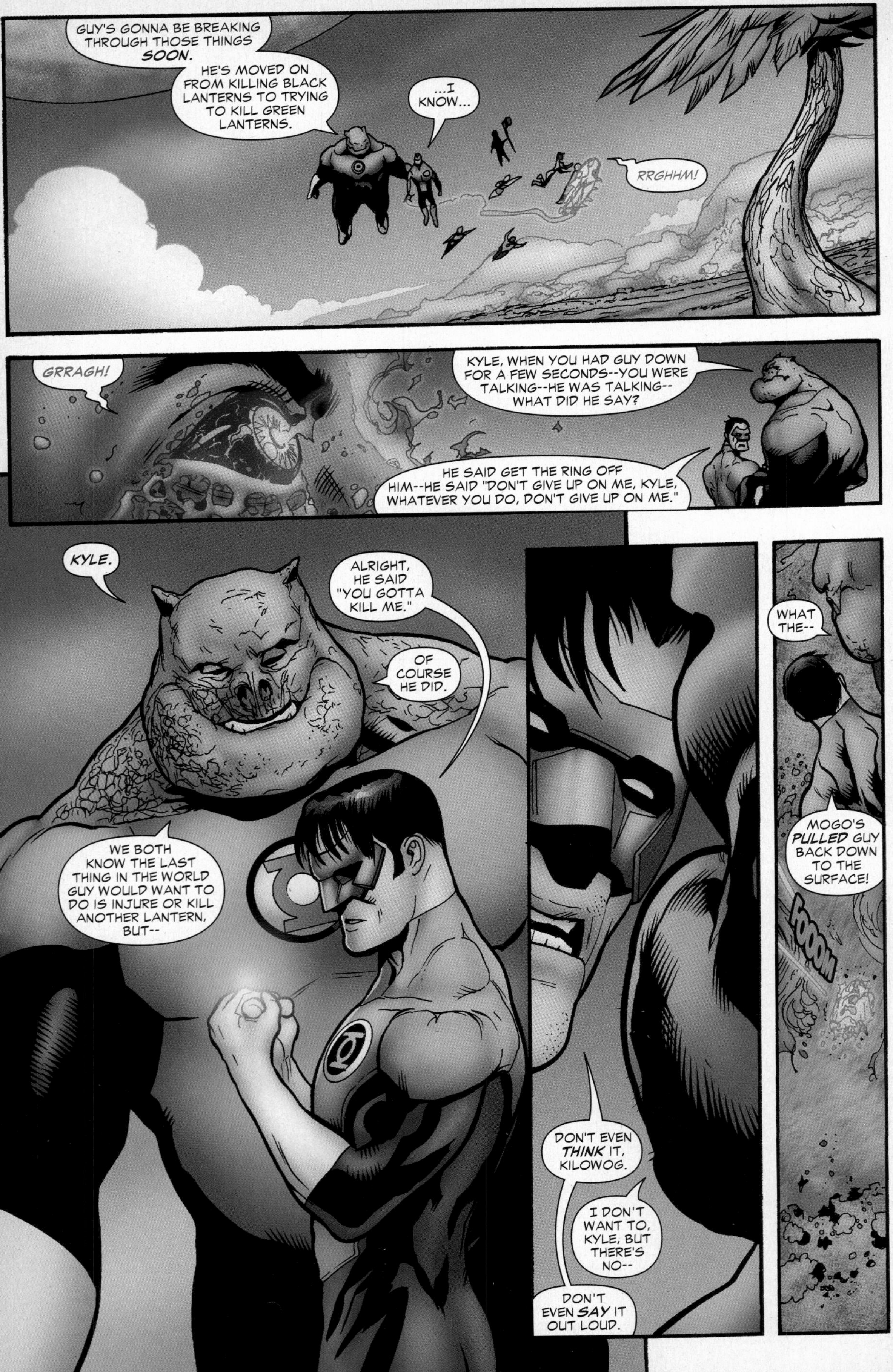
GUY'S GONNA BE BREAKING THROUGH THOSE THINGS SOON.
HE'S MOVED ON FROM KILLING BLACK LANTERNS TO TRYING TO KILL GREEN LANTERNS.
...I KNOW...
RRGHHM!
GRRAGH!
KYLE, WHEN YOU HAD GUY DOWN FOR A FEW SECONDS--YOU WERE TALKING--HE WAS TALKING--WHAT DID HE SAY?
HE SAID GET THE RING OFF HIM--HE SAID "DON'T GIVE UP ON ME, KYLE, WHATEVER YOU DO, DON'T GIVE UP ON ME."
KYLE.
ALRIGHT, HE SAID "YOU GOTTA KILL ME."
OF COURSE HE DID.
WE BOTH KNOW THE LAST THING IN THE WORLD GUY WOULD WANT TO DO IS INJURE OR KILL ANOTHER LANTERN, BUT--
DON'T EVEN THINK IT, KILOWOG.
I DON'T WANT TO, KYLE, BUT THERE'S NO--
DON'T EVEN SAY IT OUT LOUD.
WHAT THE--
MOGO'S PULLED GUY BACK DOWN TO THE SURFACE!
FOOOM

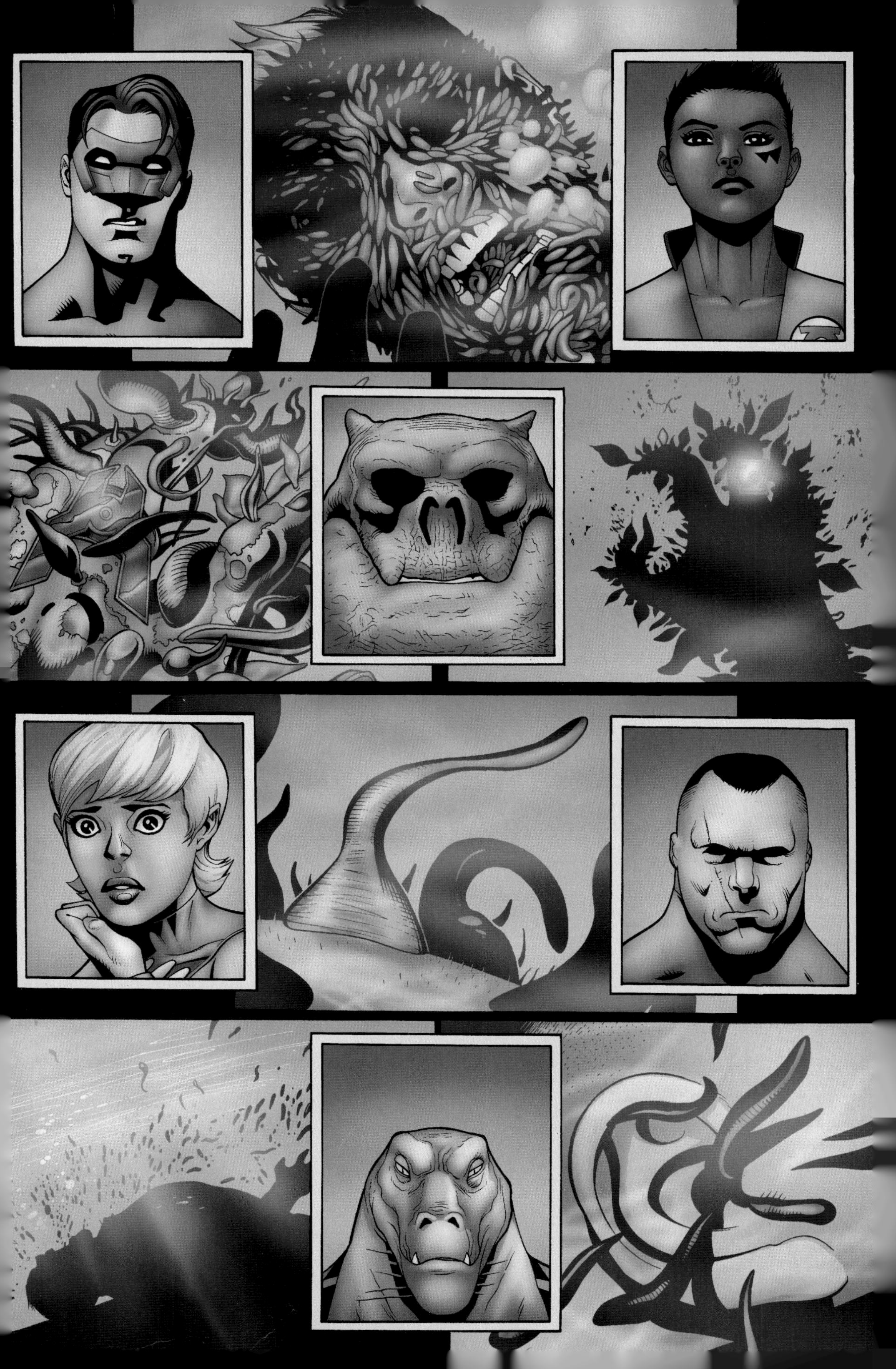

SON OF A BITCH!

GUY.

...H-HEY...

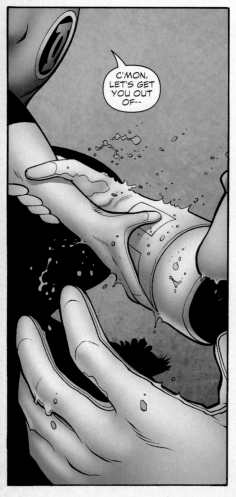

C'MON, LET'S GET YOU OUT OF--

--THERE.

I HAVE DONE ALL THAT I CAN, YET THERE ARE STILL TRACE AMOUNTS OF TOXIC RED LANTERN BLOOD COURSING THROUGH YOUR SYSTEM.

AS THE INDIGO LANTERN STATED, ONLY THE LIGHT OF A BLUE LANTERN CAN COMPLETELY ERADICATE THE EXPOSURE TO A RED RING.

GOT IT. RED BAD, BLUE GOOD.

OKAY, I KNOW WHO SAVED MY ASS, KYLE, BUT WHO SAVED YOURS?

MIRI. THE STAR SAPPHIRE.

GOOD GOING, KID. YOU GOT YOURSELF AN OPEN TAB AT WARRIORS BAR FER LIFE.

FOOD AND BOOZE MIND YA, NOT JUST--

I APPRECIATE THE GESTURE BUT--

UNNN.

WHAT IS IT, MUNK?

WE NEED TO RETURN TO OA IMMEDIATELY.

I SENSE REVERBERATIONS IN THE TIME/SPACE CONTINUUM--MEMBERS OF THE INDIGO TRIBE ARE AT THIS MOMENT LOCKING IN ON YOUR CENTRAL POWER BATTERY.

THEN LET'S STOP BURNING DAYLIGHT AND GO ROLL OUT THE GREEN CARPET...

GREEN LANTERN CORPS 46

Cover by Patrick Gleason and Rebecca Buchman with Randy Mayor

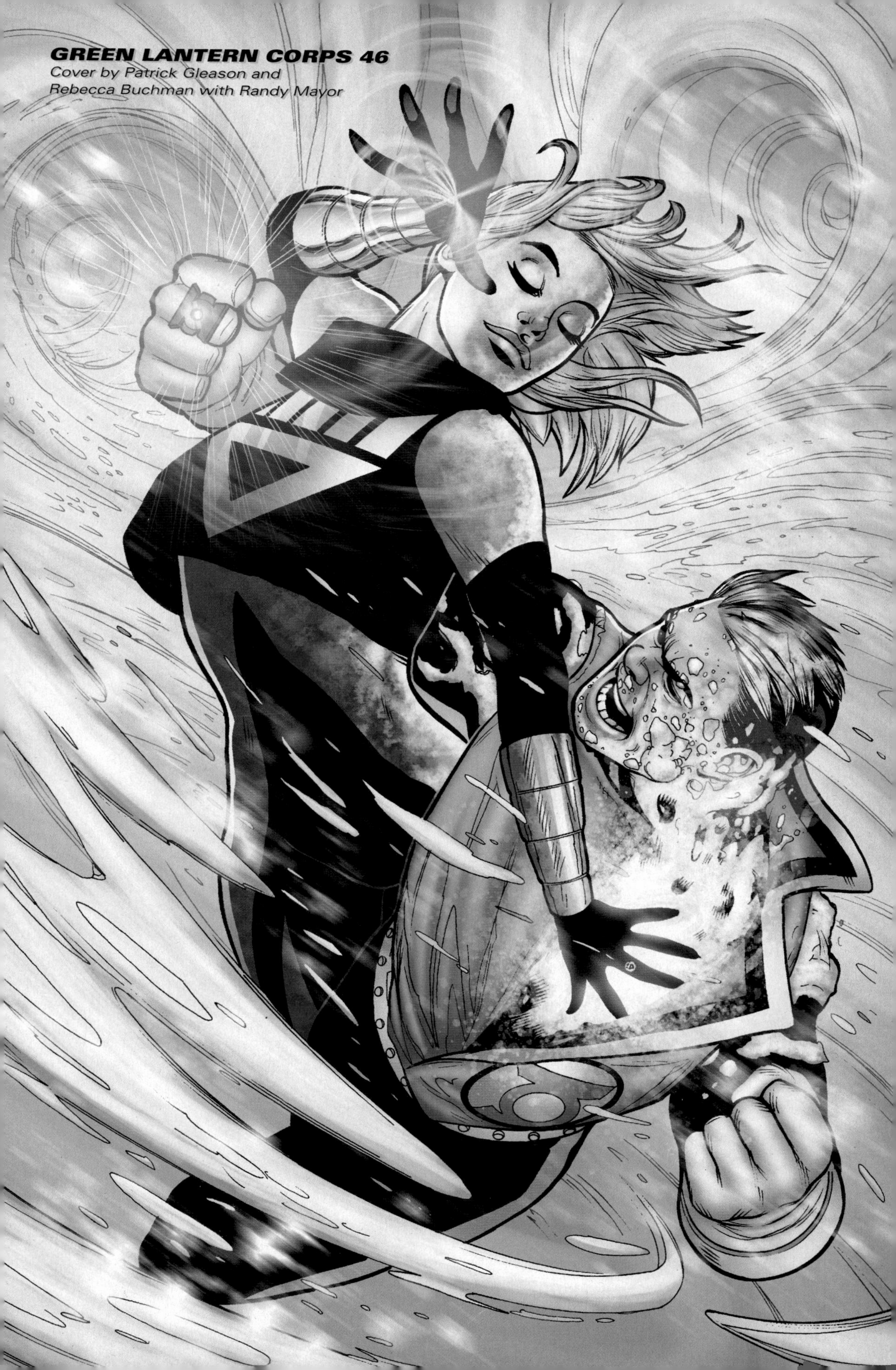

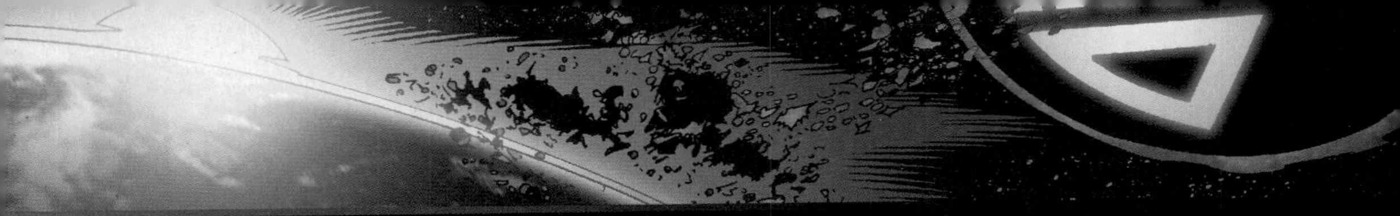

BLACK DAWN

PATRICK GLEASON
PENCILS

REBECCA BUCHMAN
KEITH CHAMPAGNE
TOM NGUYEN
INKS

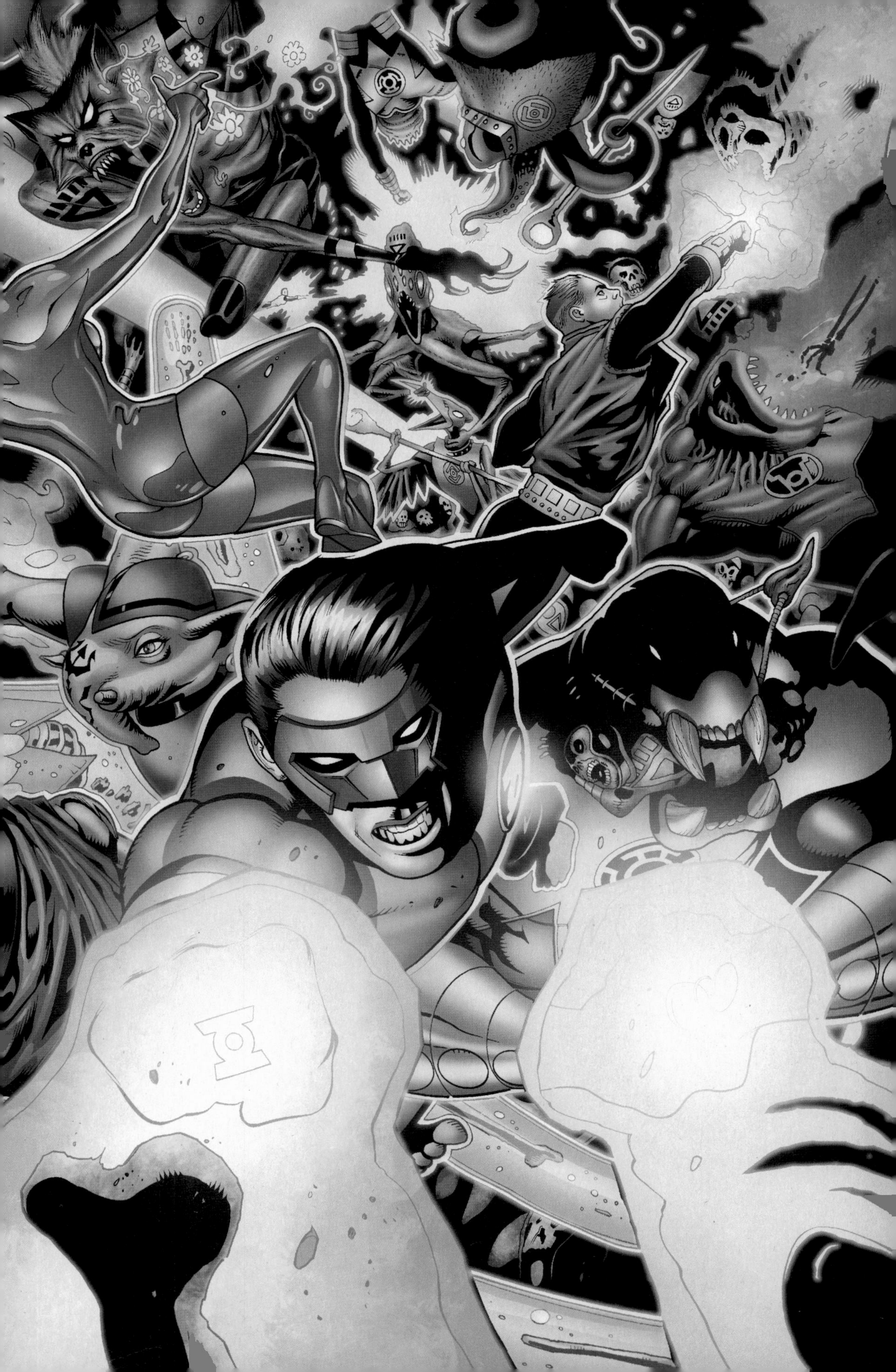

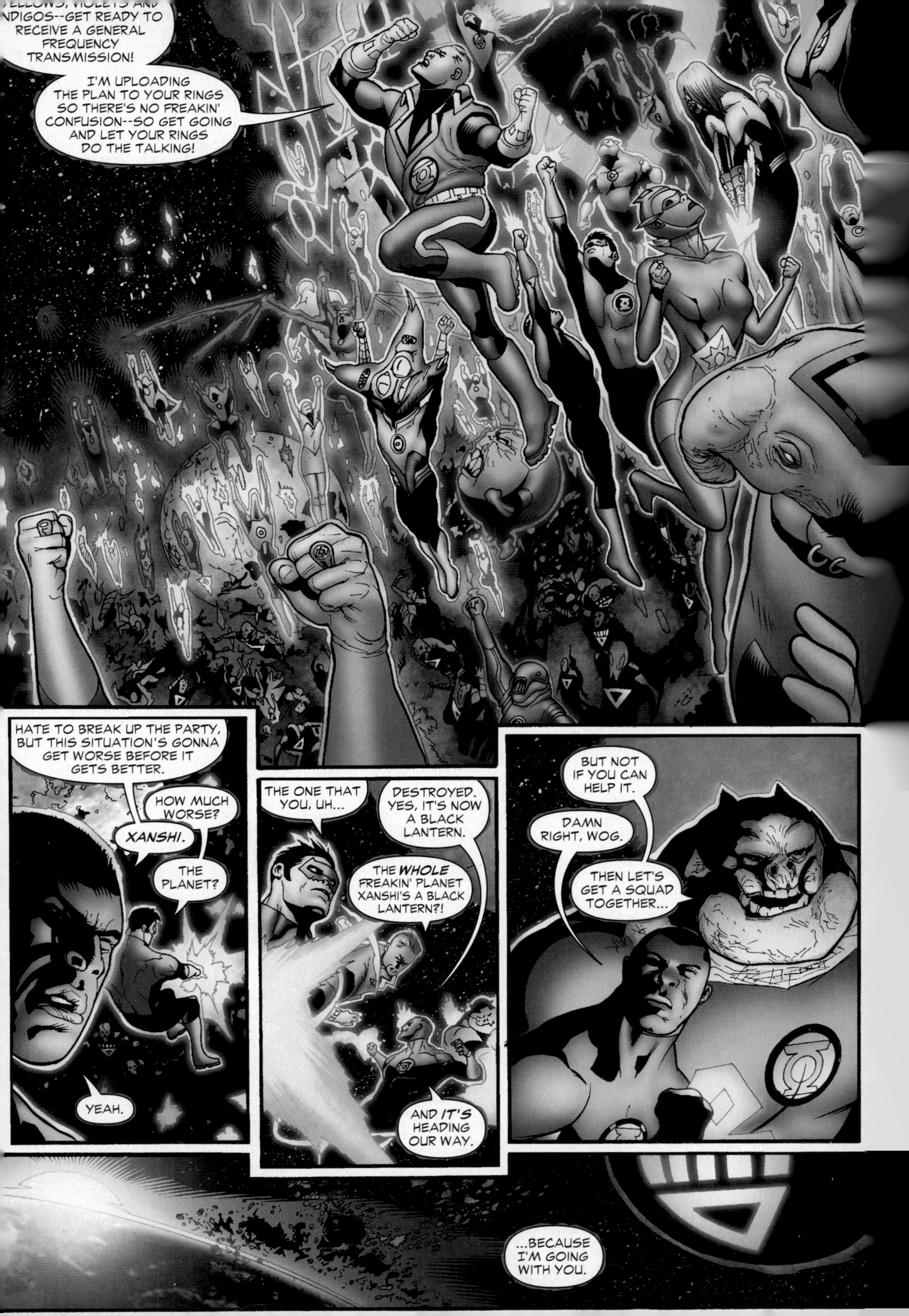
YELLOWS, VIOLETS AND INDIGOS--GET READY TO RECEIVE A GENERAL FREQUENCY TRANSMISSION!
I'M UPLOADING THE PLAN TO YOUR RINGS SO THERE'S NO FREAKIN' CONFUSION--SO GET GOING AND LET YOUR RINGS DO THE TALKING!
HATE TO BREAK UP THE PARTY, BUT THIS SITUATION'S GONNA GET WORSE BEFORE IT GETS BETTER.
HOW MUCH WORSE?
XANSHI.
THE PLANET?
YEAH.
THE ONE THAT YOU, UH...
DESTROYED. YES, IT'S NOW A BLACK LANTERN.
THE WHOLE FREAKIN' PLANET XANSHI'S A BLACK LANTERN?!
AND IT'S HEADING OUR WAY.
BUT NOT IF YOU CAN HELP IT.
DAMN RIGHT, WOG.
THEN LET'S GET A SQUAD TOGETHER...
...BECAUSE I'M GOING WITH YOU.

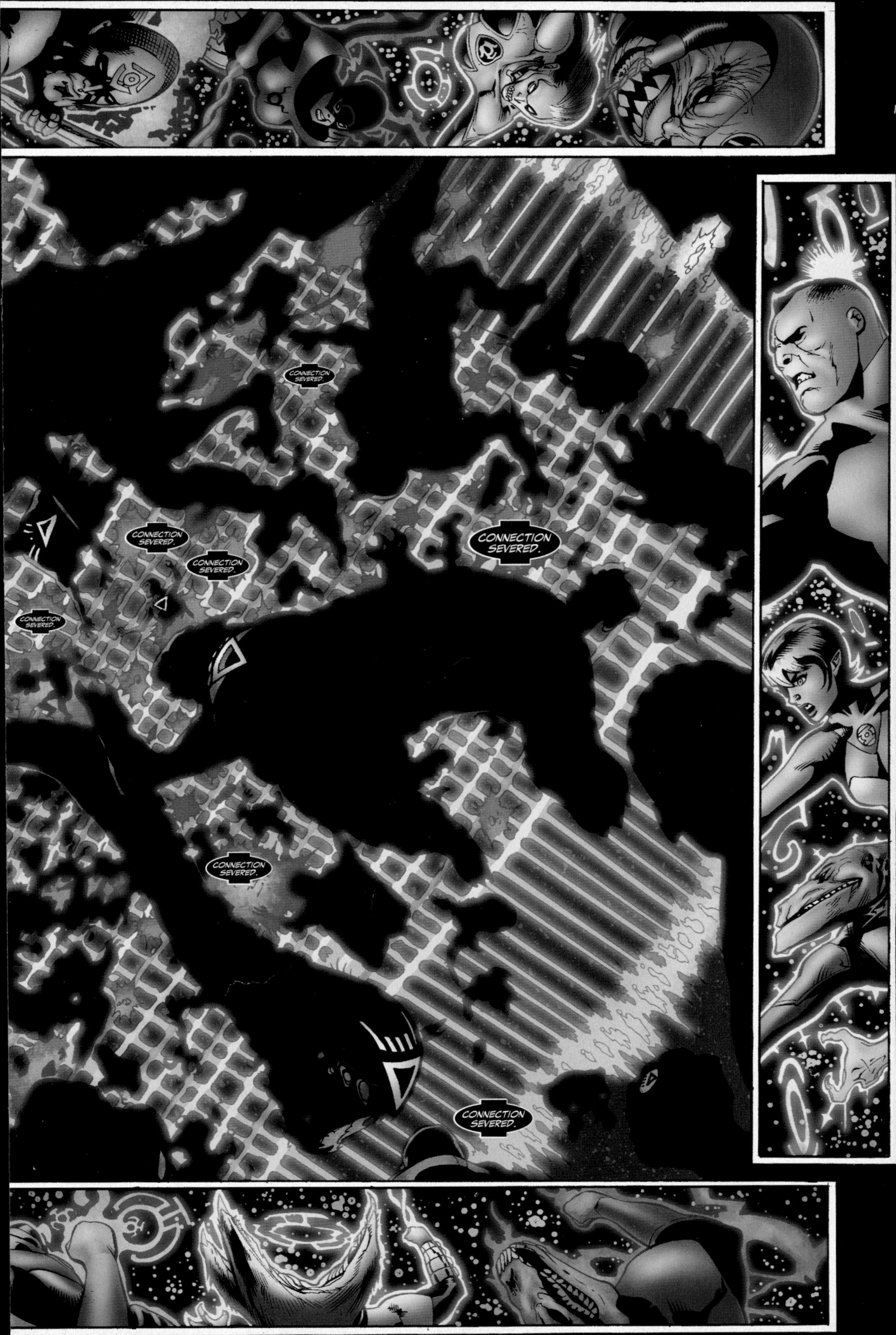

CONNECTION SEVERED.
CONNECTION SEVERED.
CONNECTION SEVERED.
CONNECTION SEVERED.
CONNECTION SEVERED.
CONNECTION SEVERED.
CONNECTION SEVERED.

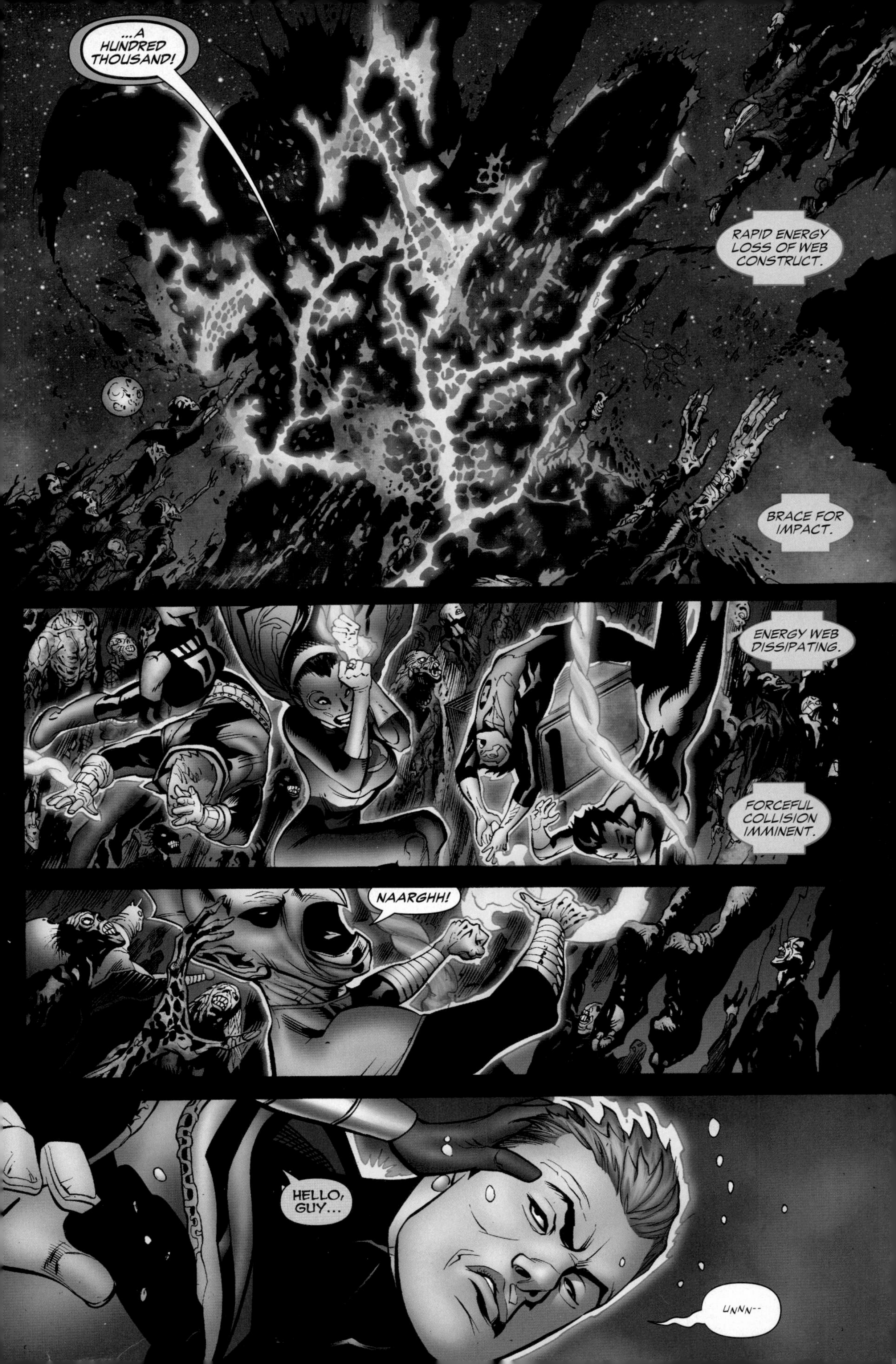
...A HUNDRED THOUSAND!
RAPID ENERGY LOSS OF WEB CONSTRUCT.
BRACE FOR IMPACT.
ENERGY WEB DISSIPATING.
FORCEFUL COLLISION IMMINENT.
NAARGHH!
HELLO, GUY...
UNNN--

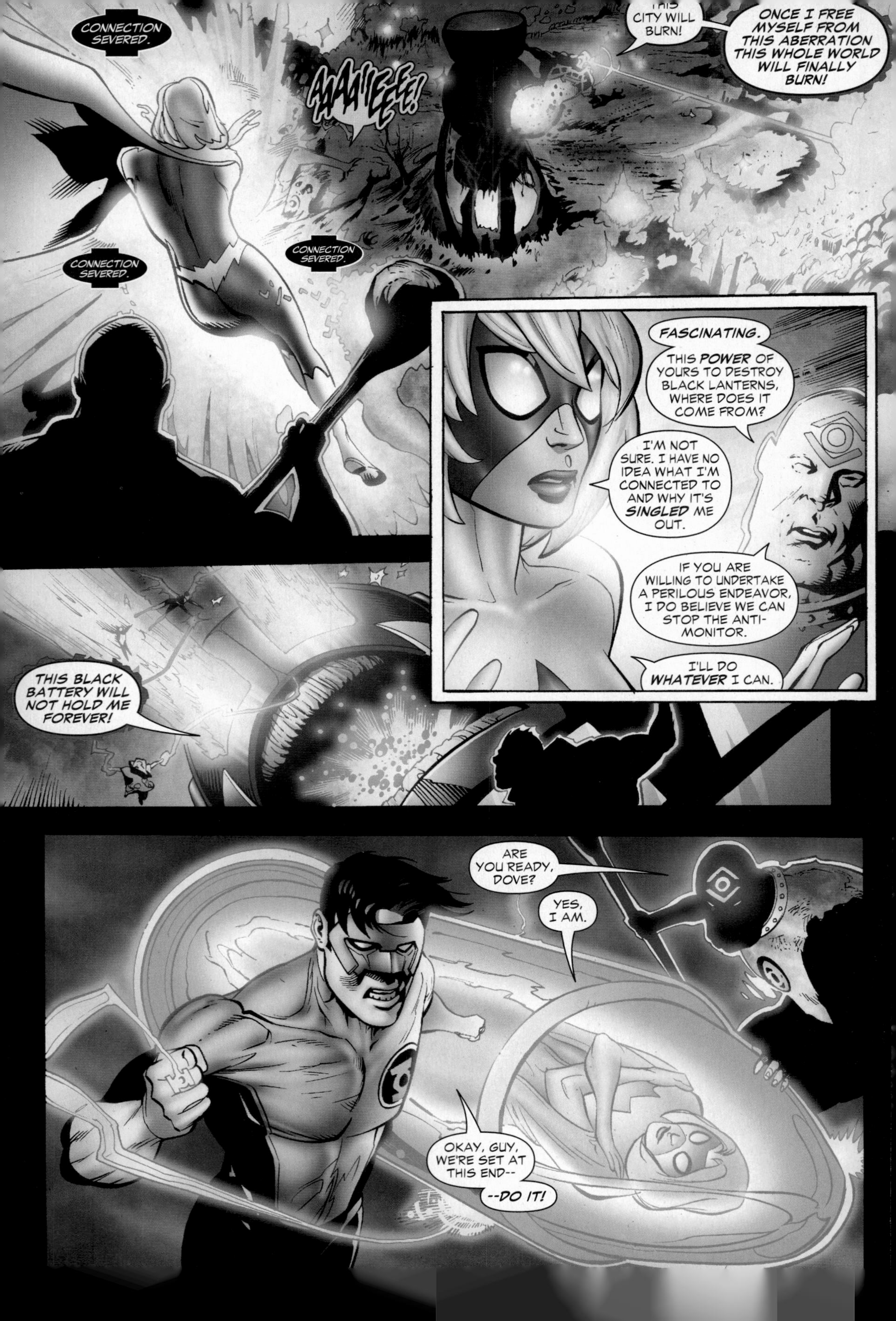
CONNECTION SEVERED.
AAAAIIEEEE!
THIS CITY WILL BURN!
ONCE I FREE MYSELF FROM THIS ABERRATION THIS WHOLE WORLD WILL FINALLY BURN!
CONNECTION SEVERED.
CONNECTION SEVERED.
FASCINATING.
THIS POWER OF YOURS TO DESTROY BLACK LANTERNS, WHERE DOES IT COME FROM?
I'M NOT SURE. I HAVE NO IDEA WHAT I'M CONNECTED TO AND WHY IT'S SINGLED ME OUT.
IF YOU ARE WILLING TO UNDERTAKE A PERILOUS ENDEAVOR, I DO BELIEVE WE CAN STOP THE ANTI-MONITOR.
I'LL DO WHATEVER I CAN.
THIS BLACK BATTERY WILL NOT HOLD ME FOREVER!
ARE YOU READY, DOVE?
YES, I AM.
OKAY, GUY, WE'RE SET AT THIS END--
--DO IT!

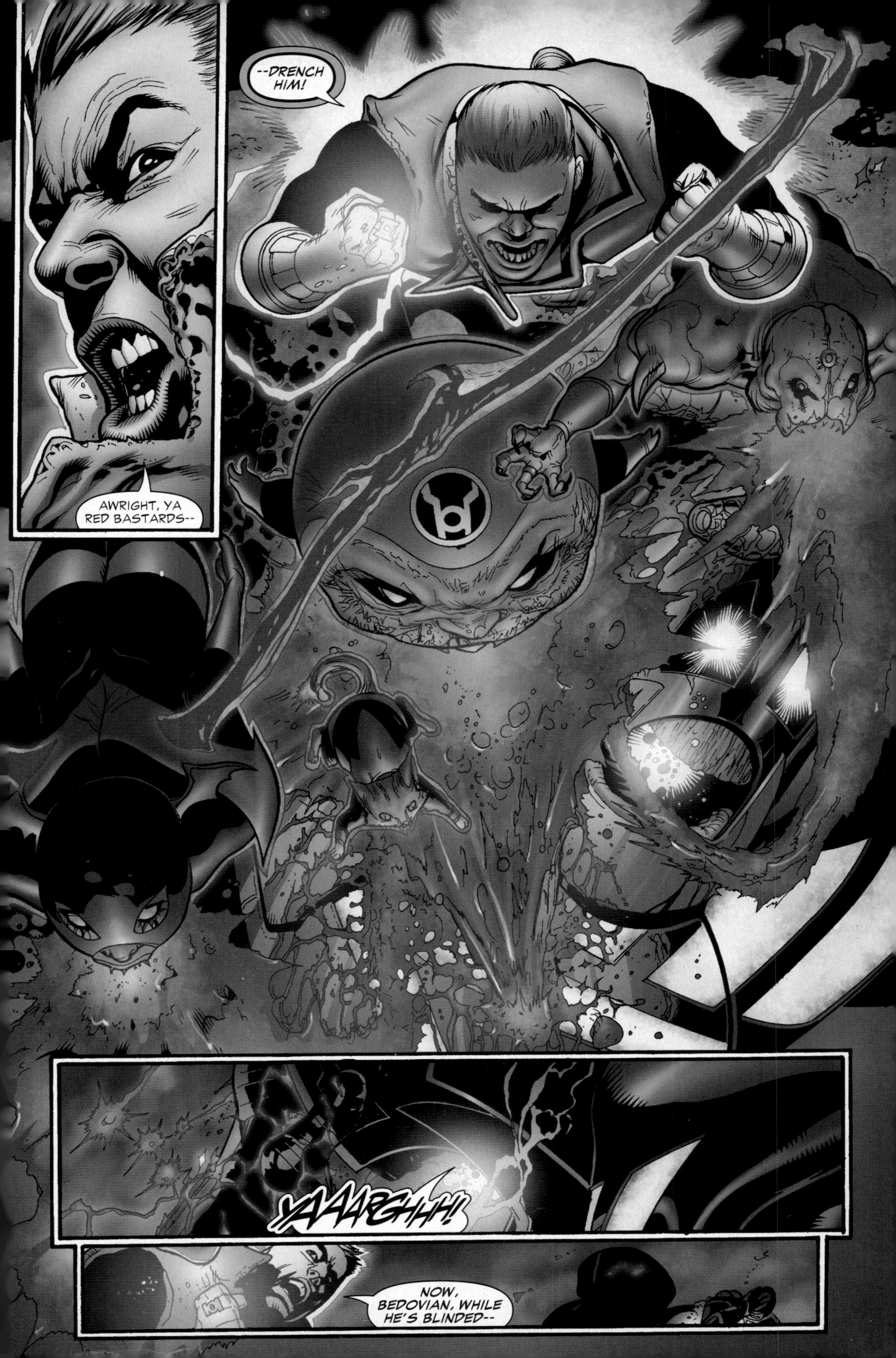
AWRIGHT, YA RED BASTARDS--
--DRENCH HIM!
YAAARGHHH!
NOW, BEDOVIAN, WHILE HE'S BLINDED--

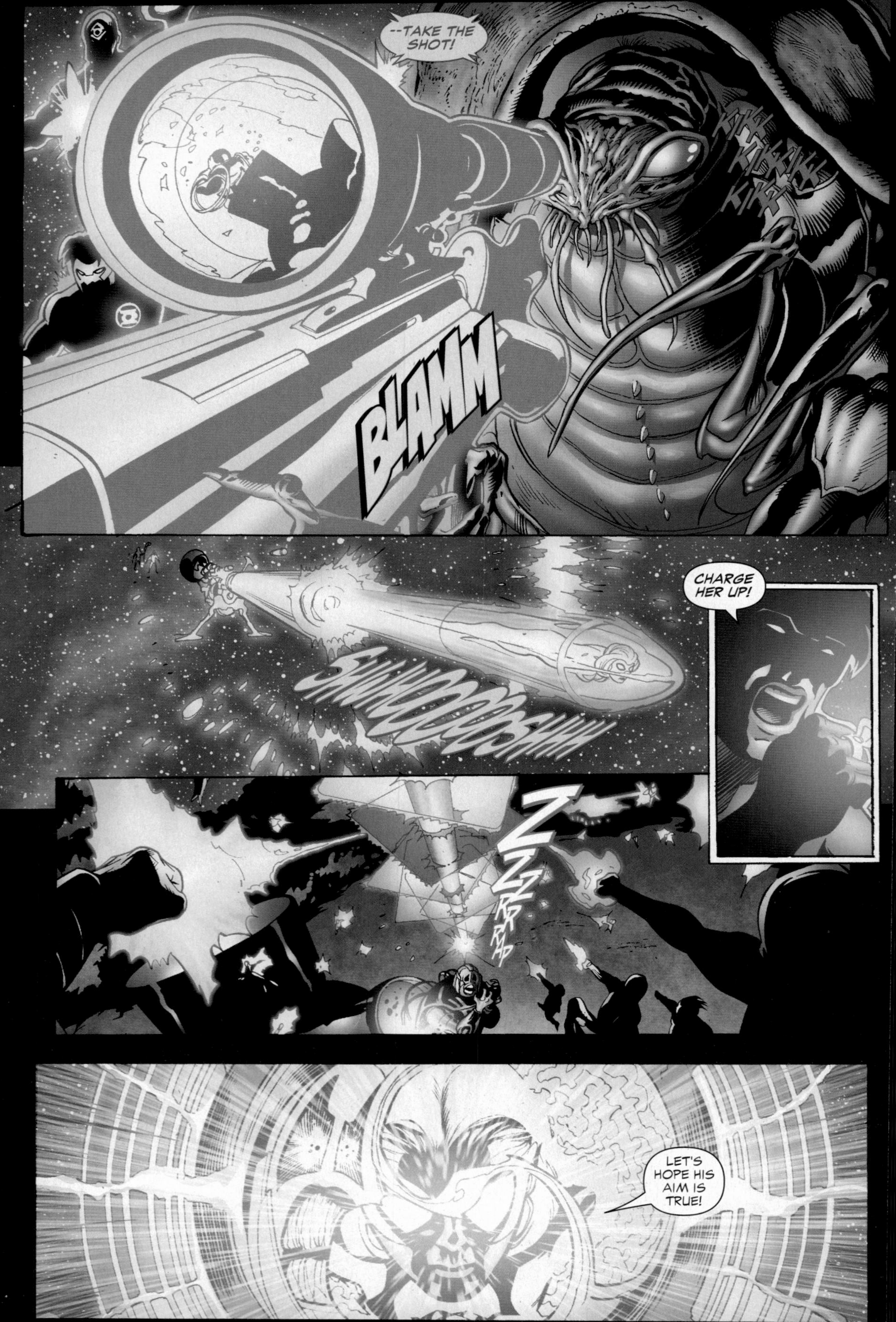
--TAKE THE SHOT!
BLAMM
CHARGE HER UP!
LET'S HOPE HIS AIM IS TRUE!

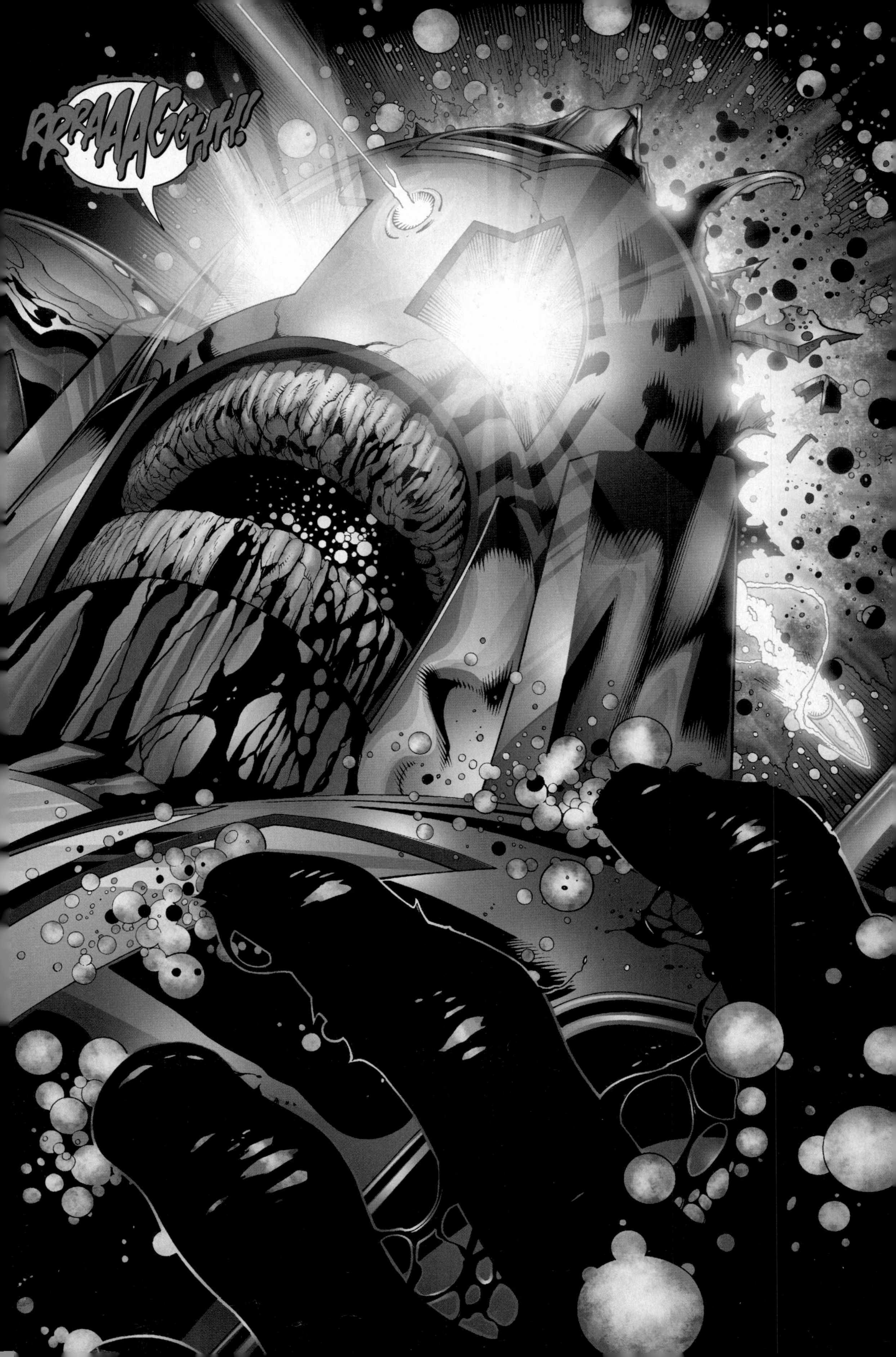
RRRAAAAGGHH!

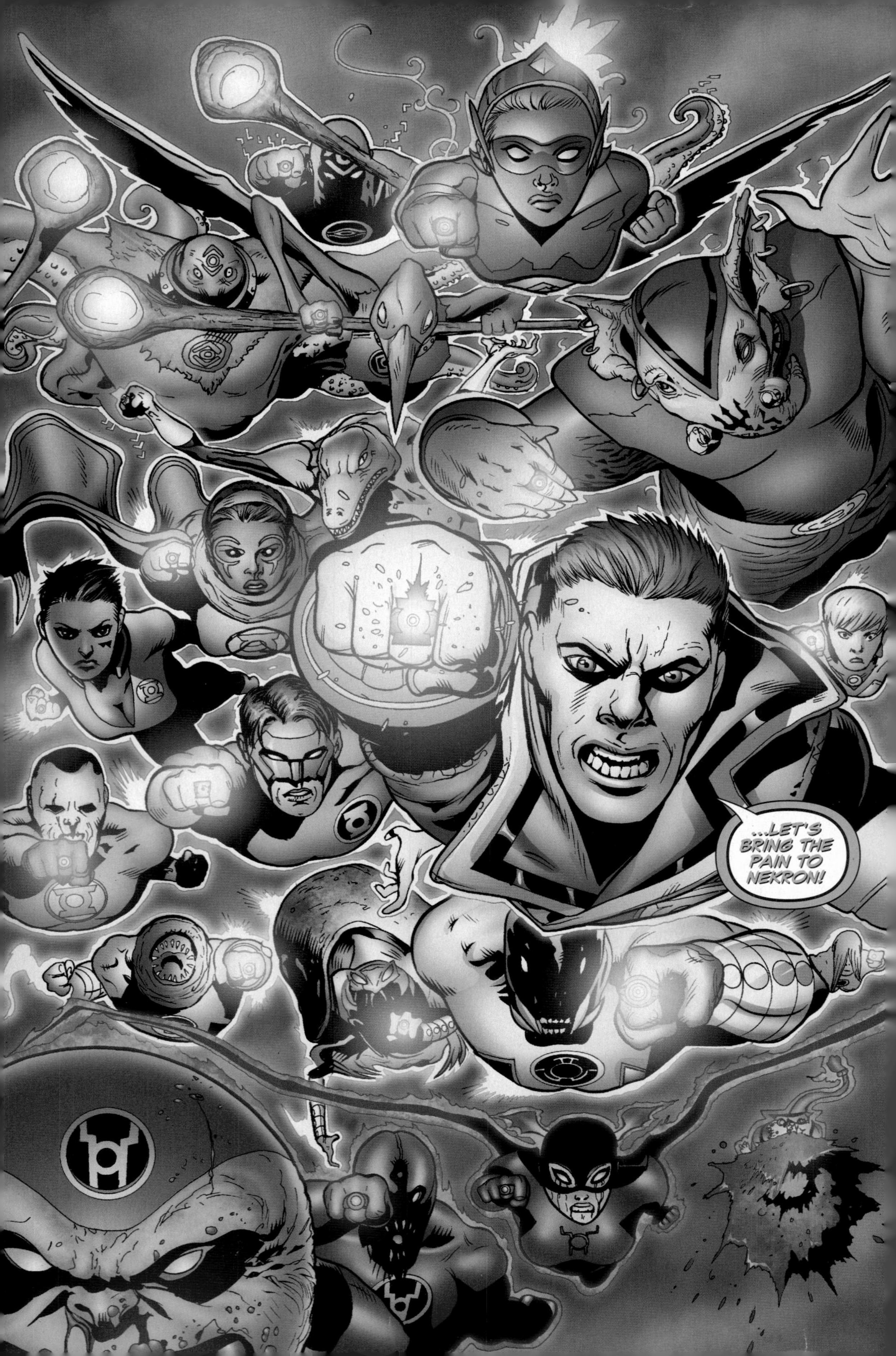
...LET'S BRING THE PAIN TO NEKRON!

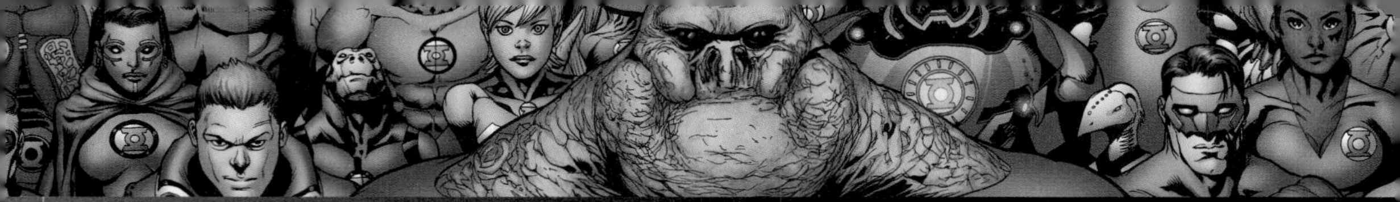

GOODBYE DARKNESS

PATRICK GLEASON
PENCILS

REBECCA BUCHMAN
TOM NGUYEN
KEITH CHAMPAGNE
MARK IRWIN
INKS

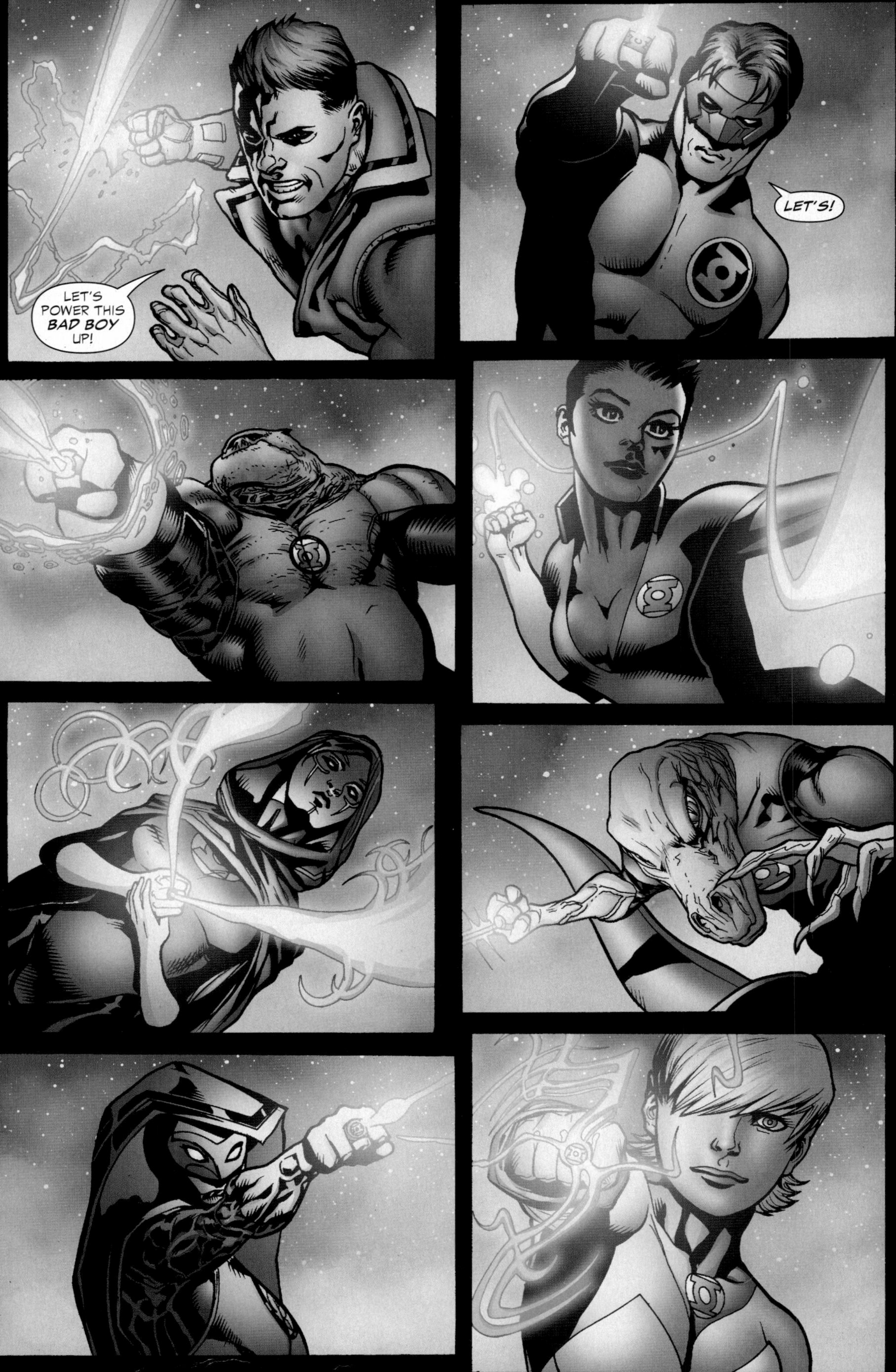
LET'S POWER THIS BAD BOY UP!
LET'S!

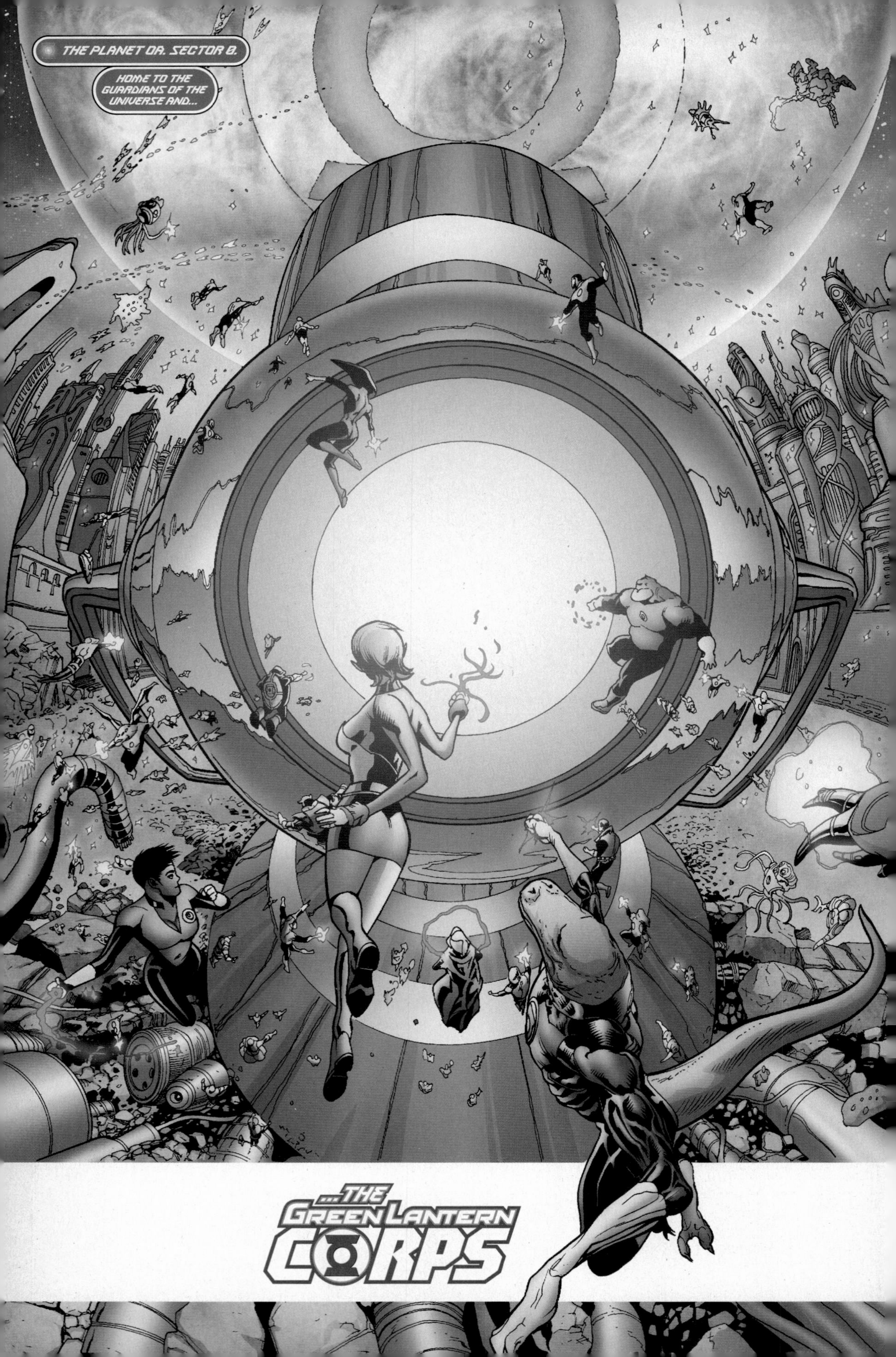
THE PLANET OA. SECTOR 0.
HOME TO THE GUARDIANS OF THE UNIVERSE AND...
...THE GREEN LANTERN CORPS

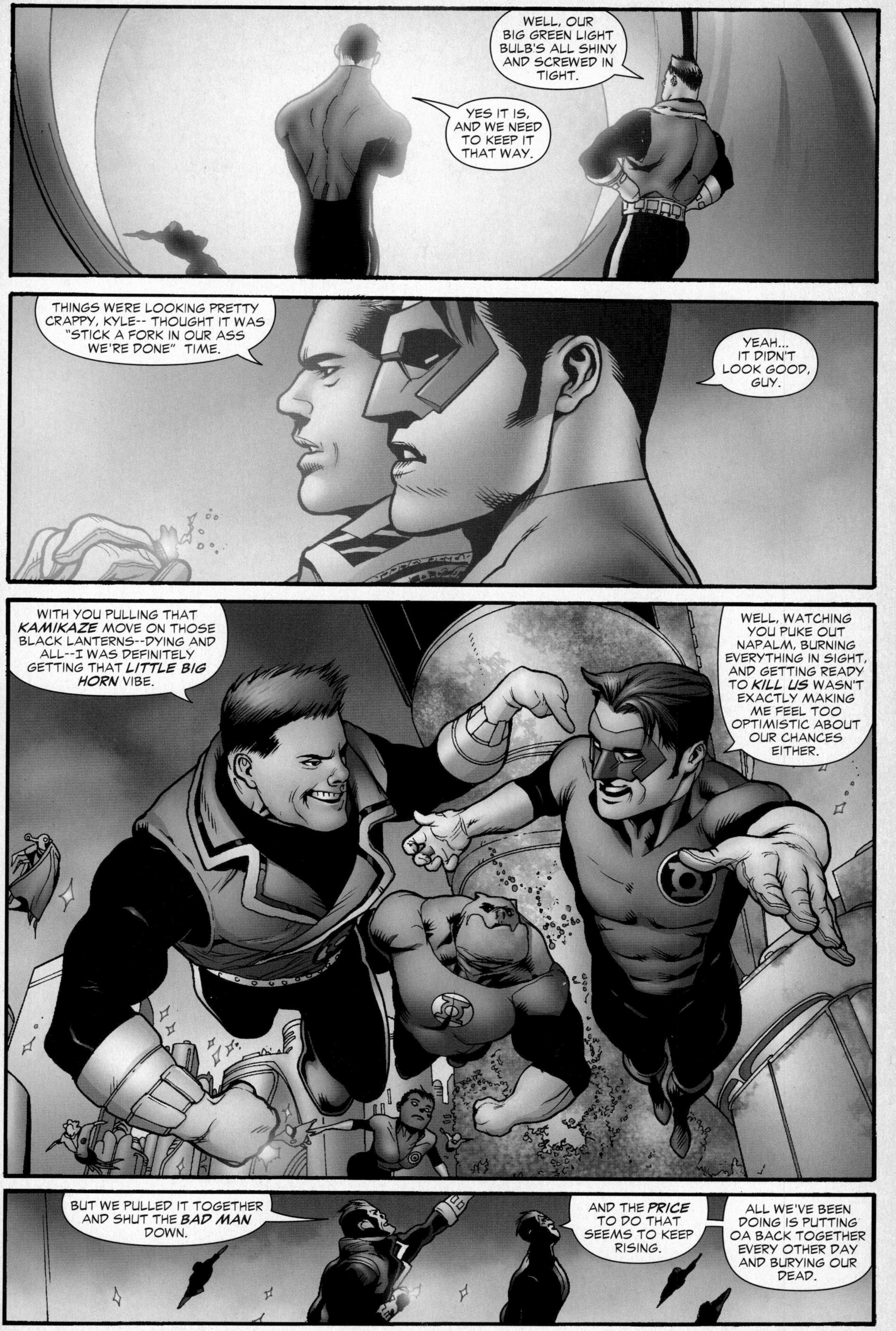
WELL, OUR BIG GREEN LIGHT BULB'S ALL SHINY AND SCREWED IN TIGHT.
YES IT IS, AND WE NEED TO KEEP IT THAT WAY.
THINGS WERE LOOKING PRETTY CRAPPY, KYLE-- THOUGHT IT WAS "STICK A FORK IN OUR ASS WE'RE DONE" TIME.
YEAH... IT DIDN'T LOOK GOOD, GUY.
WITH YOU PULLING THAT KAMIKAZE MOVE ON THOSE BLACK LANTERNS--DYING AND ALL--I WAS DEFINITELY GETTING THAT LITTLE BIG HORN VIBE.
WELL, WATCHING YOU PUKE OUT NAPALM, BURNING EVERYTHING IN SIGHT, AND GETTING READY TO KILL US WASN'T EXACTLY MAKING ME FEEL TOO OPTIMISTIC ABOUT OUR CHANCES EITHER.
BUT WE PULLED IT TOGETHER AND SHUT THE BAD MAN DOWN.
AND THE PRICE TO DO THAT SEEMS TO KEEP RISING.
ALL WE'VE BEEN DOING IS PUTTING OA BACK TOGETHER EVERY OTHER DAY AND BURYING OUR DEAD.

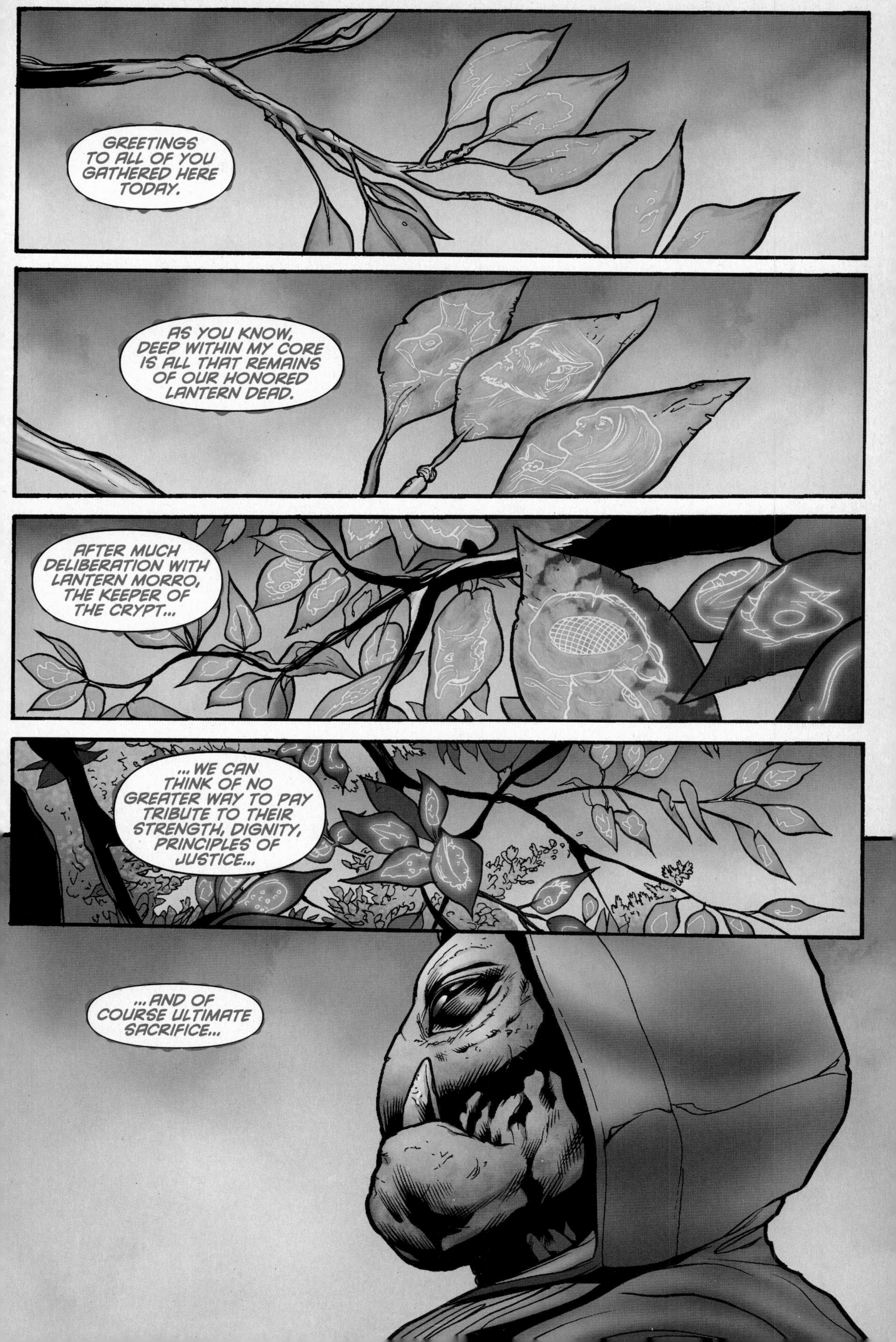
GREETINGS TO ALL OF YOU GATHERED HERE TODAY.
AS YOU KNOW, DEEP WITHIN MY CORE IS ALL THAT REMAINS OF OUR HONORED LANTERN DEAD.
AFTER MUCH DELIBERATION WITH LANTERN MORRO, THE KEEPER OF THE CRYPT...
...WE CAN THINK OF NO GREATER WAY TO PAY TRIBUTE TO THEIR STRENGTH, DIGNITY, PRINCIPLES OF JUSTICE...
...AND OF COURSE ULTIMATE SACRIFICE...

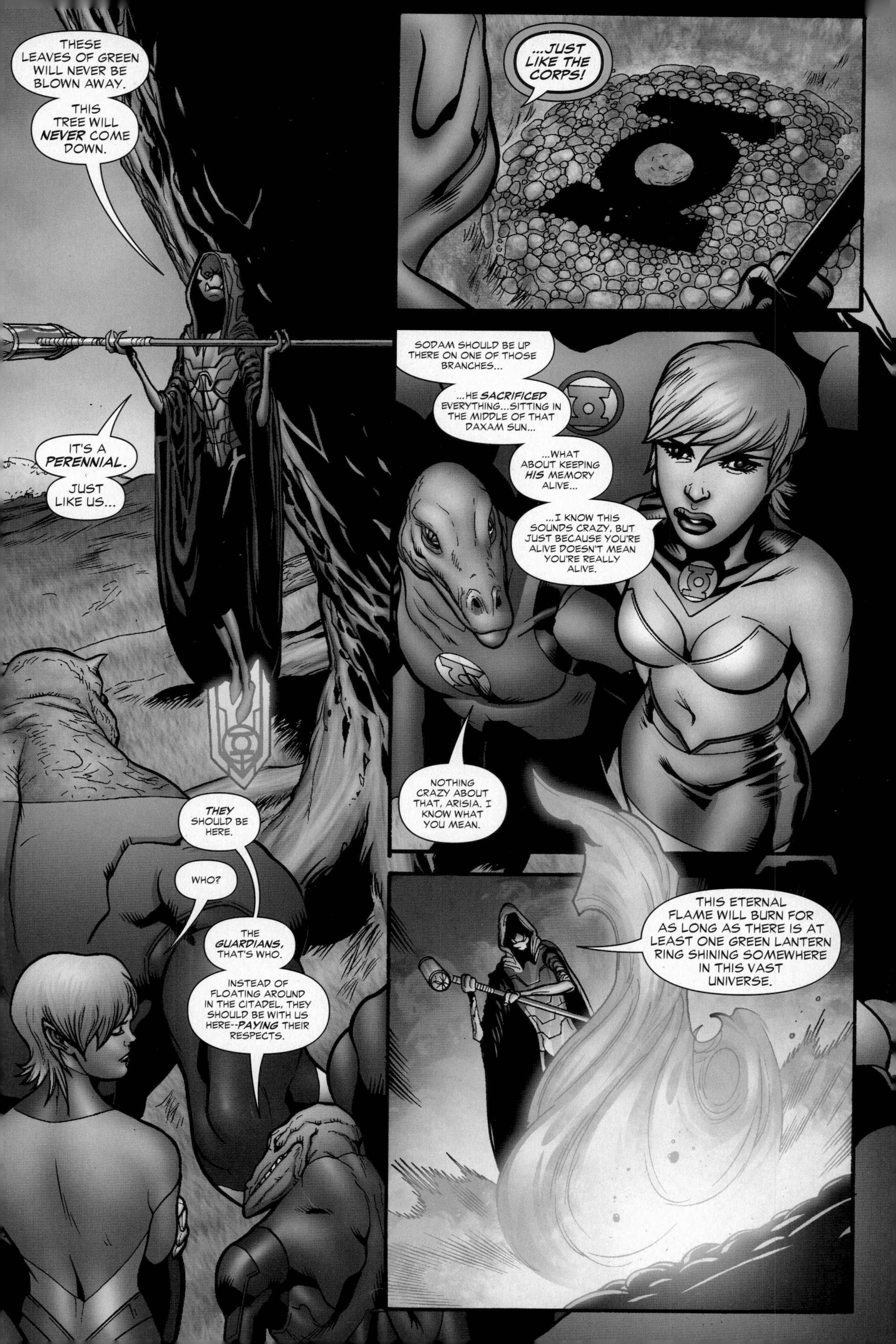
THESE LEAVES OF GREEN WILL NEVER BE BLOWN AWAY.
THIS TREE WILL NEVER COME DOWN.
...JUST LIKE THE CORPS!
IT'S A PERENNIAL.
JUST LIKE US...
SODAM SHOULD BE UP THERE ON ONE OF THOSE BRANCHES...
...HE SACRIFICED EVERYTHING...SITTING IN THE MIDDLE OF THAT DAXAM SUN...
...WHAT ABOUT KEEPING HIS MEMORY ALIVE...
...I KNOW THIS SOUNDS CRAZY, BUT JUST BECAUSE YOU'RE ALIVE DOESN'T MEAN YOU'RE REALLY ALIVE.
NOTHING CRAZY ABOUT THAT, ARISIA. I KNOW WHAT YOU MEAN.
THEY SHOULD BE HERE.
WHO?
THE GUARDIANS, THAT'S WHO.
INSTEAD OF FLOATING AROUND IN THE CITADEL, THEY SHOULD BE WITH US HERE--PAYING THEIR RESPECTS.
THIS ETERNAL FLAME WILL BURN FOR AS LONG AS THERE IS AT LEAST ONE GREEN LANTERN RING SHINING SOMEWHERE IN THIS VAST UNIVERSE.

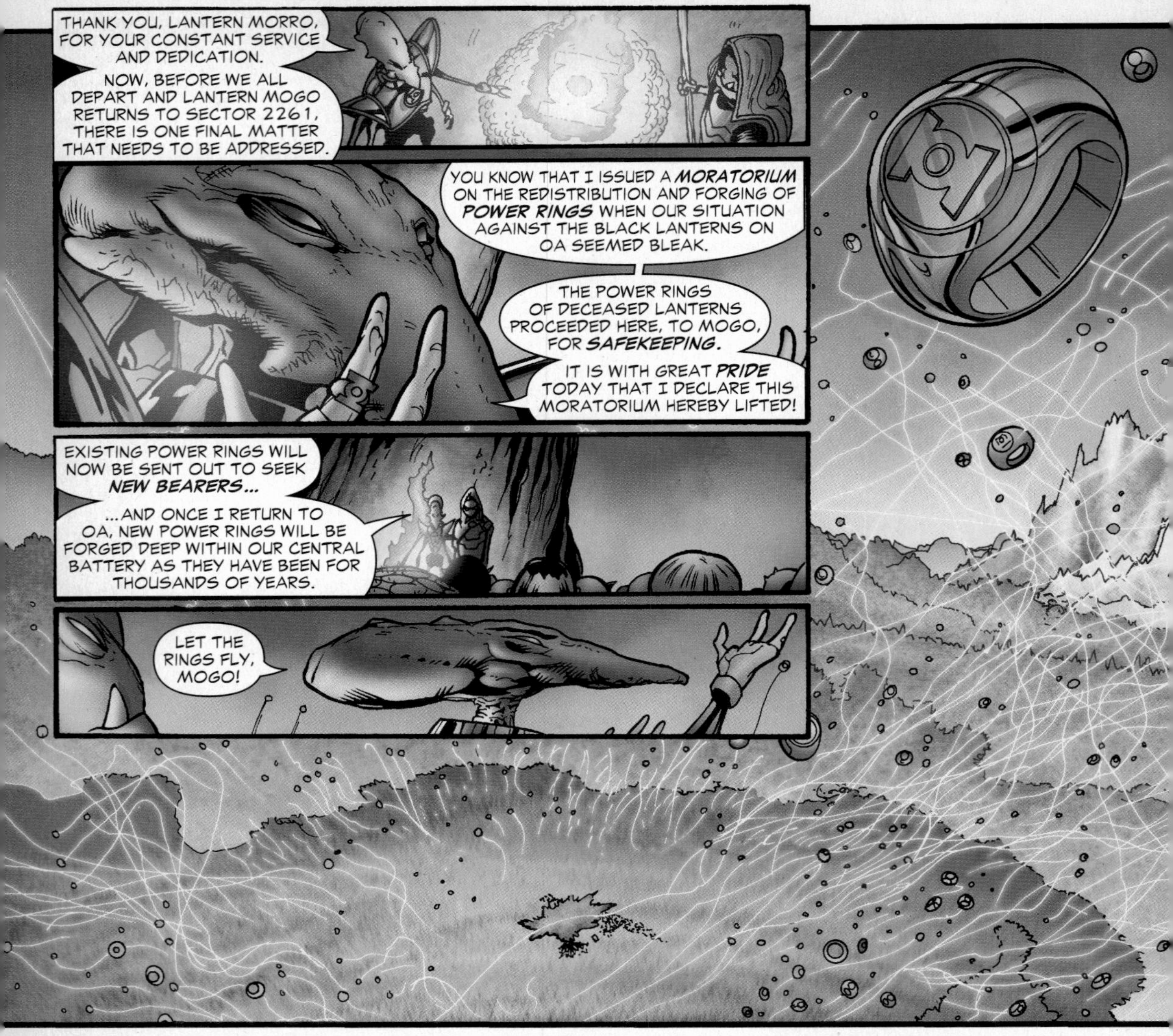
THANK YOU, LANTERN MORRO, FOR YOUR CONSTANT SERVICE AND DEDICATION.
NOW, BEFORE WE ALL DEPART AND LANTERN MOGO RETURNS TO SECTOR 2261, THERE IS ONE FINAL MATTER THAT NEEDS TO BE ADDRESSED.
YOU KNOW THAT I ISSUED A *MORATORIUM* ON THE REDISTRIBUTION AND FORGING OF *POWER RINGS* WHEN OUR SITUATION AGAINST THE BLACK LANTERNS ON OA SEEMED BLEAK.
THE POWER RINGS OF DECEASED LANTERNS PROCEEDED HERE, TO MOGO, FOR *SAFEKEEPING*.
IT IS WITH GREAT *PRIDE* TODAY THAT I DECLARE THIS MORATORIUM HEREBY LIFTED!
EXISTING POWER RINGS WILL NOW BE SENT OUT TO SEEK *NEW BEARERS...*
...AND ONCE I RETURN TO OA, NEW POWER RINGS WILL BE FORGED DEEP WITHIN OUR CENTRAL BATTERY AS THEY HAVE BEEN FOR THOUSANDS OF YEARS.
LET THE RINGS FLY, MOGO!
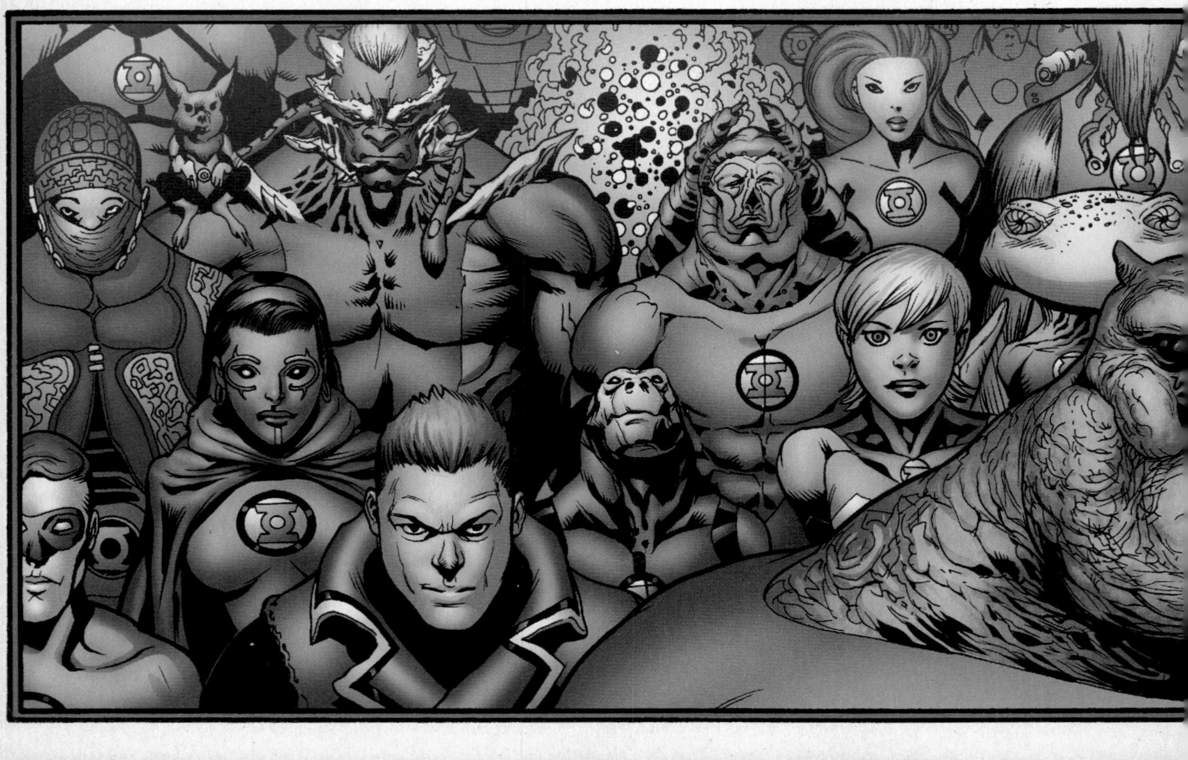

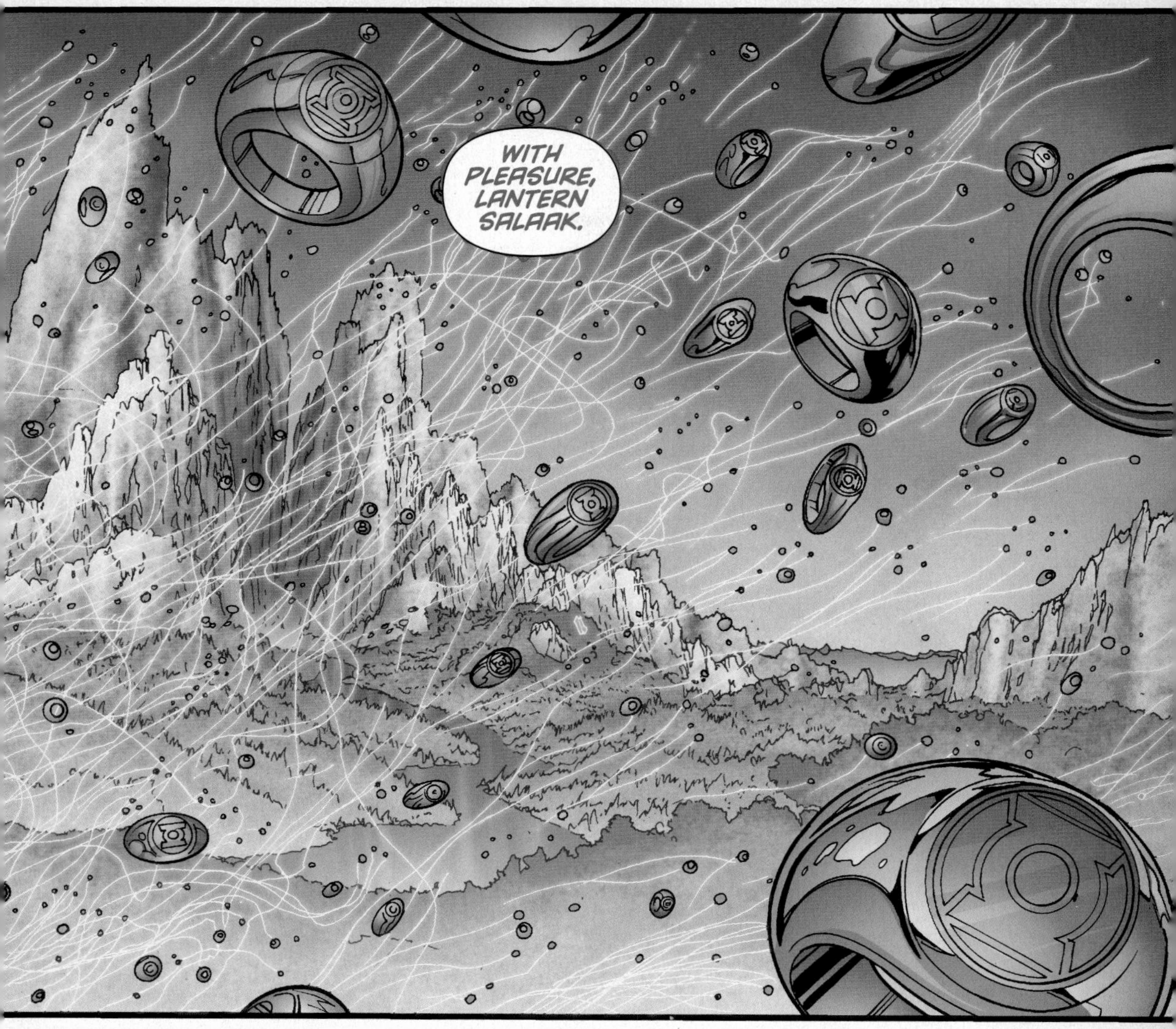
WITH PLEASURE, LANTERN SALAAK.

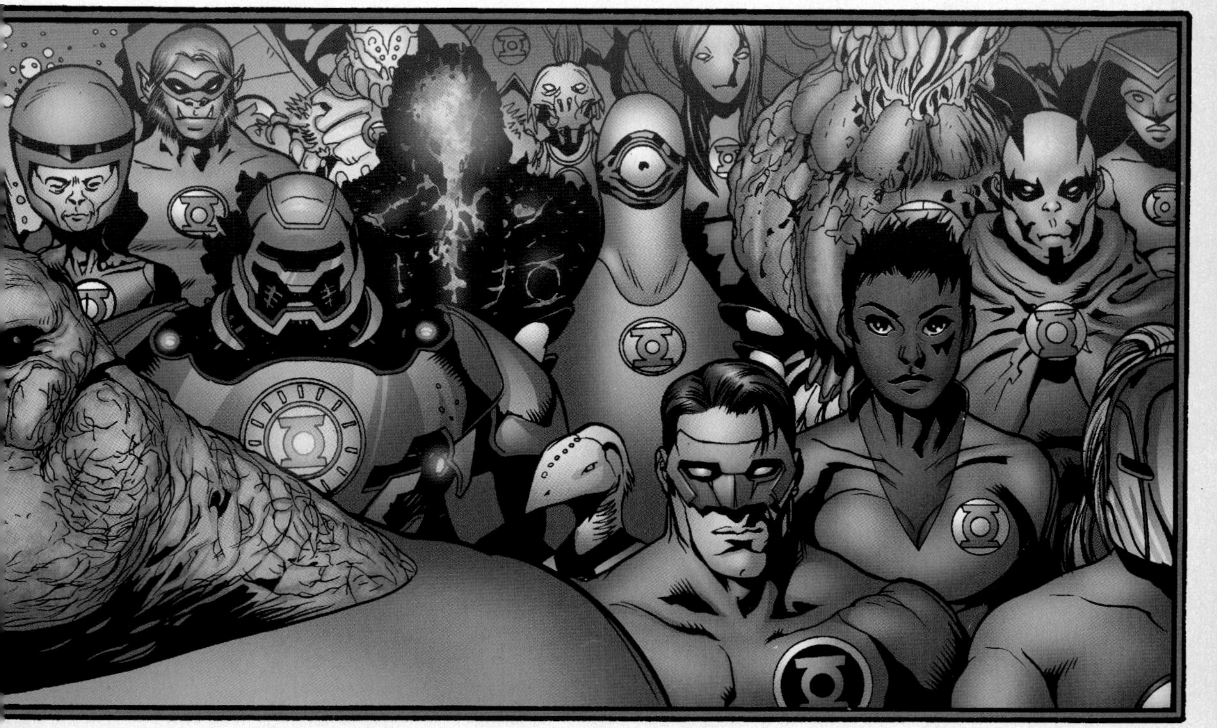

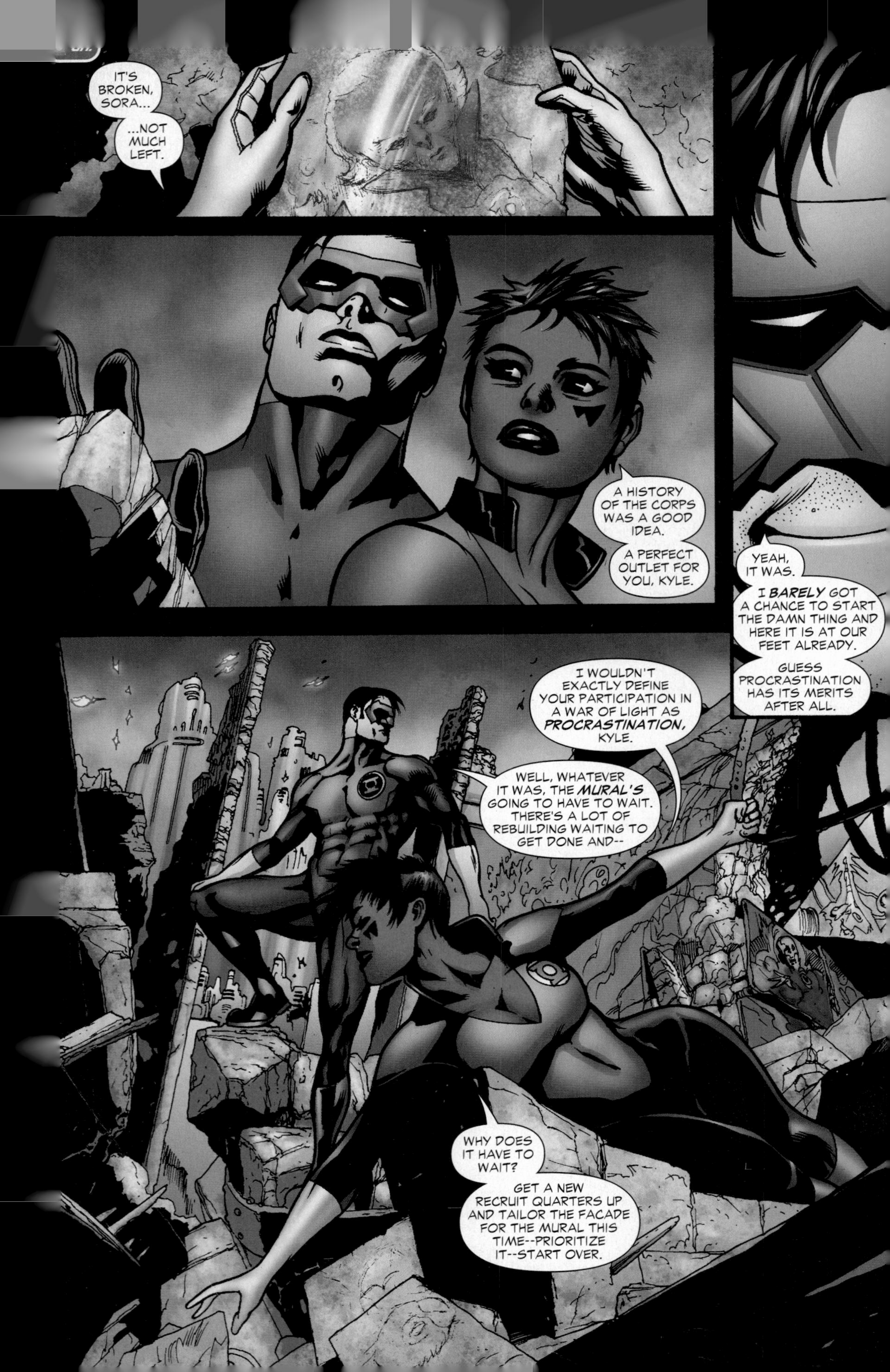
IT'S BROKEN, SORA...
...NOT MUCH LEFT.
A HISTORY OF THE CORPS WAS A GOOD IDEA.
A PERFECT OUTLET FOR YOU, KYLE.
YEAH, IT WAS.
I BARELY GOT A CHANCE TO START THE DAMN THING AND HERE IT IS AT OUR FEET ALREADY.
GUESS PROCRASTINATION HAS ITS MERITS AFTER ALL.
I WOULDN'T EXACTLY DEFINE YOUR PARTICIPATION IN A WAR OF LIGHT AS PROCRASTINATION, KYLE.
WELL, WHATEVER IT WAS, THE MURAL'S GOING TO HAVE TO WAIT. THERE'S A LOT OF REBUILDING WAITING TO GET DONE AND--
WHY DOES IT HAVE TO WAIT?
GET A NEW RECRUIT QUARTERS UP AND TAILOR THE FACADE FOR THE MURAL THIS TIME--PRIORITIZE IT--START OVER.

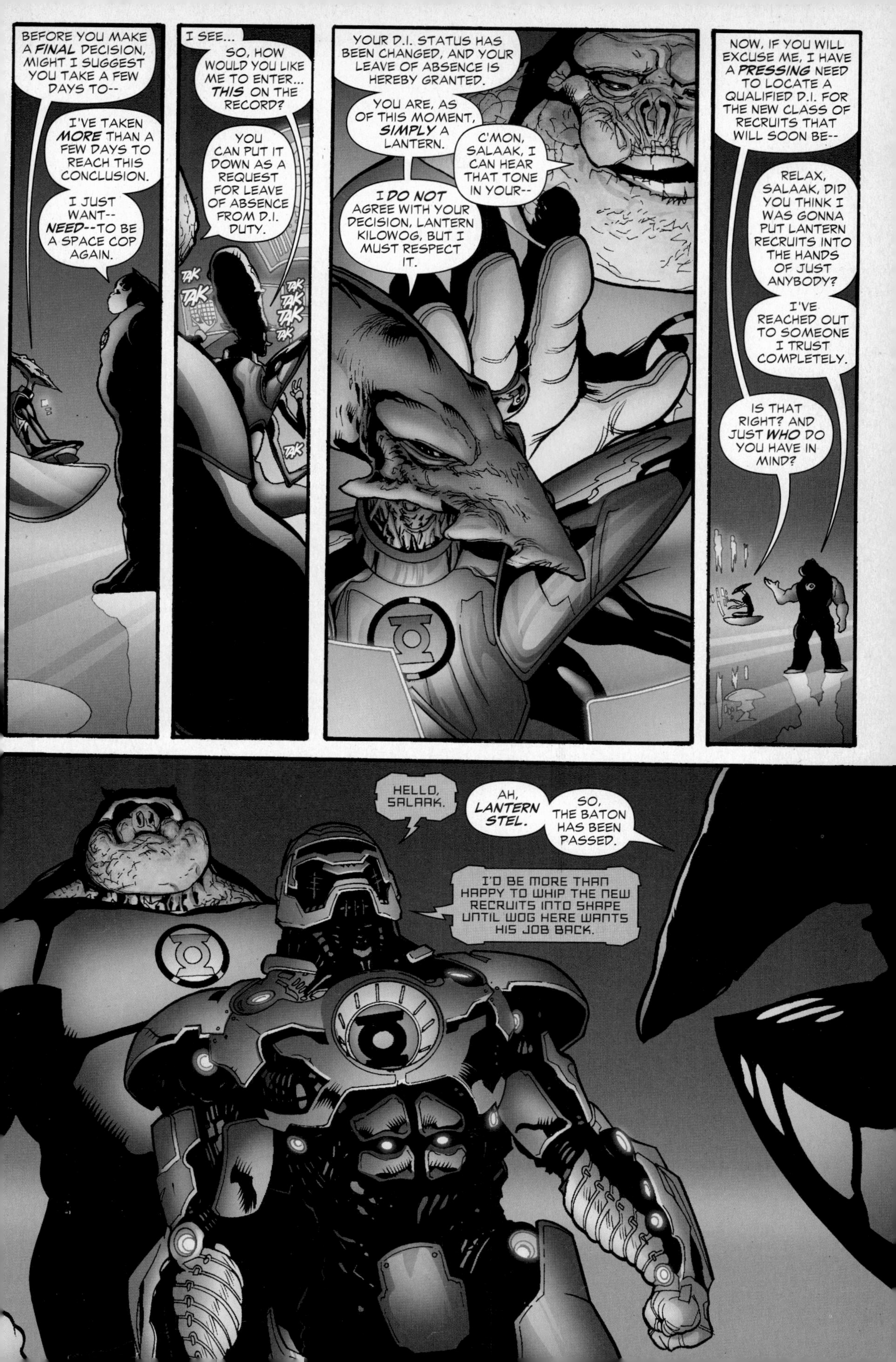

BEFORE YOU MAKE A *FINAL* DECISION, MIGHT I SUGGEST YOU TAKE A FEW DAYS TO--
I'VE TAKEN *MORE* THAN A FEW DAYS TO REACH THIS CONCLUSION.
I JUST WANT-- *NEED*--TO BE A SPACE COP AGAIN.
I SEE...
SO, HOW WOULD YOU LIKE ME TO ENTER... *THIS* ON THE RECORD?
YOU CAN PUT IT DOWN AS A REQUEST FOR LEAVE OF ABSENCE FROM D.I. DUTY.
TAK TAK
TAK TAK TAK TAK
TAK
YOUR D.I. STATUS HAS BEEN CHANGED, AND YOUR LEAVE OF ABSENCE IS HEREBY GRANTED.
YOU ARE, AS OF THIS MOMENT, *SIMPLY* A LANTERN.
C'MON, SALAAK, I CAN HEAR THAT TONE IN YOUR--
I *DO NOT* AGREE WITH YOUR DECISION, LANTERN KILOWOG, BUT I MUST RESPECT IT.
NOW, IF YOU WILL EXCUSE ME, I HAVE A *PRESSING* NEED TO LOCATE A QUALIFIED D.I. FOR THE NEW CLASS OF RECRUITS THAT WILL SOON BE--
RELAX, SALAAK, DID YOU THINK I WAS GONNA PUT LANTERN RECRUITS INTO THE HANDS OF JUST ANYBODY?
I'VE REACHED OUT TO SOMEONE I TRUST COMPLETELY.
IS THAT RIGHT? AND JUST *WHO* DO YOU HAVE IN MIND?
HELLO, SALAAK.
AH, *LANTERN STEL.*
SO, THE BATON HAS BEEN PASSED.
I'D BE MORE THAN HAPPY TO WHIP THE NEW RECRUITS INTO SHAPE UNTIL WOG HERE WANTS HIS JOB BACK.

SKRAK
SKRAK

WHAT DID *YOU* DO TO ME, ISAMOT?!

DO TO YOU? I *GAVE* YOU MY LEGS, VATH.

I DIDN'T ASK FOR THEM!

YOU DIDN'T HAVE TO.

WHAT THE HELL MADE YOU THINK I'D WANT TO WALK AROUND WITH...WITH... *THESE* FOR THE REST OF MY DAMN LIFE?!?

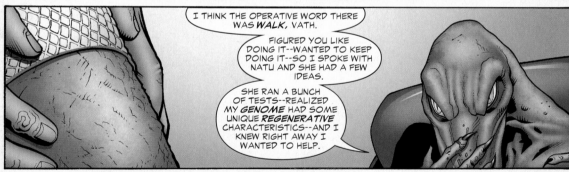

I THINK THE OPERATIVE WORD THERE WAS *WALK*, VATH.

FIGURED YOU LIKE DOING IT--WANTED TO KEEP DOING IT--SO I SPOKE WITH NATU AND SHE HAD A FEW IDEAS.

SHE RAN A BUNCH OF TESTS--REALIZED MY *GENOME* HAD SOME UNIQUE *REGENERATIVE* CHARACTERISTICS--AND I KNEW RIGHT AWAY I WANTED TO HELP.

HELP WHAT?

HELP ME LOOK LIKE A *THANAGARIAN?!?*

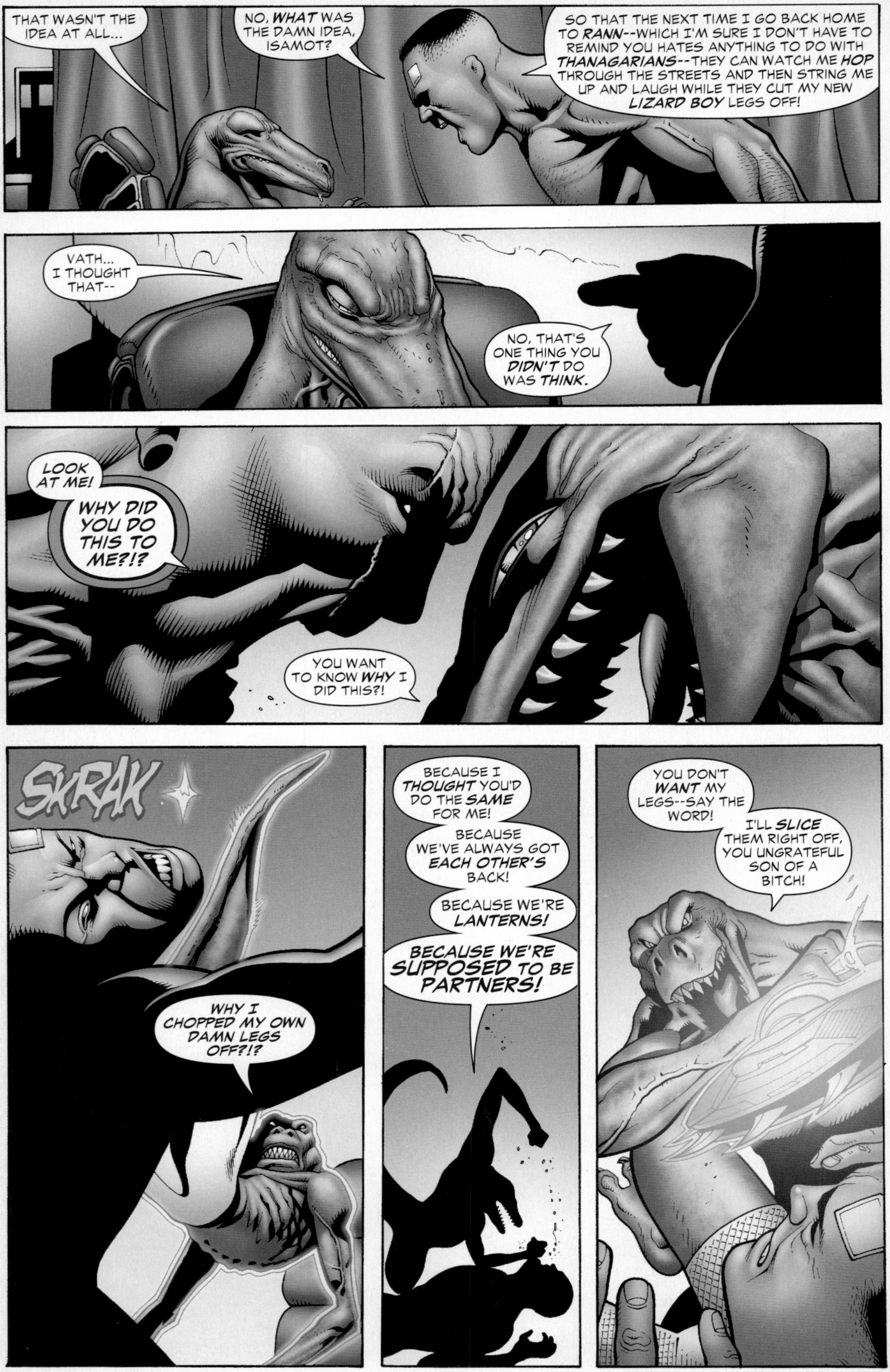
THAT WASN'T THE IDEA AT ALL...
NO, WHAT WAS THE DAMN IDEA, ISAMOT?
SO THAT THE NEXT TIME I GO BACK HOME TO RANN--WHICH I'M SURE I DON'T HAVE TO REMIND YOU HATES ANYTHING TO DO WITH THANAGARIANS--THEY CAN WATCH ME HOP THROUGH THE STREETS AND THEN STRING ME UP AND LAUGH WHILE THEY CUT MY NEW LIZARD BOY LEGS OFF!
VATH... I THOUGHT THAT--
NO, THAT'S ONE THING YOU DIDN'T DO WAS THINK.
LOOK AT ME!
WHY DID YOU DO THIS TO ME?!?
YOU WANT TO KNOW WHY I DID THIS?!
SKRAK
WHY I CHOPPED MY OWN DAMN LEGS OFF?!?
BECAUSE I THOUGHT YOU'D DO THE SAME FOR ME!
BECAUSE WE'VE ALWAYS GOT EACH OTHER'S BACK!
BECAUSE WE'RE LANTERNS!
BECAUSE WE'RE SUPPOSED TO BE PARTNERS!
YOU DON'T WANT MY LEGS--SAY THE WORD!
I'LL SLICE THEM RIGHT OFF, YOU UNGRATEFUL SON OF A BITCH!

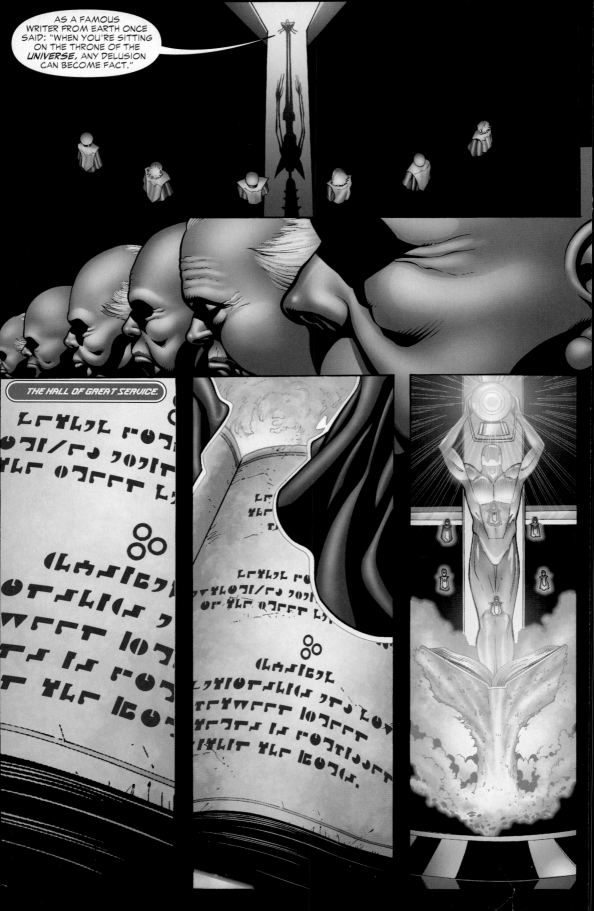

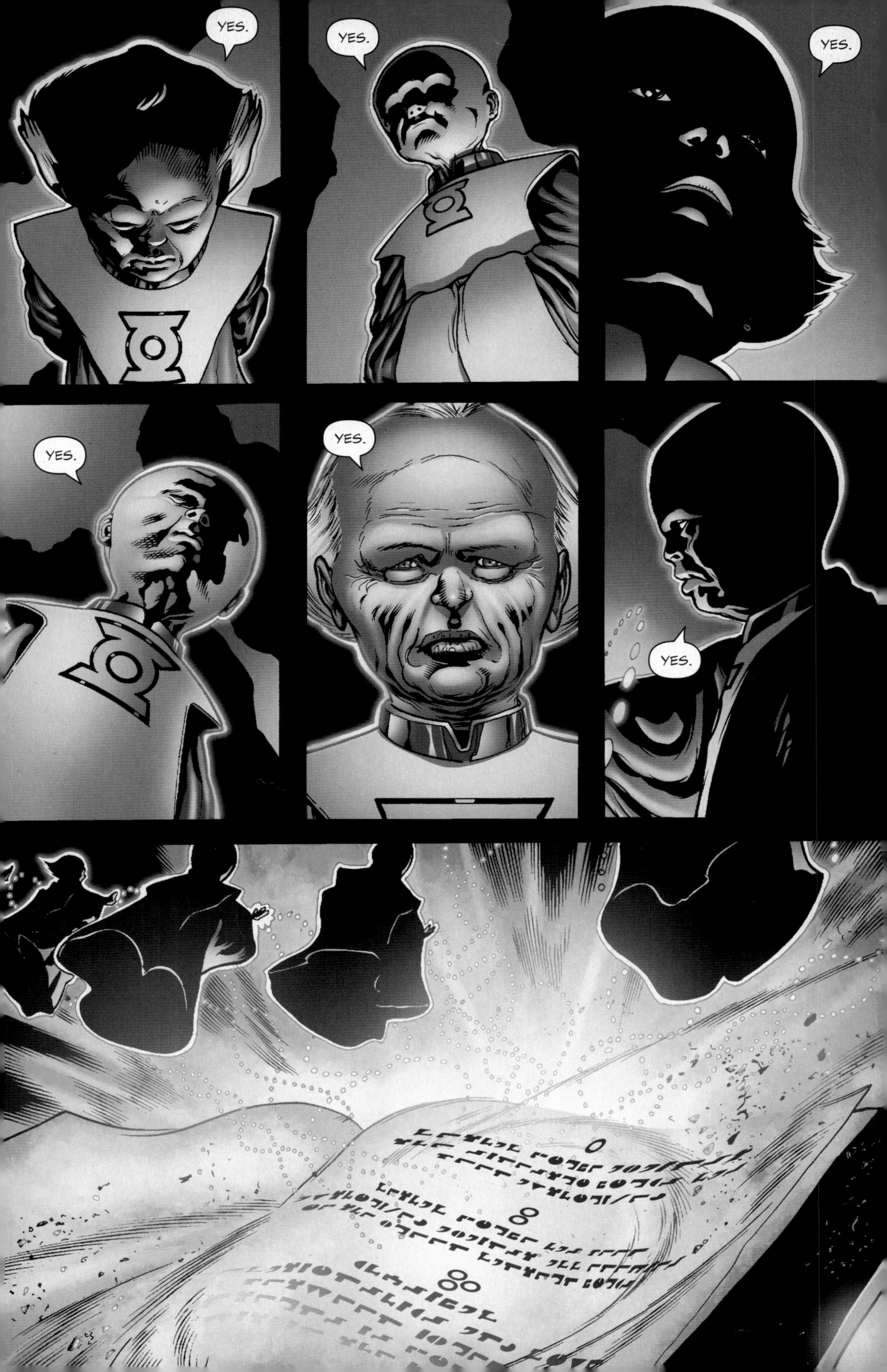
YES.
YES.
YES.
YES.
YES.
YES.

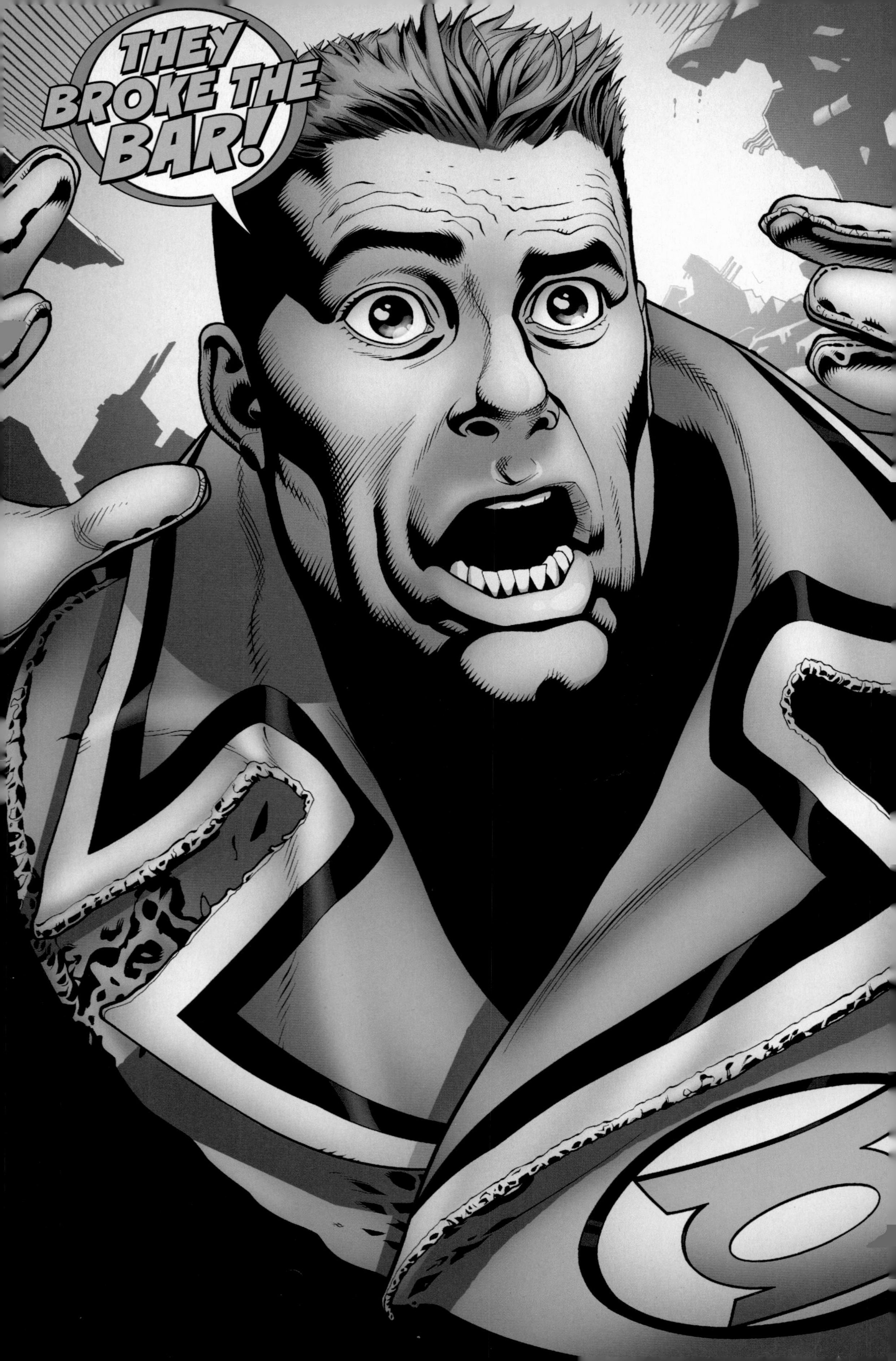
THEY BROKE THE BAR!

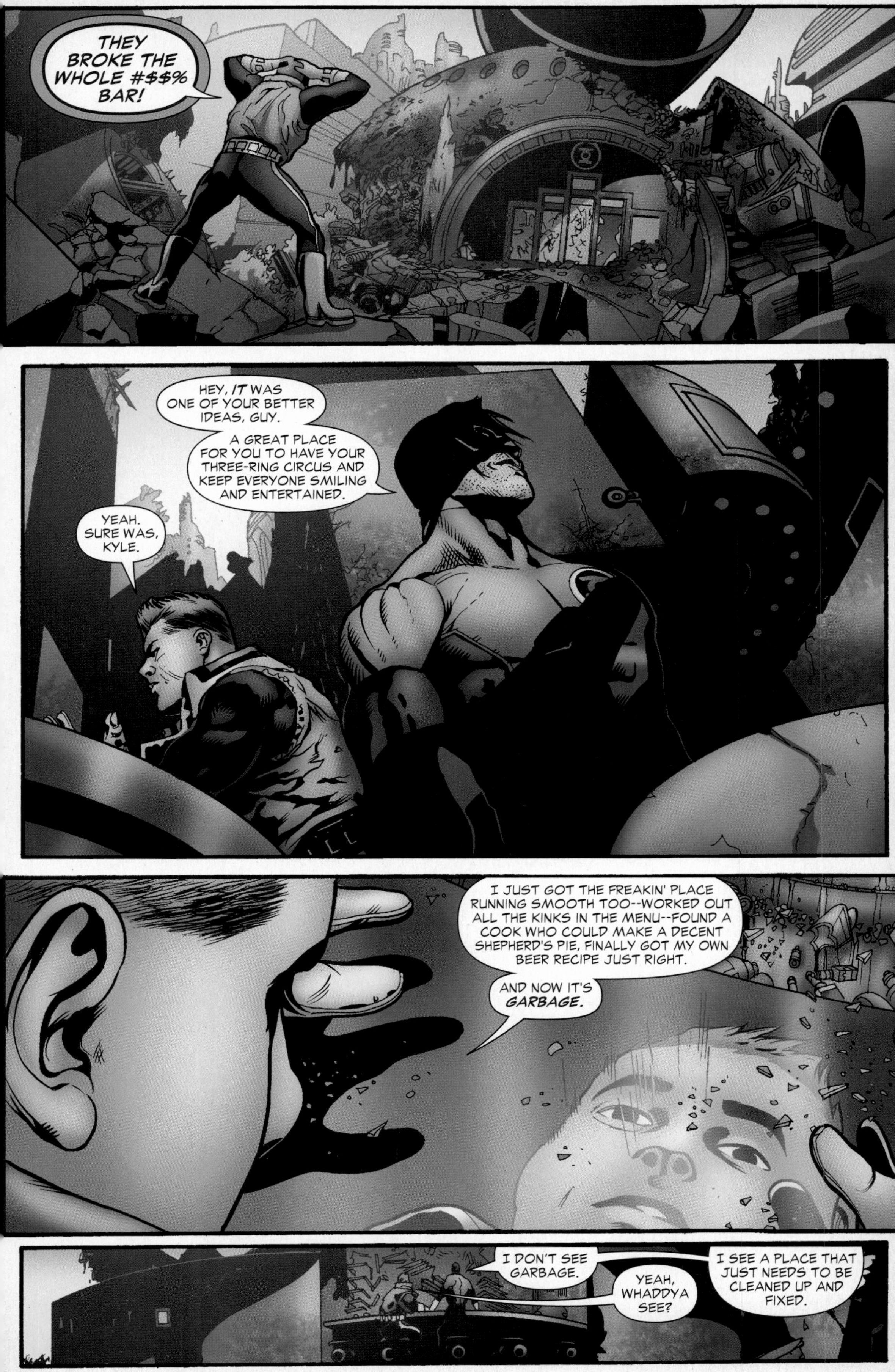
THEY BROKE THE WHOLE #$$% BAR!
HEY, IT WAS ONE OF YOUR BETTER IDEAS, GUY.
A GREAT PLACE FOR YOU TO HAVE YOUR THREE-RING CIRCUS AND KEEP EVERYONE SMILING AND ENTERTAINED.
YEAH. SURE WAS, KYLE.
I JUST GOT THE FREAKIN' PLACE RUNNING SMOOTH TOO--WORKED OUT ALL THE KINKS IN THE MENU--FOUND A COOK WHO COULD MAKE A DECENT SHEPHERD'S PIE, FINALLY GOT MY OWN BEER RECIPE JUST RIGHT.
AND NOW IT'S GARBAGE.
I DON'T SEE GARBAGE.
YEAH, WHADDYA SEE?
I SEE A PLACE THAT JUST NEEDS TO BE CLEANED UP AND FIXED.

HELL, THERE'S A LOTTA SPOTS ON OA RIGHT NOW THAT ARE WAY HIGHER ON THE PRIORITY LIST THAN THIS *ELBOW-BENDER.*

NO, THERE'S NOT.

I THINK IT NEEDS TO BE AT THE *TOP* OF THE LIST.

YOU DO, HUH? AND WHY'S THAT?

YOU CAN COUNT ON IT, CHUCKLES.

I KNOW *WE* CAN.

BECAUSE WE ALL NEED A PLACE TO COME TO MORE THAN EVER SO WE CAN *CONNECT* TO EACH OTHER WITHOUT HAVING TO BE IN THE MIDDLE OF A FIREFIGHT--

--A PLACE WHERE WE CAN FORGET ABOUT ALL THE BAD STUFF WE'RE SEEING IN EACH AND EVERY CORNER OF THE UNIVERSE EVEN IF IT'S ONLY FOR A LITTLE WHILE.

THIS PLACE IS A GOOD THING, GUY. IT'S A VALUABLE THING. AND YOU BETTER REBUILD IT.

ATTENTION ALL LANTERNS. THE THIRD LAW STATING THAT PHYSICAL RELATIONSHIPS AND LOVE BETWEEN MEMBERS OF THE GREEN LANTERN CORPS IS FORBIDDEN HAS, FROM THIS MOMENT FORTH, BEEN *REPEALED.*

ATTENTION ALL LANTERNS. THE THIRD LAW STATING THAT PHYSICAL RELATIONSHIPS AND LOVE BETWEEN MEMBERS OF THE GREEN LANTERN CORPS IS FORBIDDEN HAS, FROM THIS MOMENT FORTH, BEEN *REPEALED.*

ATTENTION ALL LANTERNS. THE THIRD LAW STATING THAT PHYSICAL RELATIONSHIPS AND LOVE BETWEEN MEMBERS OF THE GREEN LANTERN CORPS IS FORBIDDEN HAS, FROM THIS MOMENT FORTH, BEEN *REPEALED.*

HRRM.

BLACKEST NIGHT
GREEN LANTERN CORPS
VARIANT COVER GALLERY

GREEN LANTERN CORPS 40
Cover by Billy Tucci and Randy Mayor

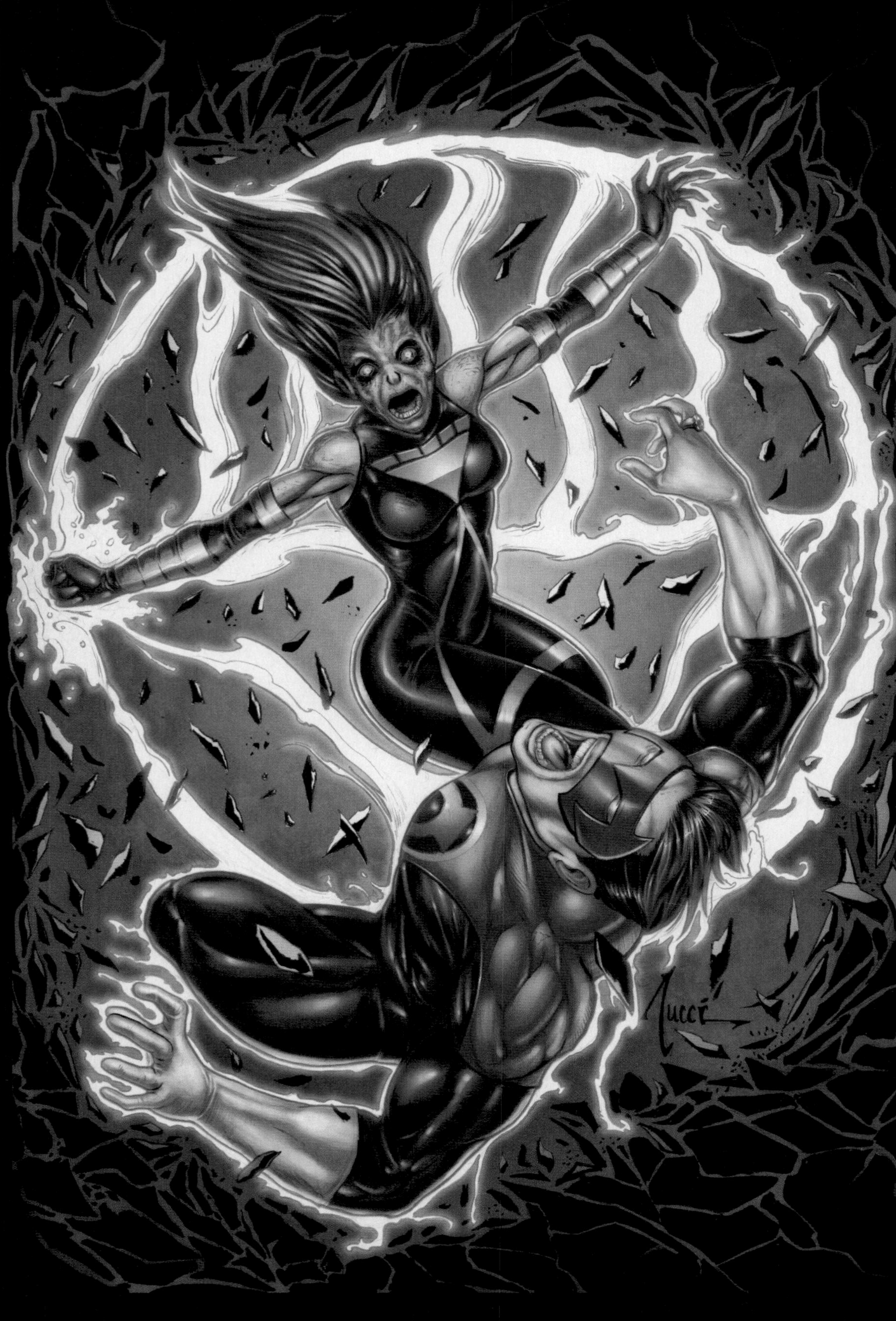
TUCCI

GREEN LANTERN CORPS 42
Cover by Greg Horn

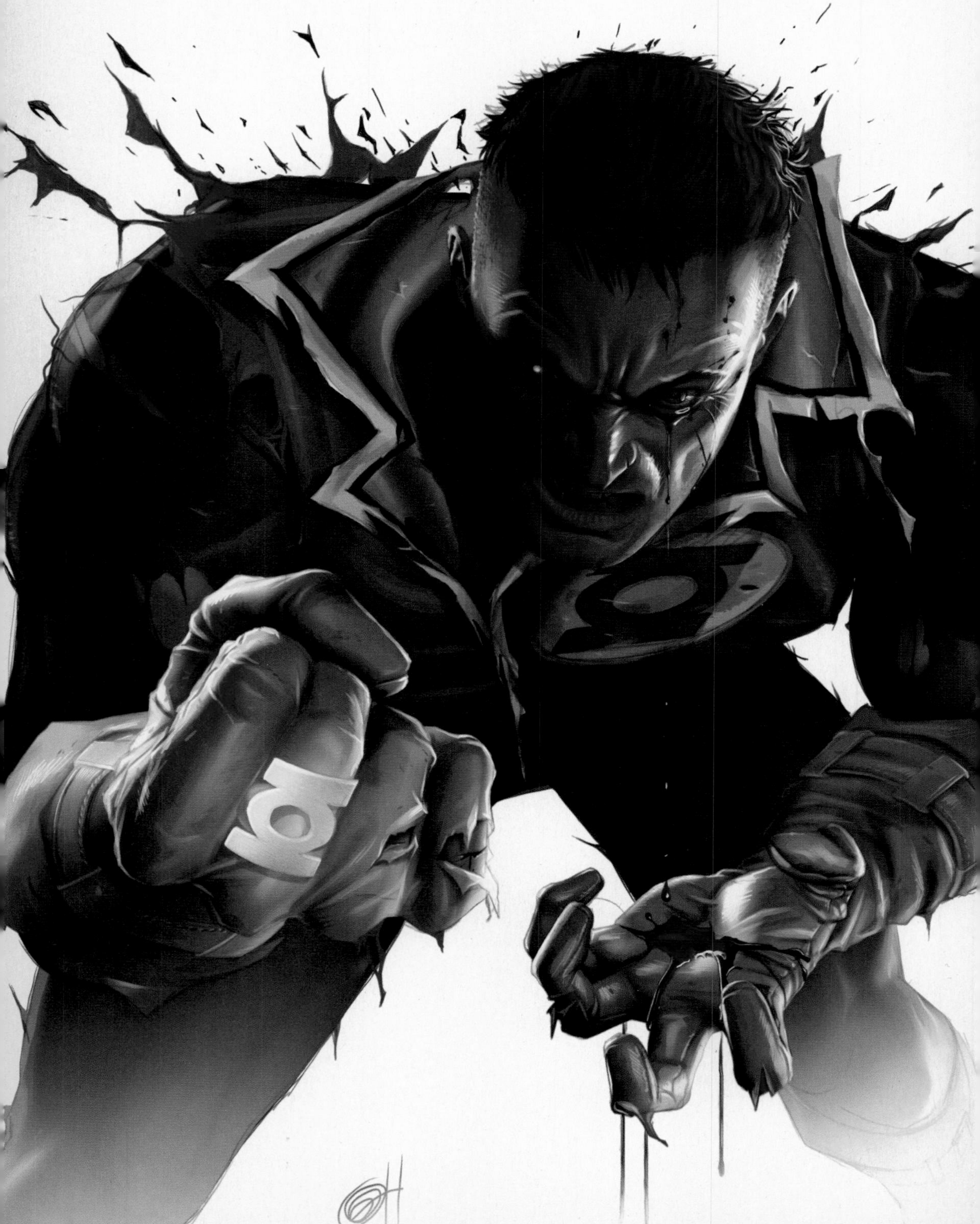

GREEN LANTERN CORPS 43
Cover by Ladrönn

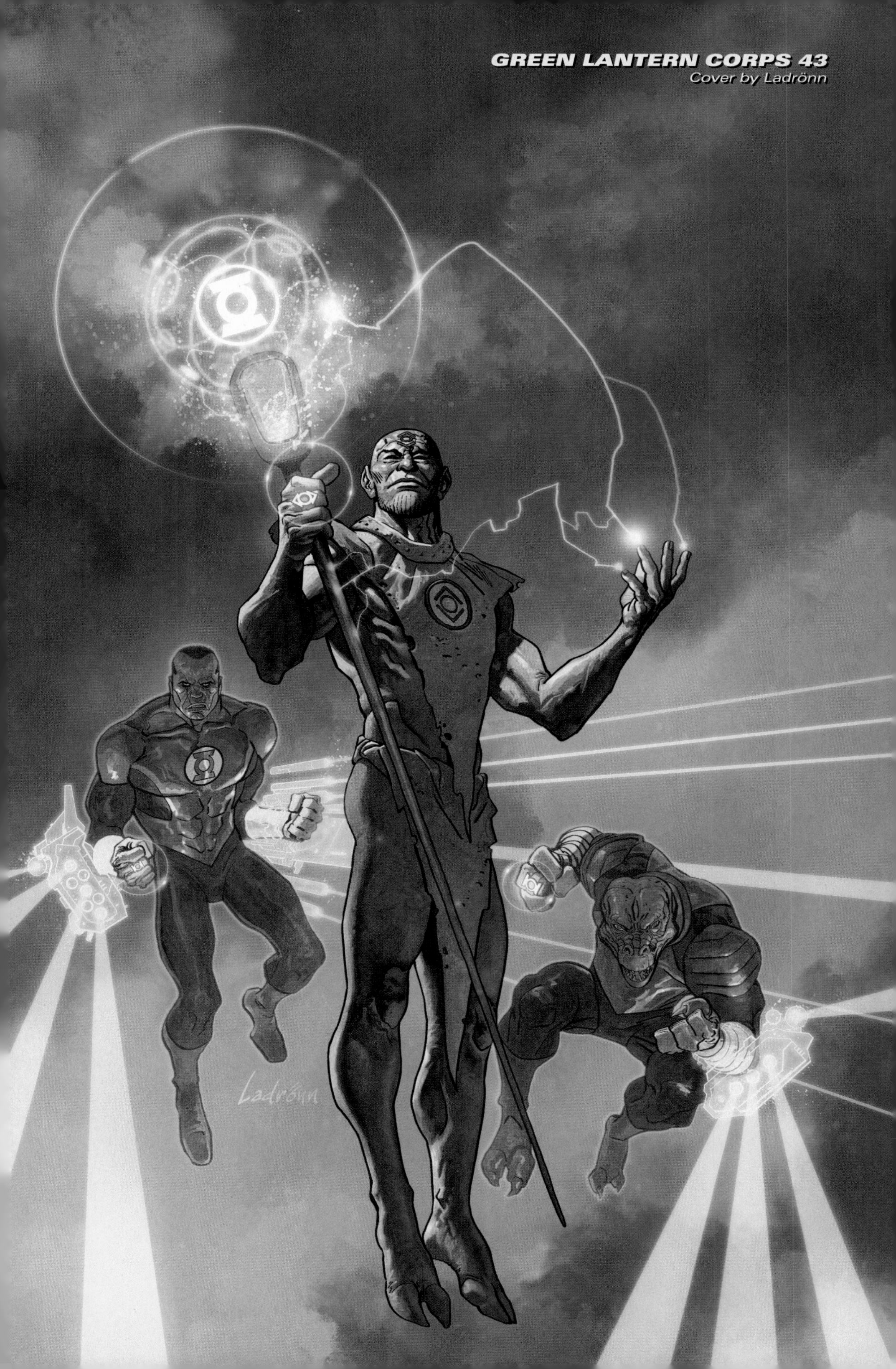
Ladrönn

GREEN LANTERN CORPS 44
Cover by Greg Horn

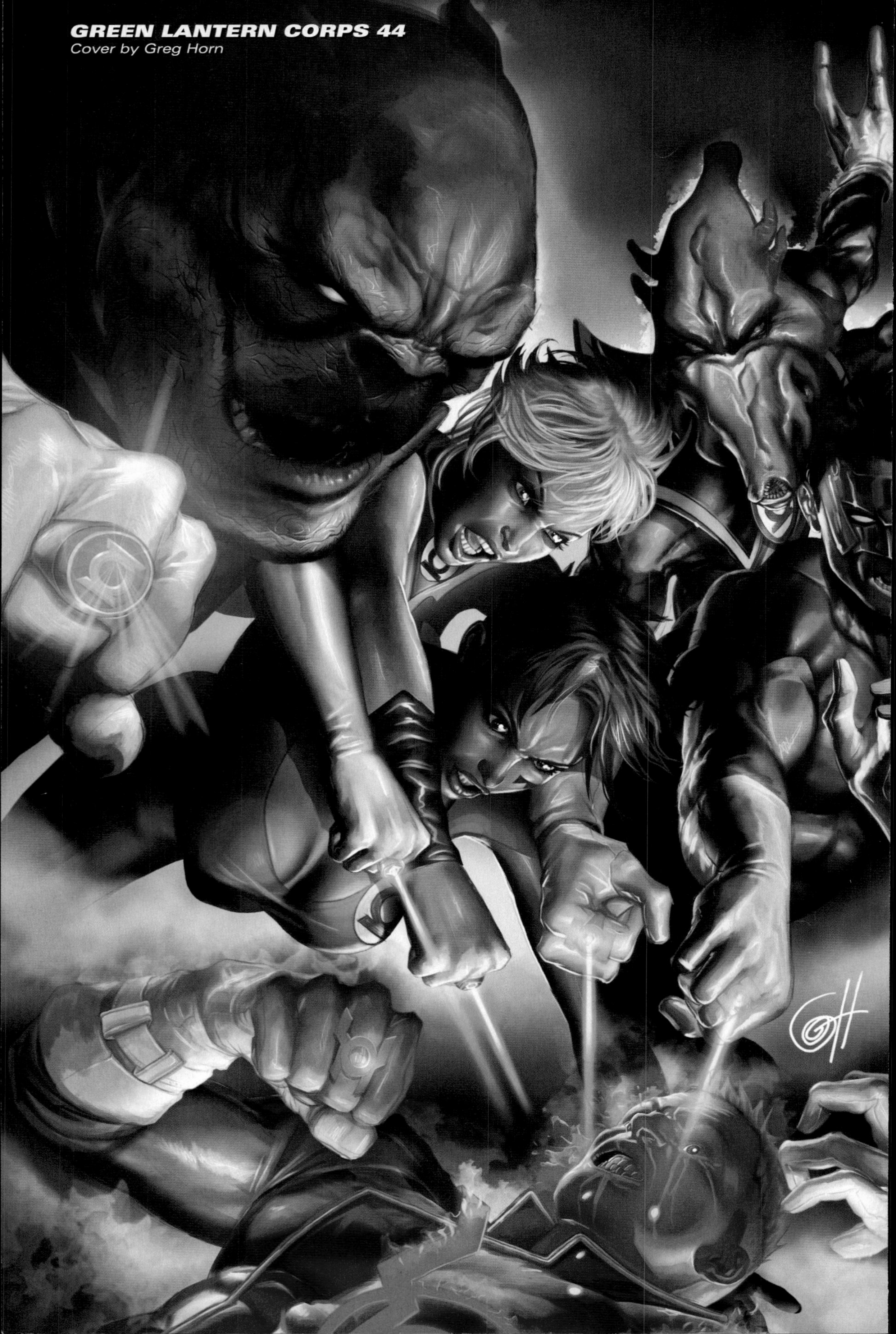

GREEN LANTERN CORPS 45
Cover by Brian Bolland

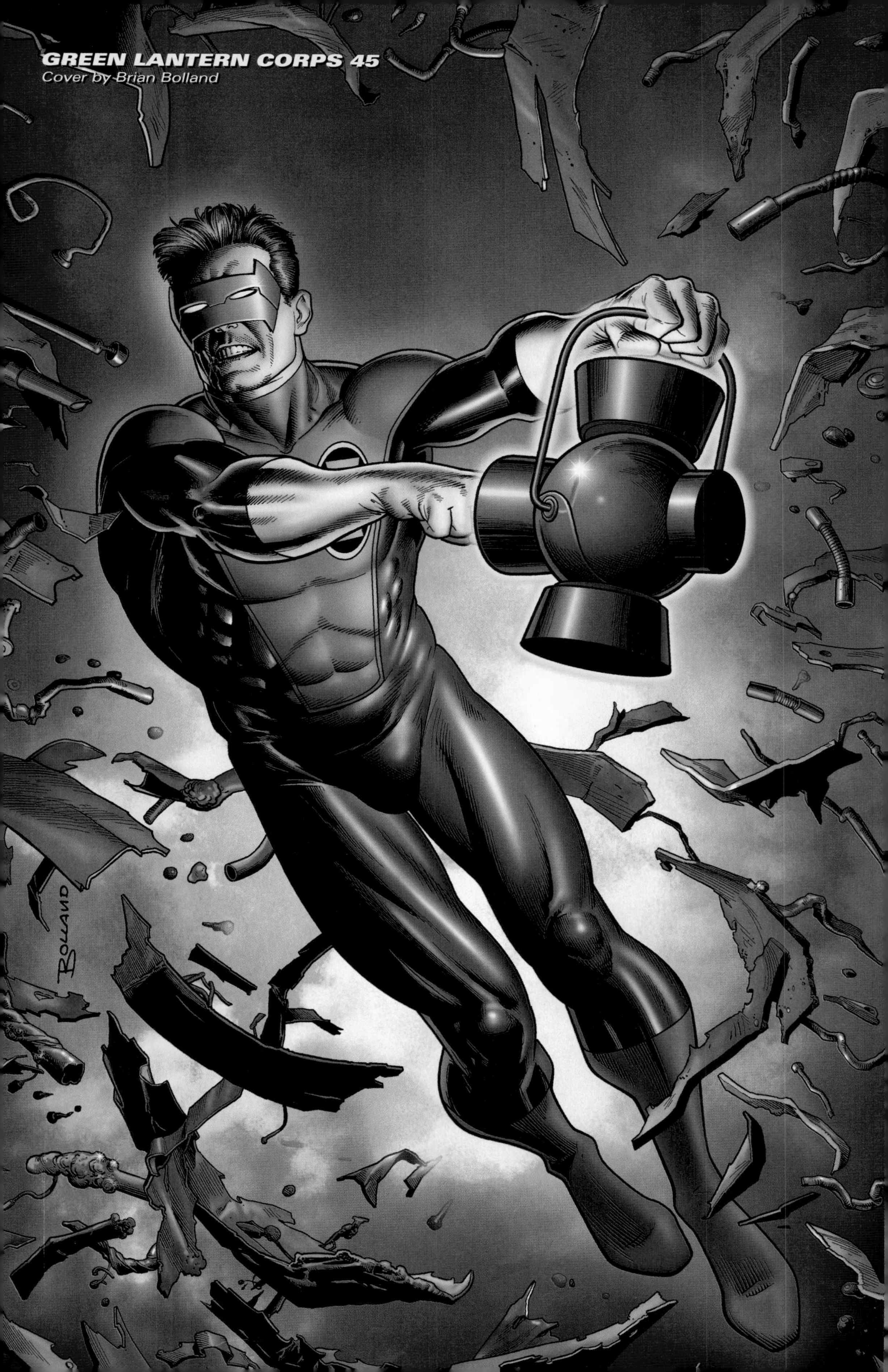
BOLLAND

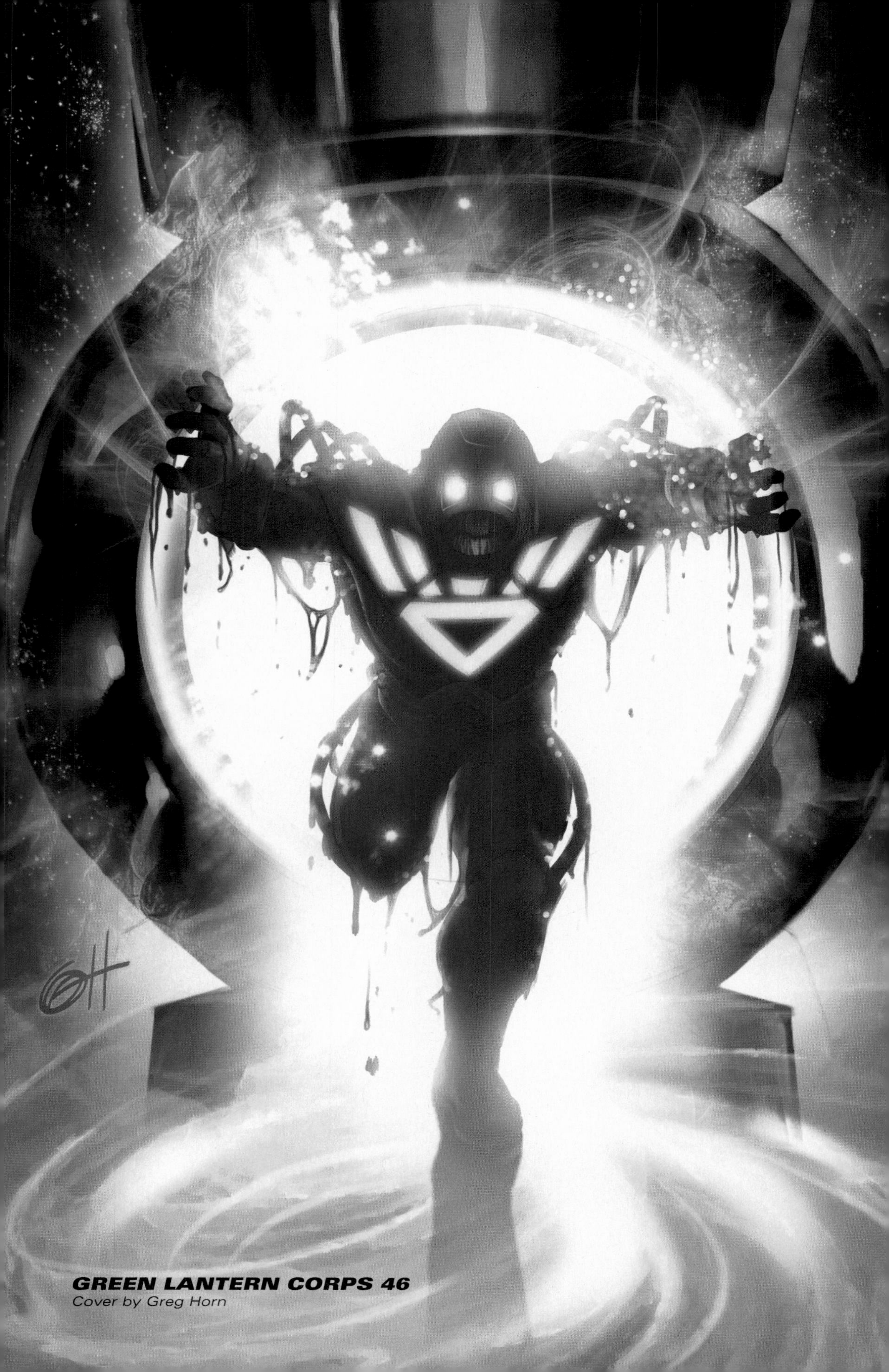

GREEN LANTERN CORPS 46
Cover by Greg Horn

GREEN LANTERN CORPS 47
Cover by Rodolfo Migliari

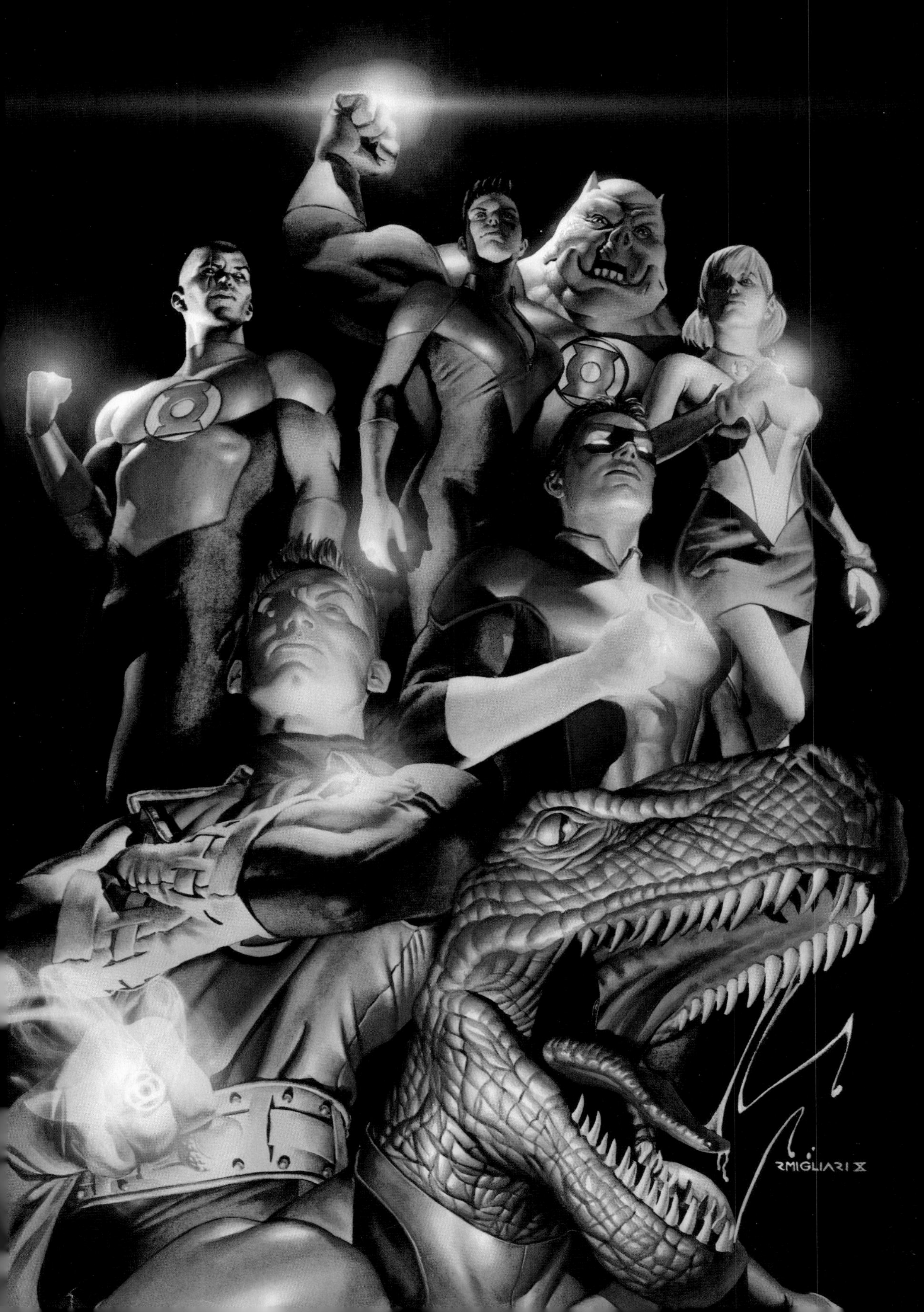
RMIGLIARI X

***BLACKEST NIGHT* —**
Unused Black Lantern Kilowog Cover

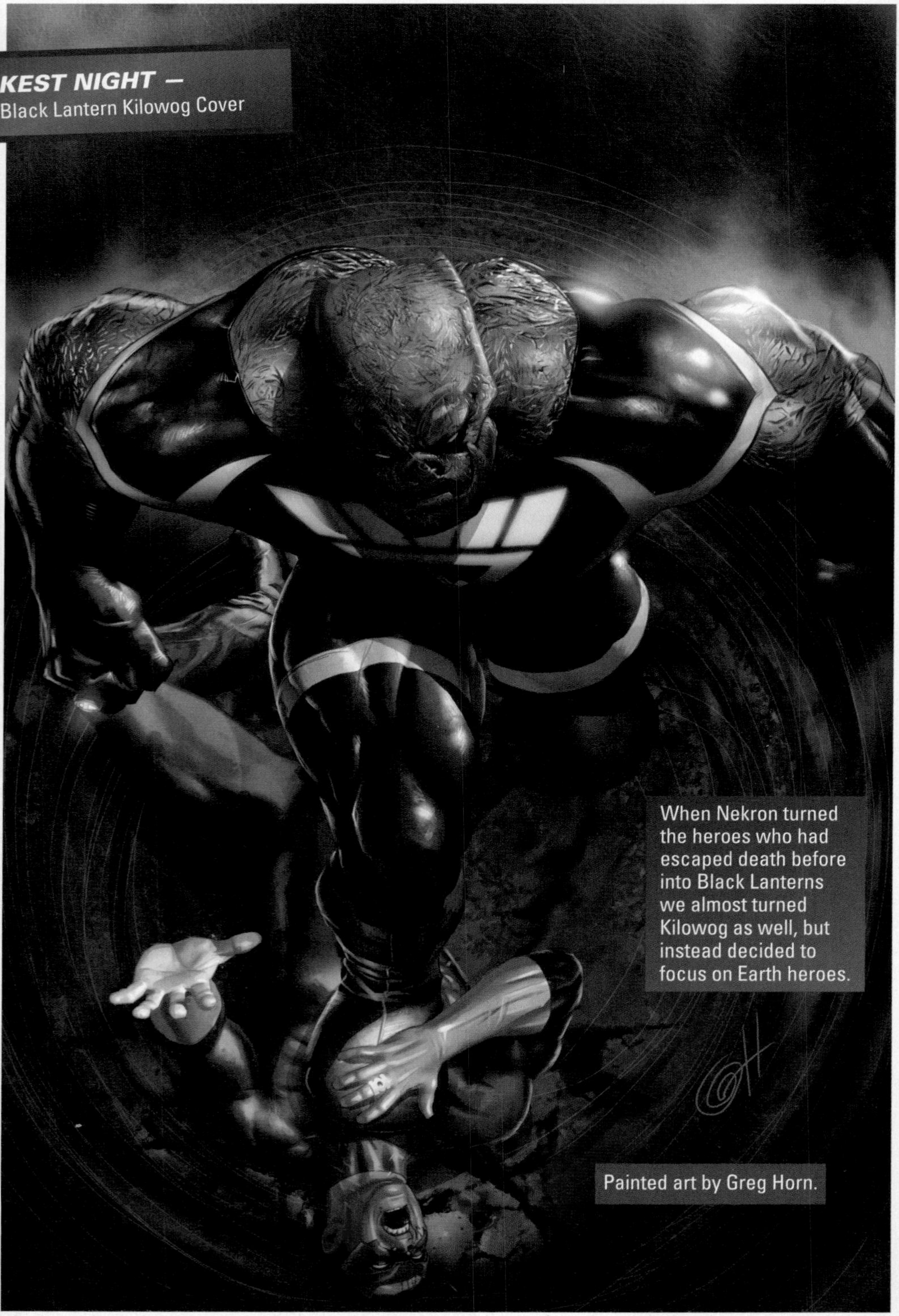

When Nekron turned the heroes who had escaped death before into Black Lanterns we almost turned Kilowog as well, but instead decided to focus on Earth heroes.

Painted art by Greg Horn.

BLACK LANTERN ICE

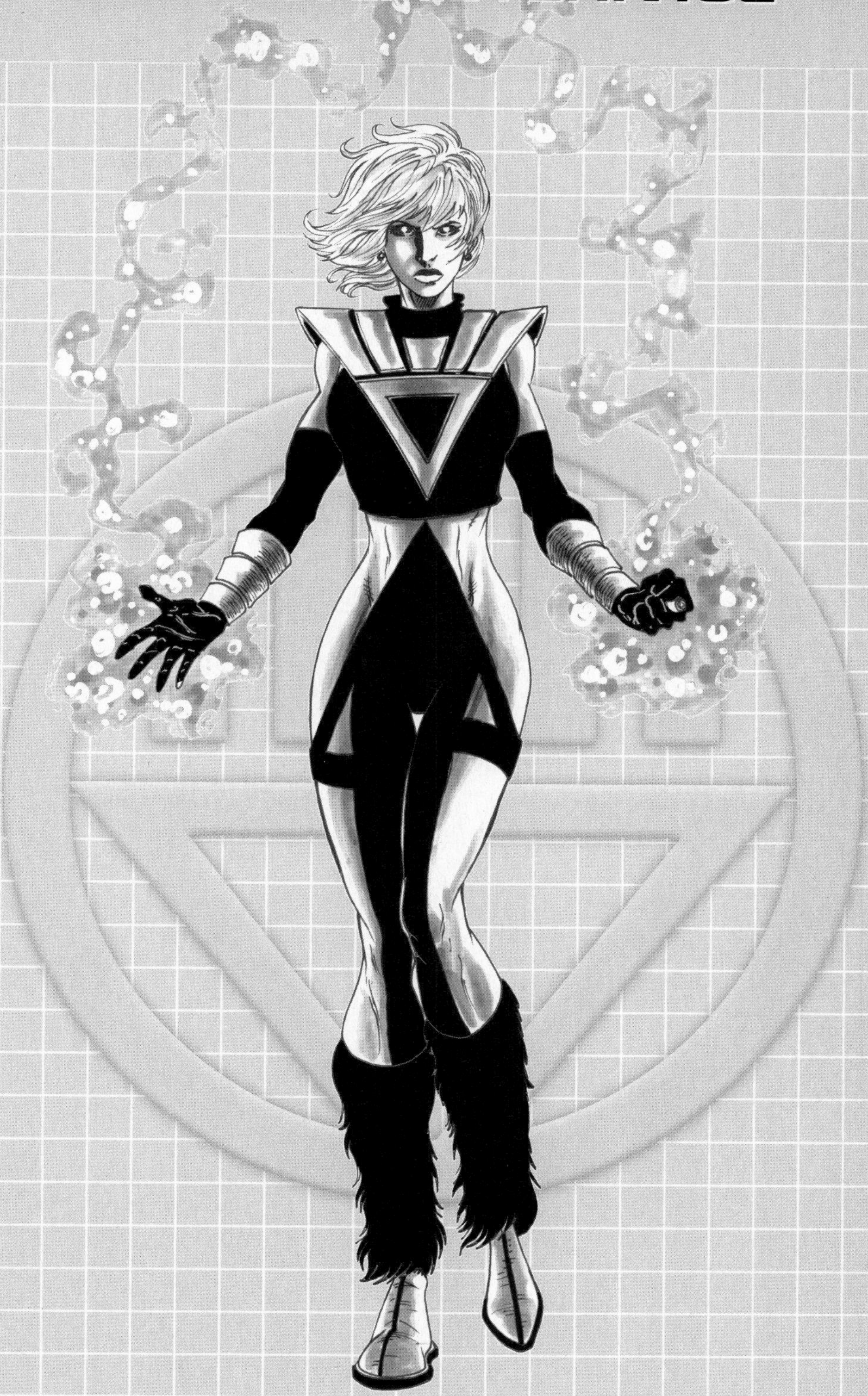

ALTER EGO: TORA OLAFSDOTTER
TORA'S POWERS ARE SUGGESTED BY HER NAME. BUT HER FREEZING ABILITIES COULD NOT HELP HER WHEN SHE WAS MURDERED BY THE OVERMASTER. ICE WAS MYSTERIOUSLY RESURRECTED, ALLOWING NEKRON TO GAIN A HOLD ON HER, TRANSFORMING HER INTO A BLACK LANTERN WHOSE MAIN GOAL IS THE DESTRUCTION OF HER BELOVED GUY GARDNER.

Design by Joe Prado

BLACK LANTERN JADE

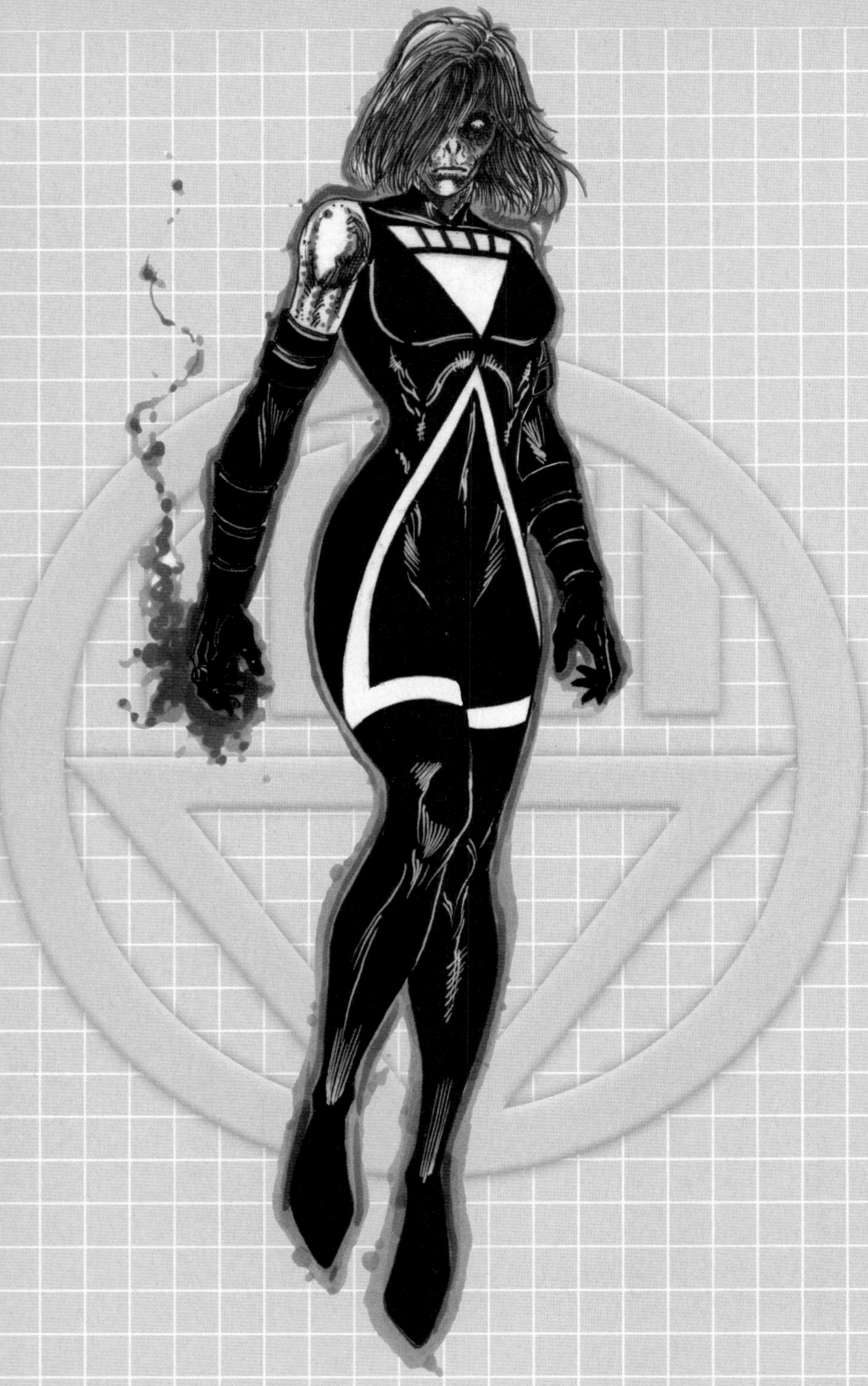

ALTER EGO: JENNIFER-LYNN HAYDEN

JADE, A FORMER GREEN LANTERN AND THE DAUGHTER OF ALAN SCOTT, MET HER END AT THE HANDS OF ALEXANDER LUTHOR, JR. RETURNING AS A BLACK LANTERN, JADE HAS SET OFF AFTER HER FORMER BOYFRIEND, KYLE RAYNER.

Design by Joe Prado

BLACK LANTERN KILOWOG
UNUSED

ALTER EGO: GREEN LANTERN
THE DRILL SERGEANT OF THE GREEN LANTERN CORPS WAS SLAIN BY THE PARALLAX-POSSESSED
HAL JORDAN BUT WAS LATER RETURNED TO THE LAND OF THE LIVING BY KYLE RAYNER AND
GANTHET. NEKRON WAS UNABLE TO TURN KILOWOG AS HE WAS NOT ON EARTH AT THE TIME
OF NEKRON'S STRIKE.

Design by Joe Prado

RED LANTERN GUY GARDNER

ALTER EGO: GREEN LANTERN
GUY GARDNER BELIEVES HIMSELF TO BE THE GREATEST GREEN LANTERN OF THEM ALL. HIS WILLPOWER LITERALLY SPARKS FROM THE RING, BUT HIS EGOTISTICAL PERSONALITY COULD PREVENT HIM FROM EVER REACHING THE HEIGHTS OF FELLOW EARTH LANTERN HAL JORDAN. HIS INTENSE ANGER GOT THE BETTER OF HIM WHEN HE BELIEVED THAT HIS COMRADE KYLE RAYNER WAS DEAD, ALLOWING HIM TO BE OVERTAKEN BY A CRIMSON RING OF RAGE.

Design by Patrick Gleason

BIOGRAPHIES

PETER J. TOMASI

Peter J. Tomasi was an editor with DC Comics for many years where he proudly helped usher in new eras for GREEN LANTERN, BATMAN, and JSA. He is now solely devoting all his time to writing comics and screenplays, having worked on such DC titles as GREEN LANTERN CORPS, BATMAN: BLACKEST NIGHT, THE OUTSIDERS, NIGHTWING, BLACK ADAM, and the critically acclaimed graphic novel LIGHT BRIGADE along with many other stories. His current projects include GREEN LANTERN: EMERALD WARRIORS and co-writing the bi-weekly series BRIGHTEST DAY.

PATRICK GLEASON

Patrick Gleason's career in comics has included work for Marvel and Image Comics. He is most noted for illustrating DC Comics' AQUAMAN, the relaunch of the Green Lantern Corps mini series, RECHARGE, and the regular ongoing GREEN LANTERN CORPS series. He is currently working on the follow-up to BLACKEST NIGHT, BRIGHTEST DAY.

REBECCA BUCHMAN

Rebecca Buchman has been involved with the comics industry since 2007 and lives in the Atlanta, Georgia metropolitan area. She learned her craft by studying under inker Dexter Vines. When she's not working on comics, Rebecca can be found kayaking, skiing and motorcycling.

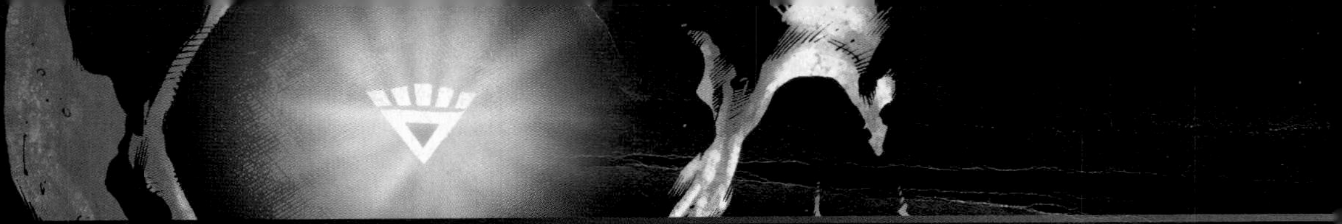